For Zannes

THE BORDERS OF NORMAL

A Clinical Psychiatrist De-Stigmatizes Paranormal Phenomena

MANUEL MATAS, M.D.

*Thank you for
your sharing

Manuel Matas*

 FriesenPress

Suite 300 - 990 Fort St
Victoria, BC, V8V 3K2
Canada

www.friesenpress.com

ISBN
978-1-5255-0455-6 (Hardcover)
978-1-5255-0456-3 (Paperback)
978-1-5255-0457-0 (eBook)

1. BODY, MIND & SPIRIT, PARAPSYCHOLOGY

Distributed to the trade by The Ingram Book Company

For Anna and Sylvia

Contents

INTRODUCTION   ix

Chapter 1: Paranormal or Normal: Beyond Stigma   1

Chapter 2: Near Death, Out of Body, After Death   27

Chapter 3: Between Skepticism and Belief   45

Chapter 4: Information Transfer: ESP, Telepathy, Precognitive Dreams, Premonitions, Predestination   65

Chapter 5: Limitless Mind, Limited Body, and the Rule of Four   95

Chapter 6: *All experience is an arch*: Empiricism vs. Rationalism   115

Chapter 7: Psychedelics: Expanding the Mind   131

Chapter 8: Paranormal Activity: Mediums, Channels, Spirit Guides, Guardian Angels, and Some Theories about Reincarnation   147

Chapter 9: *Stone walls do not a prison make*: A New Reality   175

Epilogue: Blood and the Dominion   189

Further Reading   197

Bibliography   203

Acknowledgments   233

The best physician is also a philosopher.

—Galen of Pergamon (129–c. 210 CE)

Greek physician, surgeon, philosopher, personal physician to Roman Emperor Marcus Aurelius. His theories influenced Western medical science for fifteen centuries.

INTRODUCTION

I refuse to commit the fashionable stupidity of regarding everything I cannot explain as a fraud.

—Carl Jung, Swiss psychiatrist (1875–1961)

I have been a clinical psychiatrist for forty years. For most of my professional career, I worked in university teaching hospitals. I published peer-reviewed articles in psychiatric journals and presented papers at national psychiatric conferences. I was seen as a fairly traditional, medical-model psychiatrist.

My primary concern throughout my psychiatric career was always to provide the best possible care for my patients and the best possible education for my students. I was not a proponent of talking about spirituality in psychiatry, with patients or with students, although I was always open to discussion. Throughout my life, however, I have had many experiences that could be called strange, weird, unusual, extraordinary, paranormal, anomalous, psychic, spiritual, mystical, or mysterious, depending on your point of view.

These experiences were all completely spontaneous, neither planned nor desired. One time I saw an apparition in my bedroom. Another time I left my body and found myself floating on my bedroom ceiling. When I was a second-year medical student, I dreamt the respirology exam the night before the exam. Many years later, I saw the angels at my father's funeral.

I have almost died many times. Although I have not had a typical near-death experience, I can say, in all humility, that I have had glimpses into the world beyond space and time. Without even trying, I saw, heard, and felt things that lit up my mind. I did not go looking for Spirit. Spirit came calling for me.

These events inspired a quest in me and set me on a spiritual path. I could not ignore the strange and mysterious things that were happening to me. I wanted to know what was causing them. Every once in a while, something startling happens to us which shakes us up and wakes us up from our nine-to-five, humdrum, routine existence. As we live our lives, we often suspect there must be more to this life than meets the eye. We are not wrong. My quest confirmed my suspicion.

It is a fact that we have the ability to contemplate other worlds which co-exist and overlap in time and space with our own physical plane of existence. We know that mental, emotional, and spiritual realms are out there, but most of us don't usually think about them as we go about our busy lives. We are aware of the world of ideas, the world of emotions, and the world of spirit. How many other worlds are out there?

There are many paradigms describing the various levels, dimensions, or planes of existence that surround us. To name a few: the astral, causal, and etheric planes; personal consciousness, the personal unconscious, and the collective unconscious; the intermediate state between this world and the next world, which precedes life and follows death, known as *Bardo* in Indian and Tibetan Buddhism; the four worlds or spiritual realms of Kabbalah, which in descending order are Atzilut (Emanation), Beriah (Creation), Yetzirah (Formation), and Asiyah (Action); the seven heavens through which the Prophet Muhammad ascended; and the nine circles of Hell in Dante's *Inferno*.

Just outside conscious awareness, many of us have had a sense of other worlds which, from time to time, intrude and make their presence known. There is often a conspiracy of silence that discourages a frank and open discussion of these ideas, which are often dismissed out of hand. It is well past time to draw back the veil of silence that surrounds these other worlds.

Paranormal and psychic experiences are not necessarily spiritual or supernatural in origin. They may be interpreted in many ways. Atheists, agnostics, and believers all experience paranormal, psychic, spiritual, and mystical phenomena, which may arrive bidden or unbidden. These experiences can occur once in a lifetime or repeatedly. Even if such an occurrence happens only once, it can have a life-long impact.

For some, words like "psychic" and "paranormal" are fraught with negative baggage engendered by an assortment of fakes, frauds, and charlatans. Still, what people today call "paranormal" is actually quite normal, and being psychic or sensitive or intuitive is simply another way of being in the world.

The Borders of Normal deals with the field of study known as meta-psychiatry (literally: "beyond psychiatry"). Meta-psychiatry represents the confluence of psychiatry with spirituality and metaphysics, which is the philosophy of being and knowing.

Just as there are various schools of psychiatry, there are also different schools of meta-psychiatry. I see meta-psychiatry as a field of study that does not conform to any particular religious dogma, ritual, or belief. Stanley R. Dean, clinical professor of psychiatry at the University of Florida and editor of *Psychiatry and Mysticism* (1975), used the term meta-psychiatry to describe the branch of psychiatry that studies psychic phenomena. He saw meta-psychiatry as the base of a pyramid whose other sides were psychiatry, parapsychology, philosophy, and mysticism. Meta-psychiatry includes elements of both transcendental and transpersonal psychology as it involves the study of our need for transcendence and also explores the meaning of experience beyond the personal.

Transcendental psychology is the field of study that deals with self-knowledge and self-actualization. In Abraham Maslow's hierarchy of universal human needs, our need for transcendence is crucial. It is universal, found at all times, in all cultures. Transcendental psychology has its roots in transcendentalism, an American 19th-century philosophical movement whose major writers included Henry David Thoreau, Ralph Waldo Emerson, Emily Dickinson, and Walt Whitman. These writers believed that we acquire knowledge not just through our five senses but also through our sixth sense, intuition. They combined contemplation of nature with direct knowledge of the world of spirit and were skeptical of established religions. They thought a church hierarchy was unnecessary as each individual has the capacity to attune to the divine within.

Transpersonal psychology is the branch of psychology that explores the nature of experience beyond the personal, extending outward towards the world, the cosmos, and all of humanity. It studies mystical experiences, trance states, peak experiences, and cosmic consciousness.

I have always been more drawn to the joy and beauty of life than to the mundane world of weights and measures. The idea that there is more to this life than meets the eye is not just idle speculation. It is a longing, an outcome fervently to be desired. Until recently, I kept my personal experiences mostly to myself; however, after surviving a life-threatening illness, leukemia; after a successful stem cell transplant from an anonymous donor; and after seeing the angels at my father's funeral, I decided to go public and share my experiences, in order to fight the stigma surrounding paranormal phenomena that is so prevalent in our society. I wanted people to know that it's okay to have these experiences and it's okay to talk about them. It's perfectly normal. There is no reason to feel embarrassed or ashamed. Nor is there any reason to feel proud or special. All in all, it's simply part of life.

My intention in writing this book is to normalize the paranormal and to show that phenomena we often label abnormal or paranormal are actually normal. Using a bell curve, we can see that there is a wide range of normal human behavior. Through an exploration of historical, psychological, social, and cultural trends, we will see that so-called paranormal phenomena, such as near-death and out-of-body experiences, visions, voices, precognitive dreams, and so on, have been found in every society, throughout human history.

By referring to both the scientific literature and the popular culture, I will show how pervasive paranormal phenomena have become in our own society. I will also examine some of the philosophical and metaphysical underpinnings of psychic and paranormal phenomena. Along the way, I will share a few personal anecdotes about my own experiences with these phenomena, in order to fight the stigma that attaches to the paranormal. When more people start to accept and share their own experiences, they will more readily accept themselves and others.

Chapter 1: Paranormal or Normal: Beyond Stigma

Mine eyes have seen the glory of the coming of the Lord.

Julia Ward Howe's "Battle Hymn of the Republic" was first published in the *Atlantic Monthly* in 1862. Howe said the words came to her in a rush, in the early hours of the morning, as she lay in bed waiting for the dawn. When she wrote, "Mine eyes have seen the glory..." she was not talking about seeing with her eyes. She was talking about seeing with her imagination, her inner vision, her mind's eye. The Battle Hymn was sung by both sides in the American Civil War. It has stood the test of time. More than 150 years after it was written, "The Battle Hymn of the Republic" was sung by the Brooklyn Tabernacle Choir at President Obama's second inauguration.

Paul McCartney wrote "Yesterday" the same way. The song came to him all at once, in a flash. It is one of the most successful and most widely covered songs in the history of popular music.

Creative people have visions. They are visionaries. They exist in every field of human endeavor, from music to art to literature, from science to medicine, psychology, biology, philosophy, and beyond. They see things in their minds' eyes through imagination and inspiration. But visions can also be more literal. A person may *actually* see things that others cannot, as I have done on a couple of occasions. Once, when fully awake, I saw an apparition in my bedroom. Another time, I saw two angels at my father's funeral, one on either side of the casket. I can still see them in my mind's eye, but when I first saw them, they were right there in front of me.

"If you see something, say something" is usually an appeal for people to report suspicious behavior. It can apply in this context too. People who see things that they consider abnormal often don't say anything because they are worried about what other people will think. They should say something anyway. It is helpful to talk openly about paranormal phenomena in order to de-stigmatize, process, and normalize these events.

Throughout recorded history, many people have seen things that were not visible to others – from biblical prophets like Ezekiel and Daniel to Catholic saints like Francis of Assisi and Joan of Arc; from creative geniuses like Fyodor Dostoyevky and Pablo Picasso to modern-day visionaries like Elon Musk and Steve Jobs. We say these people are marching to a different drummer. Creative people have visions. Some of them started seeing things when they were young children, and their parents often didn't know how to react.

Though William Blake (1757–1827) was unrecognized in his lifetime and lived in poverty, today he is considered a genius and one of the greatest painters, engravers, and poets of the Romantic Age. He said that he saw God when he was four and that he started seeing angels when he was eight. His father used to beat him every time he said he saw an angel because, as the father said, he was trying to teach his son not to lie.

William S. Burroughs (1914–1997), American author, painter, artist, and leading member of the Beat Generation, had childhood visions that stimulated his lifelong interest in altered states of consciousness.

Claire Danes (1979–) one of the most acclaimed actresses of her generation, also had visions. As a child, she was terrified by ghosts and gargoyles that she saw emerging from the woodwork and the showerhead. These terrifying visions eventually went away, but they returned when she took ecstasy.

Were these people psychotic as children? *Psychotic* means "out of touch with reality." If you can see or hear things which no one else can see or hear, you may be psychotic; alternatively, you may have a medical or emotional condition; you may be on drugs or medications that cause hallucinations; you may be withdrawing from drugs or alcohol; or you may be completely mentally and physically healthy.

It is important to distinguish the word *psychotic* from another word with the same root – *psychic*. People often use the word *psychic* to mean *intuitive* when they say, "You must be psychic." *Psychic* and *psychotic* sound alike because they are both derived from the same Greek word, *psyche,* which means "breath" or "soul." In English, *psyche* means "mind", but it can also mean "soul."

In *Freud and Man's Soul,* Bruno Bettelheim said that when Freud coined the term *psychoanalysis,* the meaning, in German, was "analysis of the soul." Freud saw the soul as the deep, hidden part of the self, which subsumes the life force.

Although there may be some overlap or blurring of boundaries between psychic and psychotic phenomena, as a rule the two are easily distinguished. In theory, there are four possibilities – a person may be psychic, psychotic, both, or neither. In practice, while there may be a few people who are both psychic and psychotic, I haven't met any. In the vast majority of cases, an individual is either psychic or psychotic or neither – but not both.

If a person sees visions or hears voices but does not otherwise show symptoms of psychosis (no thought disorder, delusions, paranoia, bizarre behavior, extreme mood swings, etc.) the person's experiences may be called paranormal or anomalous.

A diagnosis of psychosis is based in part on the severity, frequency, and nature of the symptoms; and, most importantly, on whether the symptoms interfere with the person's ability to function, at home or at work. Such a diagnosis cannot be made on the basis of a single symptom. Psychosis affects the whole person and the whole personality.

In this chapter, I describe some experiences I have had that I understand as psychic, spiritual, paranormal, or all three. I was not affected adversely by them; on the contrary, I was uplifted. My day-to-day functioning was not impaired in any way. I was able to carry on with my work and my family life without any difficulty. I can compare these experiences to having had a vivid dream then shaking it off and getting on with my day. These experiences did not disrupt my life. Indeed, they enhanced it.

When I was in my forties, I felt a hand on my shoulder one night when I was lying in bed. Technically, this sensation would be called a tactile hallucination. This was neither a hypnagogic (falling asleep) nor hypno-pompic (waking up) type of hallucination. I was wide awake. There was no medical condition to explain what had happened. All I knew was that the hand on my shoulder comforted me. It was as if I were being told, "Don't worry. Everything's going to be okay." I didn't doubt the experience or ask myself if I was going crazy. I simply had not known such things were possible.

The next day, I was more puzzled than anything. It was one of those vivid experiences that stays with you forever. Years later, I met a woman at a party who had had a similar experience. She said, "Oh, you had the hand-on-the-shoulder too?" I felt reassured. I was happy to hear that the same thing had happened to someone else. Knowing that another person had the same experience helped to normalize it. The experience remained open to interpretation. Was my mind playing tricks on me? What it a neurological event? Was it my spirit guide or "higher self" providing me with comfort and support? I don't really know, but I like to think it was the latter.

The Hermit, Rider-Waite Tarot Deck, designed by Pamela Colman Smith

A few years earlier, when I was lying in my bed, I saw an apparition in the form of the Hermit, one of the Major Arcana of the Rider-Waite Tarot deck. It only lasted a few seconds. I had been studying the Tarot at the time, so I was familiar with the image – a cowled monk, holding a lantern. I had never seen an apparition before. I was as shocked as anyone would be. But I wasn't afraid. I was in bed but not asleep, nor was I on the verge of falling asleep. I can accept that the apparition was a projection of my mind based on an image I had previously seen, but it left me emotionally stirred, and it raised questions. Why that particular image? Since there are 22 Major Arcana in the Tarot, why did my mind choose to project the Hermit? Was there a message?

Though I did not hear a voice, I did receive a message, through a process I was later to learn is called "thought transfer." Without speaking, the apparition conveyed two distinct messages: "It's okay" and "You're okay." The experience was very strange, yet strangely comforting. Even though I had never heard of thought transfer before, when it happened to me, I knew immediately what it was. I should add that both the apparition and the hand on my shoulder came to me at moments of extreme stress, distraction, and dislocation.

Many years after seeing the apparition in my bedroom, I came across a passage in Jonathan Lethem's great novel *Dissident Gardens* that resonated with me because it conveyed a similar message to the one I had received in my bedroom. In the novel, Sergius is an eight-year-old boy whose parents were helping the Sandanistas in Nicaragua. The boy had been left at a Quaker boarding school, where one of his teachers gave him a book to read about a boy called Pedro, who was able to communicate with his dead brother.

> Three weeks in a row, Sergius brought the Mexican book to Sunday meeting and, after a certain interval of silence and a spontaneous message or two from a teacher or an older kid, stood and cleared his throat and read aloud the story of Pedro at the graveside. See, he intended the message to say, *it's okay.* The dead are still around. And *I'm okay.* You don't have to feel sorry for me. [Italics mine]

Carl Jung saw the Hermit as an archetype of the wise old man. He described the Hermit as "the archetype of the spirit… the pre-existing meaning hidden in the chaos of life." I hadn't read this before I had the vision, but it seemed to fit with my experience. I discovered my brain had a built-in, self-comforting mechanism, a way to find comfort in the "chaos of life."

At a time of great personal upheaval, my personal unconscious was able to tap into the collective unconscious and the world of spirit in order to gain comfort and support from the archetypal image of the wise old man who brings meaning to a world of chaos.

As Jung wrote: "Man always feels the need of finding an access through the unconscious to the meaning of an actual condition, because there is a sort of correspondence or likeness between the prevailing condition and the condition of the collective unconscious."

The Hermit was my first "vision," but it was not my last. About ten years after the Hermit appeared in my bedroom, I saw the angels at my father's funeral. I know it sounds strange, but I actually saw them zoom into the funeral home on a beam of light through a window near the ceiling. They were the most beautiful creatures I had ever seen.

There were two angels. They were identical. Each one had long, dark blond hair, long white robes, and large white wings. I could not say if they were male or female. There was one on either side of the casket. They were huge. They seemed to fill the room, from floor to ceiling. The thought came into my mind that they were "ministering angels." I had the idea that they were ministering to my father, to help him make the transition from this world to the next, also known as *Yenne Velt* (the other world) or *Olam haBa* (the world to come).

At the time, I was not familiar with the concept that there are different kinds of angels. I subsequently learned that angels are usually seen as messengers, but there are different kinds of angels and ministering angels were one kind. Subsequently I came across the Hebrew prayer *Shalom Aleichem*, the English translation of which goes as follows:

Peace be unto you, O ministering angels, messengers of the Most High.

Forms of Hallucination

We need to distinguish between hallucinations that are symptoms of a psychotic illness, and visions, voices, or other perceptive and sensory phenomena which are not psychotic but may occur at times of stress, isolation, or grief. Psychics may attribute their sensory experiences to the spirit world, but their spirituality is vastly different from the distortions of spirituality that can be seen in persons who suffer from mental disorders.

Psychotic patients may demonstrate symptoms of religiosity; however, the symptoms would not be considered spiritual in any way. As a psychiatrist for many years, I had the opportunity to work with many severely disturbed psychotic patients, some of whom had religious delusions. They may have said they heard messages from God, or they may have believed that they *were* God. Manic patients often thought that they had god-like powers, knowledge, or influence (called "delusions of grandeur").

Schizophrenic patients have what is called a thought disorder, in form and content. Their speech may be fragmented and incoherent because of loosening of associations between one thought and the next. They may hear their thoughts out loud (thought echoing); they may say they can read other people's minds or that other people can read their minds (thought broadcasting); they may believe that other people put thoughts into their head or take thoughts out of their head (thought intrusion and thought extraction or thought withdrawal); or that they are being controlled or manipulated by outside forces (delusions of control).

Persons with schizophrenia may appear to be mumbling or talking to themselves, when they are in fact talking to their voices. Hearing or seeing things that other people cannot hear or see (auditory and visual hallucinations) are common psychotic symptoms, but as we have seen, hallucinations by themselves are not sufficient to make a diagnosis of schizophrenia.

Psychics may appear to have the ability to read people's minds, as they often come up with personal information about the person they are reading that they would have no way of knowing. They may appear to have special powers, to see into the future, or to hear and feel things that other people cannot see, hear, and feel (clairvoyance, clairaudience, and clairsentience, respectively). However, their appearance, behavior, and conversation are otherwise normal.

Psychic mediums say they communicate with spirits of the dead and receive messages from the spirit world. Trance channels claim to speak in the voice of discarnate entities while in a trance state. People with near-death experiences often report contact with the spirits of deceased relatives and feelings of bliss and joy that may resemble the euphoria seen in hypomanic patients.

While there may be a passing resemblance between psychotic symptoms and the paranormal phenomena reported by psychics and mediums, and by other people under special circumstances, the similarities are more apparent than real. There are major differences, both qualitative and quantitative, between psychic and psychotic phenomena.

Qualitatively, visions and voices experienced during mystical revelations or spirit visitations tend to be calming and peaceful; psychotic hallucinations, on the other hand, are more likely to be frightening and disturbing.

Quantitatively, a person may have a mystical, paranormal, or spiritual experience once or twice in a lifetime; people who have psychotic symptoms due to schizophrenia, mania, dementia, or delirium may be hallucinating constantly, every minute of every day.

There are other differences between psychotic and non-psychotic hallucinations as well. Schizophrenic patients often hear more than one voice. They may hear dialoguing voices talking to each other about the individual in an insulting way. Their voices may be soft and barely perceptible, or they may be loud and screaming insults, telling the person what to do (so-called "command hallucinations").

Psychotic auditory hallucinations may not be voices at all. They may be whirring sounds, like the grinding wheels of machinery or the buzzing of insects. They may sound like mumbling or whispering in one's ear. These noises, sounds, and voices are being perceived at the same time as all the other sounds in the environment, so they are very disturbing.

Auditory hallucinations can occur in a variety of mental disorders, such as mania, psychotic depression, schizophrenia, and drug or alcohol intoxication or withdrawal. Chronic alcoholism can lead to voices that occur in a clear consciousness (alcoholic hallucinosis) or visions that occur in a clouded consciousness, such as delirium tremens (DTs) during alcohol withdrawal. The proverbial "pink elephants" seen in DTs are visual hallucinations. The visual distortions and visual hallucinations seen in delirium or drug-induced (toxic) psychosis may also be present in conversion disorder or in trance.

Karl Jaspers was a German psychiatrist and philosopher. His 1913 textbook *General Psychopathology* is considered a classic in the history of psychiatry. Jaspers defined *hallucination* as a perception without a stimulus. He said hallucinations are false perceptions, which are not in any way distortions of real perceptions. He distinguished hallucinations from illusions as follows: "*Illusion* is the term for perceptions which in fact are transpositions (or distortions) of real perceptions. *Hallucinations* are perceptions that spring into being in a primary way and are not transpositions or distortions of any genuine perception." They occur simultaneously with real perceptions.

If the wind is rustling the curtain and someone says a spirit has entered the room, that assertion would not be called a hallucination because there was a perception based on a stimulus. There may have been faulty attribution, but there was, nevertheless, a stimulus so the perception was genuine.

Eugen Bleuler (1857–1938), the Director of the Burgholzli asylum, the psychiatric hospital affiliated with the University of Zurich, first used the word *schizophrenia* in a lecture in 1908. He coined the word from two Greek words meaning "split mind," because the schizophrenic's thoughts and feelings are split off from each other. His classic textbook, *Dementia Praecox, or the Group of Schizophrenias*, was published in 1911.

As a result of Bleuler's work, *schizophrenia* replaced the term *dementia praecox* ("precocious dementia") which had been used previously. The illness had been called "precocious" because it usually starts in the late teens or early twenties. Until this distinction was made, young schizophrenic patients were considered to be in the same category as elderly demented patients.

Bleuler noted that, while schizophrenic patients usually heard voices, hearing voices, by itself, was not sufficient to make a diagnosis of schizophrenia. This is important to remember. Schizophrenia is a major mental disorder. It cannot be diagnosed on the basis of a single symptom, such as hearing voices. There needs to be a constellation of symptoms in order to meet established diagnostic criteria, and the symptoms need to interfere with the individual's ability to function.

Unfortunately, people have sometimes been misdiagnosed on the basis of one isolated symptom. In 1973, American psychologist David Rosenhan designed an experiment in which eight "pseudo-patients" (including himself) were told to present themselves to various emergency departments at hospitals across the United States and say that they were hearing voices. Even though their thoughts, speech, and behavior were perfectly normal in every way, except for the complaint of hearing voices, all eight were admitted to hospital, diagnosed with schizophrenia, and given medication (which they didn't take). On a side note, the other patients in the ward knew they were faking their symptoms. They fooled the doctors, but they couldn't fool the patients.

The late Oliver Sacks wrote extensively about hallucinations in his book *Hallucinations* (2012). He listed the following causes of non-psychotic hallucinations: sleep or dream deprivation, especially if combined with exhaustion or severe physical stress; drug or alcohol intoxication; and withdrawal from drugs or alcohol.

Drugs that produce hallucinations, through intoxication or withdrawal, include prescription drugs, such as antidepressants, anti-anxiety medications, and sleeping pills. The anti-malarial drug Lariam (mefloquine) can cause frightening hallucinations and vivid dreams. Other medical causes of hallucinations include migraine headaches, Parkinson's disease, temporal lobe epilepsy, fever, dementia, and head injury.

Many brain disorders, not just schizophrenia and delirium, are character-ized by hallucinations. Ten percent of patients who have major depression with psychotic features hear voices, as do 21 percent of manic patients and 41 percent of combat veterans with PTSD (post-traumatic stress disorder).

Olfactory hallucinations (affecting the sense of smell) are found in a variety of medical conditions, including migraine, Parkinson's disease, head injury, stroke, and temporal lobe epilepsy. Olfactory hallucinations are considered to be a particularly malignant symptom if they are found in schizophrenia.

Migraine sufferers may have Lilliputian visual hallucinations. They may see tiny images of people or animals, or they may see shimmering arcs of light. Patients with Charles Bonnet syndrome, a condition associated with visual loss due to age-related macular degeneration, glaucoma, or cataracts may report complex visual hallucinations. They often say they are seeing tiny aliens. Even elderly patients who are blind can develop bizarre visual hallucinations.

Although visual loss and hearing loss are most often associated with per-ceptual illusions, distortions, or hallucinations, the loss of any of the five senses can lead to hallucinations. Ten to twenty percent of patients who are visually impaired develop visual hallucinations. The same percentage of people who have lost their sense of smell will develop olfactory hallucina-tions. Loss of the sense of taste can lead to gustatory hallucinations. Tactile hallucinations can appear after the loss of the sense of touch. Olfactory, gustatory, or tactile hallucinations may be present in temporal lobe epilep-tic seizures or auras.

Sacks wrote that his patients who saw musical notes, numbers, or letters had to have seen these things previously in order to hallucinate them. There was a personal and experiential component to his patients' hallucinations. Musicians saw musical notes, mathematicians saw mathematical formulas, and so on. His observation is consistent with my vision of the Hermit since I was studying Tarot at the time and was familiar with the image.

Matt Whelan, in an essay about trekking through the foothills of the Himalayas, wrote that a shortage of food caused him to hallucinate:

> Food became the stuff of fantasy, and sometimes hallucination. Rocks began to look like potatoes and the sweat pouring off people's brows became condensation sliding down the sides of a cold can of cola. People's fingers began to look more and more like sausages, and sometimes I could hear them sizzling in the midday heat.

Lack of food determined the content of his auditory and visual hallucinations, but it was severe stress, sensory deprivation, isolation, and monotony that produced his hallucinations in the first place.

Wanderers through the desert may see an oasis that turns out to be a mirage. Prisoners in solitary confinement can experience a phenomenon known as "prisoner's cinema." Sailors, marathon runners, long distance truck-drivers, and jet pilots sometimes respond to the monotonous landscape with visual hallucinations. The visual hallucinations experienced by long-distance truck drivers can also be caused by drugs such as methamphetamine, which some long-distance truck drivers take to stay awake. Long, uninterrupted silences that are experienced in sensory deprivation tanks or in meditation retreats can also lead to auditory hallucinations.

Cocaine can lead to tactile hallucinations such as a feeling of bugs crawling under the skin, a condition known as *formication* or *coke bugs*. The sensation of infestation is a tactile hallucination; the associated false belief is a delusion, known as *delusional parasitosis*. It can lead to severe excoriation of the skin if the afflicted individual scratches frantically to get the bugs out. These types of hallucinations are clearly psychotic. They are extremely unpleasant and not easily confused with the type of pleasant sensory illusions or distortions one finds in non-psychotic hallucinations.

Prevalence of Hallucinations

Hallucinations are much more common than people tend to think. One reason is that people don't usually talk about their hallucinations unless they are directly asked or encouraged to do so. Over the years, there have been many community surveys to determine the prevalence of hallucinations in the general population. Their findings have remained consistent over time.

As far back as the late 19th century, researchers in England circulated a questionnaire to 17,000 people asking if they had ever seen or been touched by an inanimate object or heard voices when no other person was present. After they excluded anyone with obvious medical or psychiatric problems, they found that ten percent of those surveyed said they had hallucinations; three to four percent of the population said they heard voices. A significant minority of the voices had spiritual, religious, or supernatural content.

In 2009, Dr. Emmanuel Stip and his colleagues at the University of Montréal published research into the incidence of psychotic symptoms in the general population. Their study was based on a literature review of psychotic features in non-clinical populations. They found that there was a continuum between normality and pathology and that psychotic symptoms such as hallucinations were often transitory and situational.

They distinguished psychotic from non-psychotic symptoms in various ways. Hallucinations that were part of a psychotic illness were usually threatening, frequent, and intrusive. They tended to be very distressing. Hallucinations in the non-clinical population, on the other hand, tended to be infrequent, mostly positive, and non-threatening. A very common non-psychotic hallucination would be the experience of hearing one's name being called out loud. You turn around and no one is there. Most of us have had this experience from time to time. It is quite normal. The realization that hallucinations are fairly common in the general population should encourage people to be more accepting of their occasional hallucinations and more willing to talk about them.

Visions of Deceased Loved Ones

Death-related or grief-related visions are an entirely different order of phenomena from hallucinations produced by brain pathology or mental disorders. Some people understand death- and grief-related visions simply as internally generated, not as external events. Others, however, experience these phenomena as messages from another world, the world of spirit, or the afterlife. The phenomenon itself is not controversial, only its interpretation.

The content of the vision is as important as the context, for it is often a reflection of the circumstances of the person who sees the vision. A grieving widow, for example, is far more likely to see her late husband in her bedroom than to have a vision of Whitney Houston. Her vision of a familiar person, not a stranger, could be considered a normal part of grieving. If a widow hears her late husband's voice out loud, or sees him in her bedroom at night, or feels his presence, this would not be considered psychotic or even unusual. If she had a vision of Whitney Houston, on the other hand, that would be considered bizarre and possibly psychotic.

Someone who hears voices or sees visions may be neither psychic nor psychotic. He or she may have normal mental and physical health. Recently bereaved people often report hearing, seeing, or feeling the presence of their deceased spouses or children. They may even report having conversations with them. For them, it may be a spiritual experience, or they may call it an emotional or psychological experience. This will depend to some extent on the background of the person who has the experience.

W. Dewi Rees, a Welsh physician, published an article in the *British Medical Journal* in 1971 in which he documented his research with what he called "grief hallucinations." In his survey of 227 widows and 66 widowers, he found that nearly half of his subjects had post-death contact with their spouses in the form of abnormal perceptual experiences. He included visual, auditory, or tactile experiences as well as a sense of the presence of the deceased if it was considered real by the widow or widower; dreams of the deceased were excluded. Thirty-nine percent felt the presence of the deceased; 14 percent saw them; 13 percent heard them; 12 percent spoke with them; and three percent said they were touched by the deceased. Some widows and widowers had more than one type of perceptual experience. These patients were not psychotic. They were in good mental and physical health and their visions were not due to medication, fever, or dementia.

Rees characterized his subjects as mostly normal, stable people, from the upper social classes and above average in intelligence and education. People were more likely to have "grief hallucinations" if they had had a long, happy marriage and parenthood. Far from being frightened by their experiences, 80 percent of his patients found post-death contact to be pleasurable, helpful, and reassuring. Even so, the majority of Rees's widows and widowers did not otherwise disclose they had conversations with their deceased spouses, even to close friends and relatives.

Many years later, American sociologist and Catholic priest Andrew Greeley did a study in which he found that many widows who reported being contacted by their dead husbands said that they had not previously believed in an afterlife. Their experiences, therefore, could not be seen as confirmation of previously held beliefs. Greeley found that many people who reported paranormal experiences were not particularly religious.

The sense of a presence reported by bereaved parents and spouses is also a common phenomenon experienced by survivors of extreme circumstances. As documented by John Geiger in *The Third Man Factor: Surviving The Impossible,* many people facing death, including 9/11 survivors, polar explorers, mountaineers, astronauts, prisoners of war, and shipwreck survivors have sensed an unseen presence, a benevolent, incorporeal being, who gives them hope and guidance, and encourages them to make one last effort to survive. These reports have become so common that the phenomenon has a name: the third man factor. Whether the experience is due to hallucination, higher self, divine intervention, or neurological event is open for discussion.

Deathbed Visions

Deathbed visions (DBVs), also called pre-death visions, have been described for thousands of years, in every age and in every culture. They are not to be confused with near-death experiences (NDEs), which I discuss in the next chapter. DBVs are experienced by people just before their death. These are people who actually die. They are not resuscitated. NDEs are reported by people who were clinically dead and then were resuscitated or revived spontaneously.

William Barrett, a physics professor at the Royal College of Science in Dublin, studied psychic phenomena, such as dowsing, mediumship, and table-tapping for over 50 years. He was one of the founding members of the Society for Psychical Research (SPR), which was established in London in 1882. It was one of the first organizations to do scholarly research on psychic phenomena. Barrett edited the SPR Journal from 1884 to1899. His seminal work, *Death-Bed Visions*, was published posthumously in 1926, one year after his death.

Barrett became interested in doing a systematic study of deathbed visions in the 1920s after his wife, an obstetrical surgeon, told him about one of her patients who had died from a post-partum hemorrhage. Prior to her death, the woman, Doris, became very excited about seeing a beautiful landscape. She said her late father and her beloved sister, Vida, had arrived to take her to the other side. The surprising thing was that Doris had not been told that Vida had recently died. Due to her condition, her family had wanted to spare her the knowledge.

The same thing happened with other patients as well. Dying patients would report seeing a friend or relative at their bedside whom they thought was alive but had in fact died without the patient's knowledge.

Barrett found that dying children usually did not report seeing their parents, since in most cases the parents were still alive. Many of the dying children who saw angels expressed surprise that the angels waiting to take them to the other side didn't have wings. Deathbed visions do not always coincide with preconceived notions.

The phenomenon of deathbed visions was re-visited in 2014 by researchers at Canisius College in Buffalo, New York. They interviewed 66 terminally ill patients living in a hospice. They found that most of the patients reported seeing visions (or "visitors" as they called them) of deceased friends and relatives at least once a day. The majority of these terminal patients said their visitors felt real and their visions were comforting. As they got closer to death, the visions became more frequent.

As reported in her 2012 book *Heavenly Hugs: Comfort, Support and Hope from the Afterlife*, Carla Wills-Brandon collected nearly 2,000 cases of deathbed visions. She rejected the notion that these visions were the product of a dying brain. She noticed that the "visitors" were all deceased family and friends, even though in some cases the dying patients didn't know the "visitors" were deceased. She questioned why the dying brain didn't produce images of people who were alive, if this were strictly a physiological phenomenon. She also rejected the notion that these visions were due to medication, as the non-medicated, clear-headed dying patients had similar deathbed visions to the medicated, confused, dying patients.

Award-winning journalist Patricia Pearson used the term "near-death awareness" in her description of the visions of dying patients. She also rejected the idea that these visions were due to lack of oxygen to the brain or to medication. She observed that, in fact, the more clear-headed and the less medicated patients were the ones who were more likely to have death-bed visions. A similar observation has been made with regard to patients who report visions with their near-death experiences.

Back in the 1920s, Barrett had reported the curious finding that the dying patients' visions were often shared by medical personnel or relatives who were present at their bedside. Dying patients who reported visions were, for the most part, clear-minded and rational. There was no evidence to suggest that they were confused or that their visions were caused by a lack of oxygen to the brain. This is an interesting observation because near-death experience skeptics often claim the experience is caused by a lack of oxygen to the brain. While that theory may be somewhat plausible, surely the relatives who were gathered at the bedside or the medical personnel who shared the visions did not also suffer from lack of oxygen to their brains.

A cross-cultural study of the experiences of dying patients was done in the 1960s by Karlis Osis and Erlendur Haraldsson who studied 50,000 terminally ill patients in India and the United States. They reported the observations of more than one thousand nurses and physicians. Osis was a Latvian-born psychologist who worked as a research associate at the parapsychology laboratory at Duke University and then as Director of Research at the Parapsychology Foundation in New York. Haraldsson was Professor of Psychology at the University of Iceland. They found deathbed visions were very common for both Indian and American patients. Their findings are reported in their book *At the Hour of Death*. The most common type of vision was dead friends and relatives who came to accompany them to the other side. These bedside visions usually lasted only a few minutes.

The authors of the study reported that the patient's belief in an afterlife was not related to the occurrence of deathbed visions. The majority of patients were not taking medication which could cause hallucinations. They also reported shared visions. In one well-documented case, a dying woman's deathbed apparition was seen by three relatives. Fifty to 60 percent of the patients who were conscious at the moment of death said they saw a vision of the afterlife.

As we have seen, pathological hallucinations can be caused by both mental and physical illnesses. But deathbed visions are not caused by brain disorders or mental illness. Should they even be called hallucinations?

Now that we know how common hallucinations are in the general population, and that they are not necessarily signs of psychosis, we can either restrict the use of the word "hallucination" to indicate psychosis, or we can broaden the definition to include both psychotic and non-psychotic phenomena such as "grief hallucinations."

There is a support group in the United Kingdom called Hearing Voices Network (HVN). It offers support and advocacy for people who hear voices. Not only persons with schizophrenia hear voices. People who are not psychotic can also hear voices, but many people who hear voices are too ashamed to admit that they hear voices. For example, hearing voices can be part of the narcoleptic syndrome, but even the narcoleptics who attended the support group Narcolepsy Network were reluctant to talk about their voices because of the stigma and the fear of being labelled crazy.

Religious Visions

Anthropologist T. M. Luhrmann studied the visions and voices of American evangelicals who claimed to have had direct communication with God as part of their religious experience. She expressed her distaste for the word *hallucination*, which she found patronizing and pathologizing. She preferred the term *sensory override*, that is to say, sensory perception overrides the material evidence in these cases. She wrote that 10 to 15 percent of the general population have had similar experiences. She herself once had a vision. She reported seeing six Druids looking at her through an upper-floor bedroom window while she was doing research for her dissertation on witches and warlocks in modern-day England.

Many religious traditions report direct communication with God and angels. In the Hebrew Bible, God spoke to Moses through the burning bush. In the Koran, the Archangel Gabriel spoke to Muhammad in a cave. Francis of Assisi and Joan of Arc (Jeanne d'Arc, the Maid of Orleans) are sainted and revered figures in the Catholic Church. They also heard voices. Joan heard a voice accompanied by a blinding white light in her father's garden when she was 13. She identified the voice as belonging to the Archangel Michael. But she wasn't canonized or burned at the stake as a heretic because of her voices. Her victory over the British Army in the latter part of the Hundred Years War led to her becoming the patron saint of France; her dressing as a man led to her death as a heretic, even though she said she dressed as a man in order to avoid being raped. Her voices happened, and they were accepted.

In *Fresh Verdicts on Joan of Arc*, de Vries wrote, "No person in the Middle Ages, male or female, has been the subject of more study." Joan's short life has been celebrated from the time of her death up to and including the present day in painting, sculpture, literature, television, movies, even video games. How could a young, uneducated, peasant girl from a small rural village lead the French Army to victory over the British Army during the Hundred Years War and then be burnt at the stake as a heretic? Some events are beyond our comprehension. Her followers would claim that she was divinely inspired.

St. Francis of Assisi, in whose honor Pope Francis named himself, is the patron saint of Italy. He also heard a voice. In his case, it was coming from a crucifix, telling him to rebuild the church. Once again, it is what he did after he heard the voice, not the voice itself, that was significant.

Should we say that St. Joan and St. Francis were psychotic and that they were hallucinating, or should we say they were divinely inspired figures of destiny? Or were they just ordinary people who rose to the occasion? In my opinion, they were far from ordinary.

A school of Jewish mysticism that flourished throughout the first millennium CE is called Merkabah or Chariot mysticism. It was based on Ezekiel's vision of God descending in a chariot. The fact that Ezekiel's vision of the destruction of Jerusalem in 586 BCE came to pass lent credibility to his vision and added to his reputation as a prophet. Ezekiel's vision is still well-known today. There is even a popular folk song about it, *Ezekiel Saw the Wheel*, which was recorded by Woody Guthrie and many others.

Hans Holbein the Younger, Daniel's Vision of the Four Beasts

Raphael, Ezekiel's Vision of the Chariot

Isaiah and Daniel also had visions. Daniel's vision came to him in a dream, known as "Daniel's Dream of Four Beasts." The four beasts were a lion with the wings of an eagle, a bear with three ribs in its mouth, a leopard with four wings and four heads, and a powerful, terrifying beast, with ten horns, teeth of iron and nails of brass (Daniel 7). The beasts have been interpreted by biblical scholars as referring to the four successive empires of Babylon, Media, Persia, and the Seleucid Greeks. Because of the symbolic nature of the dream, with each of the beasts representing a successive empire, Daniel's dream was thought to be prophetic. Of course, the dream is open to interpretation.

People often have visions and receive messages in their dreams. If visions occur in dreams, we can say that Joseph's famous "seven-lean-years" dream was also a vision. The reason that a "vision" in a dream is not just called a dream is that a vision has a different quality than a dream. Visions are much more vivid than dreams. Dreams are hazy affairs, easily forgotten. Visions stay with us forever. We have a number of dreams every night (whether we remember them or not); visions are few in number.

As in Daniel's case, visions are not always pleasant or benign. They can be very frightening. This is what Daniel said about his visions:

> As for me Daniel, my spirit was pained in the midst of my body and the visions of my head affrighted me (Daniel 7:15).

> And I Daniel fainted, and was sick certain days; then I rose up, and did the king's business; and I was appalled at the vision, but understood it not (Daniel 8:27).

If Daniel's visions were frightening, Isaiah's vision about Judah and Jerusalem at the "end of days" was the opposite. He famously wrote:

> And they shall beat their swords into plowshares,
> And their spears into pruning-hooks;
> Nation shall not lift up sword against nation,
> Neither shall they learn war any more (Isaiah 2:4).

Many of the visions of Biblical prophets inspired beautiful, dream-like works of art by artists such as Leonardo, Hans Holbein the Younger, Raphael, and Gustav Doré. Isaiah's vision was the basis for the pre-American Civil War gospel song "Down by the Riverside" (*I'm gonna lay down my sword and shield/ down by the riverside*, with the refrain *I ain't gonna study war no more*). This gospel song was an anti-war song during the Vietnam War era. No matter what we may think of them, Biblical prophecies and visions have staying power. They have been passed down from generation to generation for millennia.

The Impact of Dreams and Hallucinations

There is a difference between dreams and hallucinations. Dreams occur while we are asleep; hallucinations occur while we are awake. In a dream, the dreamer is usually part of the dream, knows the people in the dream, talks to them, and interacts with them. The dream may have a hidden meaning for the dreamer. Through conflation, metaphor, and symbolism, the dream may both reveal and conceal repressed hopes, feelings, wishes, and memories.

Psychotic visual hallucinations are usually of people and places one is not familiar with. One doesn't interact with them. One just watches them, sometimes with horror and sometimes with fascination. Psychotic auditory hallucinations are somewhat different in that persons with schizophrenia, for example, may be heard talking back to their voices, so there is interaction. There is also interaction in grief hallucinations, as the bereaved widow or widower will often talk to the image of the deceased spouse. Still, one does not assume the role of an actor in a play as one does in a dream.

Nowadays, instead of calling a person who has visions a prophet, we might call him or her a visionary, or we may offer a medical diagnosis. For example, Oliver Sacks said Joan of Arc might have been having epileptic seizures. Eric Altschuler, a neuroscientist at UC San Diego, said that Ezekiel is probably the oldest recorded case of temporal lobe epilepsy. While these claims are intriguing and may even be true, there is really no way of knowing for sure whether Joan and Ezekiel were mystics or epileptics or both. Even if they were epileptic, the diagnosis of epilepsy by itself cannot account for the huge and lasting impact they have had on society, history, religion, and culture, or why other such individuals similarly afflicted have not had similar impacts.

There has been a lot of speculation about Ezekiel's vision of the chariot. It has even been cited as evidence for the existence of UFOs in biblical times! Just the fact that we are still talking about Ezekiel's vision 2,700 years after the fact says something important. We pay attention to the power of visions and dreams. Sacks says that even if ecstatic or religious visions are caused by epilepsy, that fact alone would not diminish their meaning or value to the individual. Or, I would add, to society.

The great Russian novelist Fyodor Dostoevsky was called "Russia's great prophet." He was an epileptic who had seizures with ecstatic visions. As he got older, his novels became more mystical. He described his ecstatic seizures in several of his novels, including *The Brothers Karamazov*. Einstein once said, "Dostoevsky gives me more than any scientist." So, even a known epileptic, such as Dostoevsky, can be turned in a meaningful, spiritual direction by his experiences whether they are seizure-induced or not.

Whether Joan of Arc and Fyodor Dostoevsky were epileptic is beside the point because there is no denying that they accomplished some amazing feats during their lifetimes, and we should not fall into the trap of confusing the means with the end. There are millions of people with epilepsy, but how many have led armies while teenagers or written classics of world literature?

The Need to De-stigmatize

Just as there are people who can achieve transcendence or higher states of consciousness with the use of mind-altering drugs, whether sacramental or recreational, there are also many people, throughout history, who have had mystical, paranormal, and spiritual experiences as a result of meditation, prayer, and contemplation, or even spontaneously. My own experiences have been of the latter variety.

The late Dr. Oliver Sacks wrote:

> Many cultures regard hallucinations, like dreams, as a special, privileged state of consciousness – one that is actively sought through spiritual practices, meditation, drugs, or solitude. But in modern Western culture, hallucinations are more often considered to portend madness or something dire happening to the brain – even though the vast majority of hallucinations have no such dark implications. There is great stigma here, and patients are often reluctant to admit to hallucinating, afraid that their friends and even their doctors will think they are losing their minds.

Sacks concluded that hallucinations are an essential part of the human condition. While I endorse his wish to de-stigmatize hallucinations, there is no need to glamorize them. Hallucinations can be comforting and reassuring at times, but they can also be disturbing and frightening.

Just as it would be cruel to mock or ridicule someone who is psychotic or otherwise mentally ill, it is also cruel to ridicule people who have had paranormal experiences or to suggest that their experiences were not real or were pathological. It seems to me that some of the stigma which attaches to mental illness also attaches to paranormal experience; nevertheless, more and more well-educated, highly respected professionals are reporting paranormal experiences and are willing to talk about them and write about them, thereby normalizing paranormal phenomena.

Polls about the prevalence of paranormal phenomena have been very consistent over the past 60 years. In 1952, 155 students at Duke University were asked if they had ever left their bodies; 30 percent of the students said *yes*. Another survey showed that 5 percent of the general population had had an out-of-body experience. A 1979 survey found that two-thirds of college and university professors believed in ESP. A 1987 survey found that 67 percent of Americans said they had had psychic experiences. A 1990 Gallup poll showed that 93 percent of Americans believed in one or more paranormal phenomena, including ESP, telepathy and clairvoyance.

As these figures show, paranormal events are exceedingly common. They are not fringe phenomena. Yet people still don't want to talk about their own experiences for fear of being labeled weird or crazy. When the majority of the population has had a certain type of experience, that experience cannot be called abnormal. It is perfectly normal.

Visions, voices, and the sense of a presence are commonly seen in the general (non-clinical) population, but they cannot be taken in isolation as evidence of psychosis. Since many people are not comfortable with the word *paranormal* because of the stigma attached to that word, it may be preferable just to say what happened rather than attach a descriptive label to the event.

I would like to de-stigmatize both paranormal and psychotic phenomena, and help people distinguish between them. I look forward to the day when events that are now labelled "paranormal" will be seen as normal, when the word "psychotic" is used strictly as a medical diagnosis, not as an insult or a joke, and when people can talk freely about their mystical, paranormal, anomalous, and spiritual experiences without shame or fear of being judged.

Chapter 2: Near Death, Out of Body, After Death

There is a crack in everything / that's how the light gets in

—Leonard Cohen, "Anthem"

I grew up on the Prairies. Big Sky Country. It was idyllic – except that I almost died three times by the time I turned nine. The Angel of Death first came knocking when I was in the womb. My mother had a burst appendix when she was pregnant with me. My parents were living in a small town in northern Alberta, 400 miles north of Edmonton. After the tar sands were developed, Fort McMurray turned into a boomtown, but when my parents were living there, it was a tiny village with only a few hundred souls and one small hospital. Due to the urgency of the situation, there wasn't enough time to fly my mother down south to Edmonton for her operation. Since my father was the only doctor in town, he had to perform the appendectomy on my mother at the local hospital. There was no other option. St. Gabriel Hospital was a small Catholic hospital run entirely by nuns and priests. All of the nurses were nuns. My mother told me many years later that the nuns and priests were praying continuously throughout the surgery. Traditionally, Gabriel, for whom the hospital was named, is the archangel who gives us strength.

My next encounter with the Grim Reaper occurred in Detroit when I fell out of a car. Instead of going to the lake every summer, like a lot of my friends' families, my family took what we called in those days "motor trips." My father loved to drive. We drove through the Black Hills of South Dakota to see Mount Rushmore, to Yellowstone National Park to see "Old

Faithful", and to many towns and cities. When I was seven, we drove to Detroit to see the Ford motor factory. I was sitting in the front seat of my father's Pontiac when we went over a bump in the road, my knee hit the door handle, the door flew open, and, there being no seatbelts in those days, I fell out of the car. I was lucky not to be hit by another car. I ended up with a twisted ankle, but I could have easily been killed.

My close encounters continued apace. When I was eight, I went with my family to inspect the new house we were building. It sounds funny, but I really did slip on a banana peel someone had left on the floor. I tumbled into a closet, where my leg was cut by some rusty wire. Had I fallen the other way, I would have fallen ten feet onto a concrete floor, as the stairs to the basement had not yet been built. There was just a gaping hole where the stairs were supposed to go. Another close brush with death.

Such experiences continued into adulthood. Once, driving from Toronto to Niagara-on-the-Lake to see a play at the Shaw Festival, the last thing I remembered was listening to Simon and Garfunkel's "Cecilia" on the car radio. *Cecilia, you're breaking my heart/ you're shaking my confidence daily.* Next thing I knew, I was waking up in the back of an ambulance racing to the nearest hospital, in St. Catharines. I suffered a concussion and slept for a week. Another near-miss.

Another time, after moving to Winnipeg, there was another car accident. I was driving to the lake with my daughter and her husband, going 100 km an hour, when a car up ahead drove through a stop sign at an intersection. I had to swerve into the ditch to avoid a collision. After we pulled ourselves out of our vehicle, my son-in-law said to me, "Thanks for saving my life."

Although I was near death many times, I subsequently learned that near-ness to death does not equate with the term "near-death experience" as it is described in the literature. Saying "I almost died" is, of course, not quite the same as saying I actually died, was pronounced clinically dead, and was resuscitated... and, by the way, while I was dead I went to heaven and saw the angels. Experiences of that sort are now known as near-death experiences or NDEs. Although I have never had a classic near-death experience, I did have some of the same after-effects as described by NDE survivors: decreased fear of death, increased belief in an afterlife, increased spirituality, a sense of invulnerability, and a newfound respect for destiny.

I had chronic, lymphocytic leukemia for 16 years prior to a successful stem-cell transplant. My chronic illness presented me with many challenges. My life hung in the balance more than once. Throughout the many years of my illness, I always held onto the belief that I was going to get better. Although each of my many accidents was acutely traumatic, my chronic illness was more of a long-term struggle. Overall, however, the effects were cumulative.

In spite of my never having had a classic near-death experience, I can't help but think that my numerous close calls with death must have left their mark on me, especially those brushes with death that occurred at an early age. Ordinarily, young people don't think about death and dying. We all know we are going to die one day, but for most people, death is an abstraction. It remains so until it hits you over the head. Immortality has its charms; so does vulnerability.

In my case, repeated traumas led to anxiety, but they also heightened my interest in philosophy, psychology, metaphysics, mysticism, and spirituality. People who have been battered and shattered by life often want to believe that the world they see is not the only world, that there is another world, a better world. They like to think that their suffering was not in vain, and that they could learn and grow from their experiences, no matter how grim. I count myself among them.

What is a "Classic" Near-Death Experience?

The phrase "near-death experience" has taken on a life of its own. The term, and the acronym NDE, were coined in 1975 by Raymond Moody, a psychiatrist at the University of Virginia. Dr. Moody defined near-death experiences as "profound spiritual events that happen, uninvited, to some individuals at the point of death." The key word in this definition is *spiritual*. The NDE is a transformative, spiritual event. In *Life after Life*, Moody reported on his survey of 150 survivors of life-threatening accidents or illnesses who had been pronounced clinically dead. He found consistent elements in the accounts of patients who had returned from death's door.

Dr. Moody summarized his findings in a composite vignette, as follows:

The patient hears herself being pronounced dead by her doctor. She hears a loud buzzing noise and finds herself moving rapidly through a long, dark tunnel. Once she is out of her body, she watches the resuscitation attempt. She is greeted by the spirits of friends and relatives who have already died, and encounters a "being of light" who presents her with a panoramic playback of her life, the so-called "life review." She approaches a border beyond which she cannot go if she is to return to her body. She is consumed by intense feelings of peace and joy and she wishes to go the light, but she realizes her work is not yet done, it is not her time to die, so she reluctantly returns to her body.

Once the patient is back in her body, she tells people what happened to her, but she gets frustrated because she can't find the words to describe her experience. She discovers that people aren't that interested, so she stops talking about it. Still, she is profoundly affected by her experience. Her ideas about life and death have changed. She is no longer afraid to die, she finds renewed purpose in living, she becomes less materialistic and more spiritual, and she develops a belief in the afterlife.

Dr. Moody listed 15 common NDE elements, but not every person who reported an NDE experienced all of them. In fact, no one person had more than 12. Furthermore, no one element appeared in every account and no two accounts were exactly the same. Reports of NDEs have also featured cities of light, bewildered spirits, a feeling of cosmic unity, and a realm where all knowledge exists.

Moody listed four recurrent themes for NDE survivors: frustration upon relating the experience to others; deeper appreciation of life; elimination of death anxiety; and corroboration by independent observers of the out-of-body experience. An example of such corroboration would be if the NDE survivor left her body while being resuscitated and overheard a conversation between the doctor and the nurse while out of her body, then details of the overheard conversation were later confirmed by medical personnel involved in the resuscitation. Or if, while out of her body, she noticed a broken window or a missing shingle on the roof of the hospital, which was later confirmed.

Russell Noyes, another NDE researcher, also found that NDEs changed the attitudes of people who had them. In addition to reduced fear of death, reduction in anxiety, and increased meaning in life, NDE survivors developed a sense of invulnerability, feelings of special importance or destiny, reduction in addictions, and increased belief in an afterlife.

NDE survivors became more spiritual after the NDE, but that did not translate into greater church attendance. Rather, there was a general belief that no one religion was better than any other. There was an inward feeling of closeness to God, a greater awareness of God's presence, and an embrace of unconditional love and acceptance for others.

American psychologist Kenneth Ring, founding editor of the *Journal of Near Death Studies*, found that although religion did not account for or affect the development of NDEs, religious beliefs did influence the interpretation of the experience. Atheists reported NDEs just as often as religious people. Atheists became more spiritual but not more religious.

Ring, author of two major books on NDEs, was interviewed by journalist Pierre Jovanovic, author of *An Inquiry into the Existence of Guardian Angels*. Jovanovic asked Ring, "What is the state of your own spiritual life after all these NDEs?" "They've probably made me more spiritual," Ring said. "I'm Jewish but don't consider myself a practicing Jew. Religion is a doctrine, an institution where spiritual life is not put first. After the NDE, many people become extremely spiritual but not religious."

There has been an explosion of interest in the near-death experience in recent years. Accounts of near-death experiences are now commonplace, most likely because tens of thousands of people who were pronounced clinically dead have been resuscitated, thanks to advanced resuscitation techniques in modern medicine. NDEs have been reported throughout history, in every culture, but they are becoming much more frequent.

Since the 1970s, many NDE survivors have become best-selling authors. After Betty Eadie died from a post-surgical hemorrhage and was revived, she wrote her ground-breaking memoir *Embraced by the Light* (1973) in which she described how she left her body, saw three angelic beings, went to Heaven, and returned to her body after she was told it was not yet her time.

Another popular NDE book from the seventies was *Saved by the Light* by Dannion Brinkley, who woke up in a morgue 28 minutes after he had been killed by lightning. Like Eadie, Brinkley claimed to have visited the afterlife and to have seen angels. By 2013, books about NDEs had become so popular that the *New York Times* had three books on the topic on its bestseller list at the same time – *Proof of Heaven* (Eben Alexander), *Heaven is for Real* (Todd Burpo), and *Waking Up in Heaven* (Crystal McVea). *Heaven Is For Real* sold over ten million copies, was on the *New York Times* bestseller list for over a year, and was made into a big-budget movie starring Oscar-nominated actor Greg Kinnaer. *Waking Up in Heaven* sold 13 million copies and was also made into a movie, as was Don Piper's *90 Minutes in Heaven,* which sold over six million copies and remained on the *New York Times* bestseller list for more than five years.

In the book world, these sales are considered phenomenal, almost unheard of. The immense popularity of these and similar books tells us a great deal about the zeitgeist, the spirit of the times in which we live. It indicates a widespread hunger for spiritual knowledge and a great curiosity about what happens to us when we die.

Mary Neal is an orthopedic surgeon who died after a kayaking accident in Chile in 1999. Her bestselling memoir *To Heaven and Back* recounts her adventures in the afterlife. She also said she went to Heaven and saw angels. This is a very common theme in NDE survivors.

Dr. Neal was born into a Catholic family but she had converted to Mormonism prior to her near-death experience. After coming back from the other side, her attitude towards religion completely changed. She wrote that she was more accepting of all religions. She no longer believed there was only one true religion. This shift to a more loving, more accepting attitude to people of other faiths is common amongst NDE survivors.

Ben Breedlove (*When Will Heaven Begin?*) cheated death four times as a child before he finally expired on Christmas Day, 2011, at the tender age of 18. As a teenager, he became well known for his blogs on YouTube, in which he described his thoughts and feelings about life and death. He said that, as result of his NDEs, he wasn't sad or scared about dying, and he affirmed his belief in God, angels, and heaven.

In the 1990s, pediatrician Melvin Morse studied the deathbed visions of dying children. He, like Barrett, reported shared visions, when two or more people reported seeing the same thing. According to Morse, such shared visions undermine the idea that deathbed visions are pathological hallucinations.

Morse found that NDEs were reported by almost half of the children who survived critical illnesses. His study revealed that children have similar NDEs to adults, except in two particulars – they did not generally meet friends and family members who had died (presumably because their family and friends were still alive) and they did not report a life review. One child who was brought back from the brink of death described a conversation he had with his brother on the other side. The boy had not been told his brother had died in the same car accident in which he had been severely injured, so his parents and doctors were astonished when he recounted what had happened to him while he was out of his body.

It has been suggested that NDEs are caused by cerebral anoxia, or lack of oxygen to the brain. Pim van Lommel and his colleagues in the Netherlands did a prospective study of 344 consecutive patients who were resuscitated after a cardiac arrest. They found that 62 patients (18 percent) reported near-death experiences. Van Lommel said that if NDEs could be attributed to cerebral anoxia, then most of the patients who clinically died from cardiac arrest and were resuscitated should report NDEs, not just a small percentage.

Researchers have found that the occurrence of NDEs is not related to the duration of unconsciousness, medication, lack of oxygen to the brain, prior fear of death, religious affiliation, or beliefs.

Near-death experiences have been likened to mystical or spiritual experiences, with which they have many features in common. In his 1902 book *The Varieties of Religious Experience*, William James proposed four major components of the mystical experience, as follows:

1. The person doesn't have the words to describe the experience; any description is, at best, an approximation. The experience is "ineffable."

2. The experience leads to a sudden insight/revelation into the meaning of life. This attribute is called "noetic" (derived from the Greek word for understanding).

3. The experience is short-lived but has a lasting, lifetime influence.

4. The mystic feels passive, as if he or she is not in control of the experience.

As Moody and others have reported, these descriptions could also apply to people who have had near-death experiences. In *The Way of the Explorer*, Apollo astronaut Edgar Mitchell compared the ineffable nature of a spiritually transformative experience to "the peace which passeth all understanding." (Philippians 4:7).

Robert K. C. Forman, who was Professor of Religious Studies at City University of New York and co-editor of the *Journal of Consciousness Studies*, identified what he called a Pure Consciousness Event, which he said was common to all mystical experiences. He wrote that having an experience and reading about it or learning about it later does not mean that the learning caused the experience; to think that way would be to commit a logical error known as *post hoc ergo propter hoc* ("after this therefore because of this").

Protestant theologian Judith Cressy compared NDEs to the experiences of the medieval mystics St. Theresa of Avila and St. John of the Cross. She noted that they shared ecstatic out-of-body travel, clairvoyance, loss of fear of death, visions of God, and healing transformations.

British theologian Paul Badham said the NDE is comparable to the deepest religious experience known to humanity and that modern resuscitation techniques have made available to many people a form of mystical enlightenment that was previously available only to a select few.

One way the NDE differs from the mystical experience is that the NDE arrives unheralded. It is not sought out. The mystic seeks a mystical experience through prayer, fasting, meditation, ritual, or hallucinogenic drugs, such as peyote or ayahuasca. Near-death-experience survivors, on the other hand, have had spiritual awareness thrust upon them without any preparation and they are returned to a society where such experiences are generally not valued or even, in most cases, believed.

Bruce Greyson, a Professor of Psychiatry at the University of Virginia, is known as the father of NDE research. He observed that, although the term *near-death experience* was coined in 1975, the phenomenon was well-known long before that date. He found reports of similar events in the folklore of European, Middle Eastern, Indian, East Asian, African, Native American, and Pacific cultures.

There have been many reports of NDEs in world literature, memoirs, and narrative reports. In Charles Dickens's *A Christmas Carol,* Ebenezer Scrooge underwent what sounded like a near-death experience. He was visited by four spirits, had a life review, and returned to his life determined to be a better person. After his encounters with the ghost of his old business partner and the ghosts of Christmas past, present, and future, his interests shifted from accumulating wealth to being of service.

Written in 1843, *A Christmas Carol* is, by far, Dickens's most popular novel. It has maintained its popularity for almost two hundred years. From theatre to movies, dance, public readings, radio, television, recordings, graphic novels, and school plays, *A Christmas Carol* has become ubiquitous. There have been countless adaptations, including movies, in 1935, 1951 (Alastair Sim), 1970 (Albert Finney), 1984, 1988 (Bill Murray in *Scrooged*), 2013, an animated movie (1984), a TV movie (1999), a 3D-animated movie (2009), *Mickey's Christmas Carol, The Muppet's Christmas Carol*, and on and on. There have been numerous theatrical adaptations, including a stage musical (1994) and stage readings by such prominent actors as Patrick Stewart.

Regional theatres, such as the Guthrie Theatre in Minneapolis, stage *A Christmas Carol* as an annual event. It is just as much a Christmas tradition as *The Nutcracker* ballet. When I was eight, I played the role of Tiny Tim in my elementary school production. Whatever the format, people just can't seem to get enough of it. Ebenezer Scrooge's journey from materialism to spirituality has had enduring appeal, from generation to generation, and there is no end in sight.

Although Scrooge's transformation was a work of fiction, there have been many similar factual accounts. In 1865, British surgeon Sir Benjamin Brodie described the spiritual transformation of a sailor who was rescued from near drowning. Upon his recovery, the sailor said he had been in heaven and he complained bitterly about having been rescued. His fellow sailors noticed a complete transformation in his character after he was rescued. He changed from being an ill-tempered person, who was very hard to get along with, to being one of the most well-loved and best-behaved sailors on the ship.

Albert von St. Gallen Heim (1849–1937) was a Swiss geology profes-sor in Zurich. After a fall while climbing the Alps, he had a near-death experience. In 1892, he published a collection of the experiences of fellow mountain climbers who had fallen in the Alps, workers who had fallen off scaffolds, soldiers wounded on the battlefield, and individuals who had barely survived near-drowning. It was the first modern-day account of NDEs. *Remarks on Fatal Falls* was translated into English in 1972 by Russell Noyes and Roy Kletti. All of Heim's fall victims reported that there was life after death.

One of Heim's students at the Zurich Polytechnic Institute was Albert Einstein. Two years before his death, Einstein wrote Heim a letter telling him that his lectures were "magical." He must have been intrigued by Heim's report that during his NDE time slowed down because, as we know, Einstein later postulated that what he called "spacetime" time was plastic and elastic. He correctly predicted the existence of gravitational waves, which are ripples in spacetime, a century before they were detected.

Ring also reported time distortions in NDE survivors. Only 2 percent experienced time as normal; 6 percent experienced time as extended; a large majority, 65 percent, said they had no sense of time.

A curious phenomenon related to NDEs is the reporting of visions by patients who were blind at the time. Kenneth Ring reported that 15 out of 21 blind patients who had NDEs reported fully sighted visions. Some of these patients had been blind since birth. Their visions were very similar to those reported by sighted patients. Although skeptical at first, thinking that these visions were merely dreams or the retrospective reconstruction of past events, Ring eventually found that there were clear features of the reports that could be confirmed as veridical, or verifiable, perception.

For example, a blind post-surgical patient who had an NDE was able to describe the color and the pattern of the tie his surgeon was wearing during the operation. Another patient also reported leaving her body during surgery. When she awoke from the anesthetic in the Recovery Room, she said that during surgery she had visited her sister who was in a diabetic coma in another ward. She told her nurse that her sister had died while she was there and she gave the nurse the exact time of her sister's death. Her nurse called the sister's ward and, to her amazement, confirmed the sister's death and the time of death. These reports, while anecdotal, are veridical perceptions associated with near-death and out-of-body experiences.

Dr. Sam Parnia, a critical care doctor, reported the case of a Dutch patient who had an out-of-body experience during cardiac resuscitation. When he was resuscitated, his nurses were unable to find his false teeth, which had been removed after his cardiac arrest. The revived patient told the nurses where to look for them, saying that he had left his body and had watched everything from above during the resuscitation, including where the nurse had put his dentures. This would be another example of corroboration or validation.

There has been some confusion in the NDE literature about the definition of death, as some researchers use cardiac arrest as a criterion to define death, while others use brain death. Merriam Webster defines "death" as "the irreversible cessation of all vital functions especially as indicated by permanent stoppage of the heart, respiration, and brain activity." In other words, the heart stops beating, the person stops breathing, and the EEG is flat, indicating a lack of electrical activity in the brain. The key words in this definition are "irreversible" and "permanent."

There is a problem with this definition, however. There is a folk wisdom that says, "If it walks like a duck and quacks like a duck, it probably is a duck." If a physician sees someone who has stopped breathing and whose heart has stopped beating, he will likely pronounce that person dead, once resuscitation attempts have failed or if resuscitation is not possible.

Most people who die are not hooked up to an EEG so we don't really know if their EEG is flat. Also, most people die outside of hospital and are not resuscitated. The above definition would require us to conclude that the dead person was not really dead if he or she woke up, such as the man who was struck by lightning then woke up in the morgue after being pronounced dead. But this would be post-hoc revisionism of the definition. It is a logical fallacy. In any case, the subject matter of NDE is called "near-death" not "post-death."

While the case of the Dutch patient reported by Parnia involved a person who had a cardiac arrest, NDEs have also been reported when the patient was brain-dead and the EEG was flat. These patients reported in vivid detail things that they saw or that happened while they were clinically dead. These reports were also veridical. Some persons with a skeptical bent may say that patients with NDEs are dreaming or hallucinating, but dreams and hallucinations are not possible when a person's EEG is flat and there is no brain activity.

There is a continuum between near-death experiences, out-of-body experience, deathbed visions, and communication with spirits. Some people claim to have the ability to communicate with discarnate entities. As discussed in the previous chapter, it is not at all unusual for bereaved spouses or parents to see visions or hear voices of their deceased loved ones.

After-death communication (ADC) can occur randomly and spontaneously, but it can also be guided or mediated. Psychotherapist Allan Botkin has developed a technique to induce after-death communication in his grieving clients. He uses ADC to help his clients deal with grief and trauma. He claims that ADC can be induced in the great majority of people if they are willing to try his protocol.

In her 1969 bestseller *On Death and Dying,* Swiss-American psychiatrist Dr. Elisabeth Kübler-Ross (1926–2004) pioneered the field of thanatology, the scientific study of death. At the time her book was published, doctors often wouldn't tell their patients they had cancer or that they were dying. The doctors would tell family members, but not the patients themselves because they thought the knowledge of their imminent death would be too upsetting for the patients. It was Kübler-Ross who got doctors to talk with their patients about death and dying, so we owe her a debt of gratitude.

As a resident, Kübler-Ross was appalled by the way dying patients were treated. She was instrumental in starting the hospice movement and in getting doctors to talk to their patients, not just to the relatives. Her description of the five stages of grief in dying patients – denial, anger, bargaining, depression, and acceptance – became well-known. She worked tirelessly with thousands of dying patients. Like many physicians, she was initially skeptical about anything to do with the afterlife; however, over the course of her career she collected 20,000 anecdotes of near-death experiences, and she became convinced of the reality of NDEs and the immortality of the soul. Even though she had received more than twenty honorary doctorates and was widely admired and respected, when she started to talk about NDEs, many of her colleagues thought she had lost her mind.

In her research on NDEs, she reported startling similarities across age groups and across cultures. The reports almost always included tales of being greeted by a white light and by deceased relatives. There was usually a tunnel which one was supposed to go through towards the light, and there was a feeling of bliss and unconditional love. Her description of her patients' reports of their NDEs matched very closely the results of Moody's study.

Anthropologist Christopher Carr did cross-cultural studies on NDEs. He explored the similarities and differences in the death process and near-death experience in Tibetan Buddhist and Euro-American Christian culture. He concluded that, in both cultures, NDEs provided opportunities for learning and growth, not only for the patients but also for family members and health-care providers, who reap the benefits of the NDE, the greatest of which is learning to overcome the fear of death. As a rule, NDE survivors and their families are no longer afraid to die. As we have seen, NDE survivors tend to have a renewed sense of meaning and purpose in life. They become less materialistic, more spiritual, and more altruistic.

Although the great majority of NDEs are described as peaceful, even joyful, there has been the odd report of a disturbing NDE. One of the best-known accounts of a frightening NDE was Howard Storm's description of his encounter with an evil spirit in his memoir *My Descent into Death: A Second Chance in Life*. Prior to his NDE he was an atheist; post-NDE he became a Christian pastor.

As for why certain people have frightening experiences while others feel peaceful and surrounded by love, Melvin Morse thinks our end-game is a reflection of how we lived our lives, the way we played the game. He cited a very scary NDE in a patient who had been a violent criminal throughout his life. This man died the way he lived. He lived in fear and he died in fear.

As Paul McCartney wrote in his song "The End",

And in the end, the love you take is equal to the love you make.

Moody estimated that 1 in 30 Americans either has had a near-death experience or knows someone who has had one; however, not everyone who was near death reported a classic near-death experience. The best estimate of prevalence is about 20 to 40 percent. It has been suggested that the figure isn't higher because most hospital patients are heavily medicated. Either they don't have the experience, they have the experience but don't remember it, or they don't want to talk about it because they can't find the words or else they fear being labeled crazy.

As discussed in the section on Deathbed Visions, patients who are not on medication and are not confused are more likely to report "visits" from deceased relatives, so it seems likely the same factors would be involved in patients who report NDEs. Since NDE skeptics claim that death-bed or near-death visions are due to side effects of medication, the fact that unmedicated patients are more likely to have visions undermines their argument.

If 20 to 40 percent of patients who are near death report a near-death experience, this means that the majority of patients who are resuscitated or return from the brink of death do not actually report the classic near-death experience, with the white light, the tunnel, spiritual beings, etc. This fact may account for the great deal of skepticism that surrounds near-death experience.

There may be, for many people, an inherent bias against anything to do with the paranormal. With or without any evidence, some people take the attitude, "My mind's made up. Don't confuse me with the facts." Even without this bias, however, the classic near-death experience is going to be outside of most people's experience, and that includes most attending physicians.

Other Out-of-Body Experiences

Patients with NDEs usually report out-of-body experiences (OBEs), but one does not need to be near death to be out-of-body. Only a minority of out-of-body experiences occur when one is near death. OBEs can also occur during surgery, under anesthesia; during sleep, while dreaming; during meditation; or while in a hypnotic trance. Out-of-body experiences can be spontaneous, guided, or drug-induced.

When I was in my twenties and a psychiatric resident at McGill, I did have an OBE when I was lying in bed one night in my apartment in Montréal. I was fully awake when I noticed that I was floating near the ceiling, looking down on my body in bed. It felt very strange. I wasn't at all frightened. I was just curious. What was going on? I really didn't know anything about OBEs at the time. I had not been reading about them or studying them. I didn't know anyone who had had one. I didn't even know such a thing was possible.

I later learned that the term *out-of-body experience* was introduced by George N. M. Tyrell in 1943 in his book *Apparitions*. The phrase was presented as a belief-free alternative to terms such as *astral travel, astral projection, soul travel,* or *soul walking. Astral projection,* the favored terminology in esoteric literature, has been known throughout human history, both in ancient and modern civilizations.

I eventually met other people who had had similar experiences, and I learned that OBEs are surprisingly common. It has been estimated in various studies that 10 to 20 percent of the world population has had an OBE. The figure rises to 25 percent among students.

In her ground-breaking book *The Enigma of Out-of-Body Travel* (1965) Susy Smith documented hundreds of case histories of people who reported out-of-body travel, including Goethe, Ernest Hemingway, and Carl Jung. In 1968, British philosopher Celia Green published her analysis of 400 first-hand accounts of OBEs. Robert Monroe, founder of The Monroe Institute and consciousness researcher, popularized the acronym OBE in his 1971 book *Journeys Out of the Body.*

The effect of an OBE can be profound and long-lasting. Diane Morrissey is a hypnotherapist who became psychic and started seeing auras after she had an out-of-body/near-death experience due to an accidental electrocution. She was clinically dead for 35 minutes. After she was revived and had recovered, she started giving lectures and leading workshops based on what she had learned about NDEs, OBEs, and life after death. Over the course of many years, she successfully taught more than 25,000 people how to leave their bodies during sleep.

Whether OBEs are spontaneous or induced, the effects are the same. In *Hallucinations*, Oliver Sacks described a patient who had an OBE during an epileptic seizure. Although in this case the cause was clearly organic, due to a brain disorder, the patient, in his own words, subsequently became "more spiritual, more creative, [and] more artistic."

Pioneering neurosurgeon Wilder Penfield, the father of modern neuroscience, was able to induce out-of-body experiences in his subjects by electrically stimulating the right temporal cortex. However, the fact that electrical stimulation of the right temporal cortex can produce an OBE which may be accompanied by a spiritual feeling of cosmic consciousness does not invalidate the reality of the experience itself. Our view of a beautiful sunset is processed by the visual system, including the eyes and the visual cortex in the occipital lobes of the brain, but that does not mean that the sunset arises from the occipital lobes. In other words, finding the area of the brain which processes an experience does not in any way invalidate or detract from the effects or the value of the experience.

In a similar vein, OBEs can also be induced by certain drugs. Ketamine is a dissociative anesthetic, as are PCP (phencyclidine or "angel dust") and DXM (dextromethorphan or cough syrup). These drugs can cause users to feel like they are floating and are far from their bodies. Ketamine used as a street drug is called "K" or "Special K." When users leave their bodies, the experience is referred to as "entering a K-hole."

There has been a great deal of effort spent trying to explain away NDEs and OBEs on a neurological basis. Whatever the brain function or dysfunction at the time these events occur, we should not accept strictly materialist explanations without looking at the metaphysical and teleological issues. It is clearly the interpretation of the event, rather than the event itself, that has the greatest impact on the individual.

In *Does the Soul Survive?* Rabbi Elie Kaplan Spitz wrote, "Near-death experiences point to another realm of awareness that transcends the body and the five senses, a dimension of existence that we identify with soul." Behaviorists, materialists, and reductionists will not accept a non-physical explanation for near-death experience, out-of-body experience, and after-death communication, even after all physical and materialist explanations have been found wanting.

For myself, I often wondered why I had no fear when I left my body. I think it was probably because, in retrospect, I resonated with the words of Ram Dass as related in his book *Still Here*. When he was asked about his stroke, he said, "I didn't have a stroke. My body had a stroke." If one doesn't identify with one's body or one's mind or one's personality, if one is not limited by self-centered beliefs and judgments, one is free to contemplate the mysteries of the universe on a much grander scale, and one can take a step away from fear, especially the fear of death.

Chapter 3: Between Skepticism and Belief

There are two ways to be fooled. One is to believe what isn't true; the other is to refuse to believe what is true.

—Soren Kierkegaard, Danish existential philosopher (1813–1855)

Bertrand Russell, British philosopher, atheist, and skeptic of the first order wrote in *Sceptical Essays* (1928) that while William James, the father of American psychology, preached the "will to believe," he preferred the "will to doubt." A skeptic can become a believer and vice versa. These categories are flexible, not hard and fast. One can go back and forth between skepticism and belief; one can also have shades of grey. One can be somewhat skeptical. Nevertheless, with respect to the paranormal events I discuss in this book, people have tended to fall into one camp or the other. In this chapter, I take a look at these two positions and suggest a more nuanced, respectful approach.

The Skeptics

Modern-day skeptics who dismiss or disparage anything seen as paranormal include many magicians and illusionists. Magician and escape artist Randall James Hamilton Zwinge ("The Amazing Randi") was born in Toronto in 1928. In order to expose paranormal fraud, he offered a $1-million reward for anyone who could offer scientific evidence of the paranormal. The reward remained unclaimed; however, the million-dollar reward has been dismissed as nothing but a publicity stunt, since Randi turned away several applicants and refused third-party mediation.

Randi does not like to be called a "debunker" because he says he keeps an open mind and is willing to be convinced he is wrong about the paranormal. He prefers to be called a scientific investigator. A feature documentary about Randi, called *An Honest Liar,* was released in 2014. The James Randi Educational Foundation sponsors a multi-author blog called *Science-Based Medicine*, which I found informative and worth reading. It features bloggers who are health-care consumers and health-care providers.

In a counter-challenge to Randi, Deepak Chopra released a YouTube video in which he offered $1-million to Randi or any of the other professional debunkers or investigators. He said to them, in effect, before you go around debunking paranormal phenomena, why don't you try to explain normal phenomena. He challenged his critics to explain how electrical activity in the brain translates into the experience of a three-dimensional world. He said that although neurological correlates of consciousness are well known, they cannot explain such things as thought, intuition, insight, self-reflection, creativity, or intention. He stressed that neural correlates are not causation. He called Randi and other debunkers naïve realists and self-appointed vigilantes for the suppression of curiosity.

Randi followed in the footsteps of another famous debunker, the great Hungarian-American illusionist Harry Houdini (1874–1926), who despised frauds, whether they were spiritualists, mediums, or magicians. In *A Magician among the Spirits* (1924), he attempted to debunk fakery in all its forms. He attended séances in disguise, accompanied by a reporter and a police officer.

Houdini was a member of a *Scientific American* committee that offered a $10,000 cash prize to anyone who demonstrated paranormal abilities. The prize money was never claimed. After his mother's death, he visited various mediums hoping to make contact with his mother's spirit. His failure to do so fanned the flames of his strong desire to expose fakes and charlatans who preyed on bereaved survivors, such as himself.

Penn and Teller are also famous magicians who joined the ranks of Houdini, Randi, and other conjurers who in their later years became known as debunkers. They initially entertained people with their magic tricks, but later in life they became appalled by people's gullibility.

British psychologist Richard Wiseman made a career of debunking paranormal claims. His book *Paranormality: Why We See What Isn't There* skewered bogus claims of psychic abilities. He said that many people have had the experience of thinking of someone and then the phone rings and it was the person they were thinking of, so they think they must be psychic, but they don't think of all the other times when they were thinking of a person and that person didn't call, or when someone called and they hadn't been thinking of that person. Similarly, when people have dreams that turn out to be true, they don't think of all their dreams that didn't turn out to be true.

I consider that a logical error because you can't prove a positive with a negative. One vivid dream which correctly predicts a future event is a lot more compelling than one hundred dreams which don't turn out to be true. Just because an event is rare does not mean it is not valuable. Quite the contrary. Rare jewels are more valuable than common ones. And a psychic who finds a missing child is worth her weight in gold.

Many of the famous debunkers who were skeptical of paranormal claims never had any personal experience of the paranormal themselves to challenge their argument. Experience changes everything. Wiseman cited surveys which reported that 10 to 20 percent of the population have had an out-of-body experience, but he never had one himself. Consequently, he could not imagine how such a thing felt, and he could not begin to understand the profound impact an out-of-body experience could have on a person. His explanation of out-of-body experience is that the brain is playing tricks on the mind. While it is true that OBEs can be brought on by certain drugs, such as ketamine, or by electrical stimulation of the temporal lobe, they can also arise spontaneously. Whatever the cause, the phenomenology remains the same.

Wiseman cited studies that showed that individuals who saw shapes in clouds or in Rorschach inkblots were more likely to see patterns in seemingly unrelated events. These personality traits could lead to creativity, gullibility, or both, as well as an interest in paranormal phenomena. However, the ability to see patterns is far from pathological; it is quintessentially human.

It has been said that a magician can fool a scientist, but he cannot fool another magician. Both Randi and Wiseman started their careers as stage magicians. Experts at illusion and sleight-of-hand themselves, they turned their attention to exposing fraud and deception in others. Wiseman quoted P.T. Barnum: "There's one [sucker] born every minute." Wiseman saw people who believed in the paranormal as suckers, easily deceived. Yet his anti-paranormal arguments are half-baked. For example, he downplays telepathy between twins, saying it doesn't exist, and if twins have similar thoughts and behaviors, it is because they were raised together. His theory cannot account for documented cases of telepathy between twins who were raised apart or telepathy between married couples.

The 19th-century American physician Duncan MacDougall devised experiments which purported to show that the human soul weighed 21 grams. This idea was referenced in the 2003 movie *21 Grams* which starred Sean Penn and Naomi Watts. MacDougall weighed his subjects before and after death, using patients who were moribund. Describing MacDougall's experiments, Wiseman wrote, "When each patient looked like they were just about to pop their clogs…"

Most people consider death a solemn occasion, not an opportunity for mirth or hilarity. While Dr. McDougall's experiments may seem silly to us today, Wiseman's use of the phrase "pop their clogs" betrays an attitude which seems disrespectful to human beings who are about to die. There is a difference between a light-hearted, irreverent approach and mean-spirited ridicule. It is easy to ridicule certain beliefs. After all, one-third of Americans believed that the results of the 2013 Super Bowl would be determined by God. Still, I think we should try to be respectful of people even if we don't agree with their beliefs.

Wiseman was certainly not the only one to engage in putdowns and ridicule of beliefs and believers. In the early 21st century, Daniel Dennett (*Breaking the Spell*), Richard Dawkins (*The God Delusion*), Sam Harris (*Letter to a Christian Nation, The End of Faith*), and the late Christopher Hitchens (*God Is Not Great*) were all bestselling authors and public figures collectively known as the New Atheists or the Four Horsemen of New Atheism. As a group, they reveled in mockery. Ridicule was their stock-in-trade.

Secular humanism has been called atheism's kinder, gentler cousin. It rejects religion, superstition, and the supernatural in favor of ethics based on reason, naturalistic philosophy, commitment to science, and a spirit of free inquiry. It would appear to be more inclusive, accepting, and nonjudgmental than the ethos displayed by the New Atheists.

Nevertheless, we cannot disregard the views of skeptics, regardless of their tone or demeanor. I think it is good to be skeptical, in general, and of paranormal claims in particular, but skepticism can easily turn into scorn and contempt for people whose only crime may be that they are naïve and gullible or in need of some comfort and compassion following the death of a loved one.

Not all paranormal claims are based on provable phenomena. Many are based on personal experiences, which cannot be verified or replicated. We should all have a healthy dose of skepticism, but we should at the same time try to avoid cynicism. Cynics generally believe that people are selfish and dishonest. As a rule, cynics are not happy people. They are often bitter, caustic, and sarcastic.

The essence of skepticism is doubt. Skeptics not only doubt the theory, they demand to see the evidence for the theory, and they doubt the trustworthiness of the evidence. I am all in favor of questioning both evidence and theories.

Michael Shermer was a skeptic *par excellence*. Founder of the Skeptics Society and *Skeptic* magazine, he was one of the world's best-known skeptics. He was inspired by the philosopher Paul Kurtz (1925–2012), who was known as the father of secular humanism. In 1976, Kurtz started the

Committee for the Scientific Investigation of Claims of the Paranormal (CSICOP). Craig Weiler pointed out that CSICOP was not a scientific organization and it did not do investigations. It seemed to exist mainly as a vehicle to vilify parapsychology.

CSICOP morphed into the Committee for Skeptical Inquiry (CSI), which published the magazine *The Skeptical Inquirer*. In "A Skeptical Manifesto," Shermer wrote, "All facts in science are provisional and subject to challenge, therefore skepticism is a method leading to provisional conclusions.... The key to skepticism is to continuously and vigorously apply the methods of science to navigate the treacherous straits between 'know nothing' skepticism and 'anything goes' credulity."

Shermer was warning against taking an extreme position, and I would agree with him on that point. When he gave a TED talk "Why people believe weird things" in February 2006, he talked about crop circles, UFOs, and aliens. He gave simple explanations, arguing that humans are pattern-seekers who make perceptual and cognitive errors. In his presentation, however, he picked on easy targets, like people who see the face of Jesus in a grilled-cheese sandwich. He said that he didn't mind being called a debunker because there was a lot of bunk out there. Just like the New Atheists, he used ridicule to put down believers. He invited us to laugh along with him at these poor misguided souls. Yet he himself was later to experience a severe challenge to his skepticism – on his wedding day no less!

Shermer married a woman from Germany. They were to be married at their home in Los Angeles. On their wedding day, his bride was missing her family and wishing her grandfather could be there to give her away. As the ceremony was about to begin, everybody heard music coming from the bedroom. They traced it to a chest of drawers. Shoved to the back of the bottom drawer was her late grandfather's broken transistor radio, playing a romantic love song. They had previously tried many times to fix this radio, to no avail. Hearing the romantic music coming from her grandfather's radio, Shermer's bride felt that her grandfather was with her and was giving his approval to her wedding. The radio stopped playing the day after the wedding and never worked again.

Shermer published an account of this event in the *Scientific American*, June 25, 2014, under the title "Anomalous Events That Can Shake One's Skepticism to the Core." In his article, aside from referring to these events as "anomalous," he also used words like "paranormal" and "supernatural." He wrote, "We should not shut the doors of perception when they may be open to us."

He stressed the importance of the emotional significance of such events, regardless of the cause. When the founder of the Skeptics Society suggests we should "keep an open mind" and "marvel in the mysterious," we need to take his words seriously. I admire his honesty and his willingness to be open to new data.

His use of the phrase "the doors of perception" was clearly a reference to Aldous Huxley's well-known 1954 essay "The Doors of Perception," in which Huxley described his experience with mescaline. Huxley's title harkened back to an even earlier reference, William Blake's 1793 poem, "The Marriage of Heaven and Hell," in which Blake wrote:

> If the doors of perception were cleansed everything would
> appear to man as it is, Infinite. For man has closed himself
> up, till he sees all things thro' narrow chinks of his cavern.

Shermer is not the only prominent skeptic whose skepticism was challenged to the core by personal experience. Barbara Ehrenreich is a bestselling author, scientist, rationalist, and atheist who published her long-secret account of a mysterious event that occurred when she was 17. In her 2014 book *Living with A Wild God: A Non-Believer's Search for the Truth about Everything*, Ehrenreich shared an experience in which everything she looked at was consumed by fire. She compared her experience to the Biblical story of Moses and the Burning Bush. She wrote:

> It was a furious encounter with a living substance that was
> coming at me through all things at once, and one reason
> for the terrible wordlessness of the experience is that you
> cannot observe fire really closely without becoming part
> of it.

Like most people who have had spiritually transformative experiences, Ehrenreich did not have the words to describe her feelings. She ended up using the only word that applied: ineffable.

> If there are no words for it, then don't say anything about it. Otherwise you risk slopping into 'spirituality,' which is, in addition to being a crime against reason, of no more interest to other people than your dreams.

In an interview, she confirmed that she is still an atheist. She said that, as a scientist, she didn't believe in belief. "The whole idea of belief," she said, "is wrong: don't believe – find out, know."

Although Ehrenreich said she had no words to describe her experience, she ended up, after many years, writing a whole book about it. Her experience ate away at her, and she had to get it out. Perhaps she was being disingenuous when she used the word "ineffable." In any case, like most scientists, she expressed an aversion to the concept of spirituality, which she called "a crime against reason." It's a pity, really, that the word "spiritual" carries such heavy baggage in our modern Western society. In my opinion, we need to be able to appreciate experience for what it is, the thing in and of itself, and if someone wants to call an experience mystical or spiritual, in order to express the profound joy, wonder, and awe of the occasion, so be it. No need to recoil in horror.

Just a word about the word *ineffable*, since it is often invoked when people try to describe paranormal experiences, whether near-death experience, out-of-body experience, or any strange, anomalous event. To use an analogy, we can say it is somewhat similar to trying to describe the feeling of falling in love to someone who has never been in love. We can describe our thoughts and our behaviors but find it difficult to find the words to describe our feelings. All attempts fall short. It is like trying to describe the beauty of a sunset. As we flail around trying to find the right word, we don't need to disparage other people's choice of words, even though they may not exactly line up with our own way of thinking.

Susan Blackmore is a well-known British skeptic and psychologist. After 30 years of experiments trying to prove various aspects of parapsychology, she threw in the towel and became a skeptic, indeed a leading spokesperson for the skeptical movement. Although she herself had an out-of-body experience, she was not swayed in her materialist beliefs.

She cited various explanations for events that occur during OBEs and NDEs. She included: "information available at the time, prior knowledge, fantasy or dreams, lucky guesses, and information from the remaining senses." She called near-death experiences and deathbed visions the hallucinations of a dying brain. Her decision to switch camps, from believer to skeptic, was partly because her description of what she saw when she was out of her body was not completely accurate. She saw colors on the roofs of the adjacent building, but the colors she reported were not the right ones. This discrepancy seemed to me to be a minor objection.

Michael Talbot explained this phenomenon in *The Holographic Universe*. He wrote:

> Despite the accuracy of the observations made by talented out-of-body travelers during their disembodied jaunts, researchers have long been troubled by some of the glaring inaccuracies that crop up as well. In terms of the holographic idea, one explanation may be that such out of-body travelers have not yet fully developed the ability to convert the frequencies they perceive while in a disembodied state into a completely accurate holographic representation of consensus reality. In other words, since [they] appear to be relying on a completely new set of senses, these senses may still be wobbly and not yet proficient at the art of converting the frequency domain into a seemingly objective construct of reality.

Dean Radin has pointed out that 5 of the 19 experiments Blackmore designed to test psychic phenomena for her doctoral dissertation achieved statistical significance. The odds against chance for this to happen were 500 to 1. He said that no one should expect every experiment to be successful, and if a major league baseball player like Mickey Mantle can be considered a superstar with a lifetime batting average of .298, why should a parapsychology researcher be held to higher standards?

Blackmore is probably the only person to have belonged to both the Society for Psychical Research (SPR) and the Committee for Skeptical Inquiry (CSI). Having attended both organizations' conferences and meetings, she wryly observed that believers had better parties than the skeptics. I wonder why.

Radin divided parapsychologists into three categories: scientists, who do experiments and are interested in theoretical issues; scholars, who are mainly interested in historical, philosophical issues; and therapists, who deal with the associated mental health issues. These categories are not mutually exclusive.

The Society for Psychical Research was founded in London in 1882. It had a very illustrious membership. Presidents of the Society included three Nobel laureates; a future prime minister, Arthur Balfour; great scientists, such as Sir William Crookes, who discovered the chemical element thallium; Sir J. J. Thomson, discoverer of the electron; and brilliant academics from Harvard University, such as William James and Gardner Murphy, who had the distinction of being both the President of the American Psychological Association and the President of the British Society for Psychical Research.

The American Society for Psychical Research (ASPR) was founded in 1885 by William James and others. As with its predecessor, the British SPR, there were many distinguished scientists and scholars who belonged to the organization. Both Freud and Jung were honorary members. ASPR's mandate was to do scientific research and provide educational services in the form of lectures, conferences, and information for the public. With offices in New York, the ASPR is a non-profit, tax-exempt organization that has served the public, as well as professional audiences, for more than a century. According to its mission statement, the ASPR is "a primary contemporary force for advancing our understanding of the far-reaching scientific and spiritual questions raised by the mysteries of consciousness."

Interest in parapsychology was not always viewed with such disdain as it is today. Of course, there were plenty of skeptics and cynics even then, but many physicians, psychologists, scientists, academics, and public figures were not afraid to lend their names to research on the paranormal.

Skeptics can be just as rigid as believers if they believe that science is simply the be-all and end-all of existence. While science, in itself, is not a belief, the idea that anything and everything in the world can be or will be explained by science is called *scientism*, a term which usually has pejorative connotations when used by philosophers of science. In that sense, science becomes as "ism," a rigid, codified system which allows no dissent.

Hilary Putnam (1926–2016), American philosopher, mathematician, and computer scientist, rejected scientism because of its dogmatic endorsement of the scientific method as the one and only truth and because of its reduction of knowledge to things which could be measured. This practice is known as "reductionism." In *Mathematics, Matter and Method*, Putnam wrote:

> I regard science as an important part of man's knowledge of reality; but there is a tradition with which I would not wish to be identified, which would say that scientific knowledge is all of man's knowledge. I do not believe that ethical statements are expressions of scientific knowledge but neither do I agree that they are no knowledge at all. The idea that the concepts of truth, falsity, explanation and even understanding are all concepts which belong exclusively to science seems to me to be a perversion…

Although thousands of controlled, double-blind scientific experiments have confirmed many types of paranormal phenomena, most people don't know these studies exist. If they did know about them, they would most likely dismiss them as pseudoscience. Dean Radin wrote that, by using the term "pseudoscience," believers in science or scientism reduce parapsychology to the status of "other." Since parapsychology researchers have not been part of the accepted group, they became targets for ridicule.

Another reason for non-acceptance of parapsychology research is cognitive dissonance. When strange things happen that we don't understand, we tend to dismiss them out of hand, and we make light of them. The accompanying effects are usually fear and loathing, expressed with ridicule and contempt.

Philosopher of science Paul Feyerabend rejected the distinction between science and non-science or pseudoscience because, he said, scientific theories and scientific methods are constantly changing in response to new data. Certain scientific theories and methods which once were widely accepted now strike us as quaint, if not ridiculous. Bloodletting was once widely used as a treatment for a whole host of afflictions. Phrenology used palpation of the skull to determine character traits. Phlogiston theory postulated that a fire-like substance called phlogiston was released during combustion. All of these practices and theories have been tossed into the dustbin of history.

The great physicist Max Planck once said, "Science changes funeral by funeral." As the old scientists pass away, new scientists with new ideas take their place. Feyerabend said a science that insists it has the only correct method and the only correct result is really an ideology. He said that in order not to impede scientific progress, the best possible principle one can adopt is *anything goes*. I think a better way to express that idea today would be "anything is possible" since "anything goes" sounds like permissiveness and licentiousness. "Anything is possible" is a way of looking at the world with the idea that the sky's the limit. It's like saying: Don't limit yourself. Think big! This principle applies both to scientists and non-scientists alike.

Believers in scientism, who are not necessarily scientists, think if something that they believe in has not yet been proven by science, it eventually will be. For them, science and measurement are articles of faith. Scientism has been criticized for ignoring perspective and the psychological dimension of experience, which cannot always be measured. As Einstein said, "Not everything that counts can be counted."

British novelist, science fiction writer, science writer, futurist, and inventor Arthur C. Clarke wrote, "When a scientist states that something is possible, he is almost certainly right; when he states that something is impossible, he is very probably wrong."

There is often a discrepancy between physicians and their patients on this issue. Doctors tend to be more skeptical, while patients, especially if seriously ill, often have a need to believe that anything is possible. They may even seek solace in spirituality. Many studies have shown a need to bridge the gap between patients' needs and the medical profession's skepticism on this issue.

The idea that anything is possible, even for terminally ill patients, was advanced by Dr. Andrew Weil, who documented many cases of spontaneous recovery from terminal illness in his #1 bestseller *Spontaneous Healing* (1995). My doctor told me about one of his patients who was brought to the Emergency Room from a nursing home in dire condition. She was a woman in her 80s who was extremely dehydrated. Her temperature was 30 degrees Celsius. Normal body temperature is 37 degrees. Her heart rate was two beats per minute. Normal heart rate is 70 beats per minute. She was about as close to being dead without actually being dead as one can possibly be. The family was notified that their mother was not expected to last the night and the doctor went home. The next morning the doctor was annoyed that he hadn't been called in the night by the hospital, because according to hospital protocol, he should have been called to notify him that his patient had died. Before he went to the ward, he stopped by the cafeteria to grab a cup of coffee. Lo and behold, there was his patient sitting up having breakfast. She was perfectly coherent and she was making jokes with him. The doctor was astounded. After he told me his story, he asked me, what do you call that? When I said he could call it a miracle, he said he didn't know what else to call it.

Dr. Marilyn Baetz and her colleagues at the University of Saskatchewan conducted surveys of psychiatric patients and their psychiatrists. Psychiatrists had lower levels of spiritual beliefs and practices than their patients and lower than the general public. A large percentage of patients felt their beliefs about spirituality should be included in their assessments. Baetz also explored ways to incorporate "psycho-spiritual interventions" into patient care. While most hospitals used to have chaplains to cater to their patients' religious needs, many hospitals now have "spiritual health specialists" whose remit is wider and, for the most part, free of dogma and judgment.

It is not just psychiatric patients who are interested in talking about spirituality. Surgical and medical patients also have spiritual needs and interests. Harvard-educated neurosurgeon Allan J. Hamilton wrote that premonition, superstition, faith, and hope can influence outcomes. These phenomena can be seen as positive coping mechanisms. He encouraged patients to voice their spiritual needs when they seek medical help.

In his book on coping with cancer, lung cancer survivor Greg Anderson listed spirituality as one of his eight survival strategies. He said cancer survivors generally embraced a more spiritual perspective and that the search for divinity, within and without, was for him the apex of the cancer patient's healing journey. For many people, crises such as cancer or other serious illness encourage the exploration of spirituality. I wonder if it takes a certain type of temperament or personality to be interested in spirituality. Maybe it's not a personality type, just an attitude, an idea that anything is possible, that there is more to this life than meets the eye.

Serious illness often shakes us up and forces us to re-examine our long-held attitudes and beliefs. One doesn't need to believe in miracles and angels to accept that other people have had some strange and mysterious experiences which can't always be explained by science and that people who have had these strange experiences are not necessarily emotionally challenged or mentally unbalanced.

There is a very respectable tradition of research into paranormal topics. The roster of well-known researchers in the field includes physicists, physicians, neuroscientists, psychiatrists, and psychologists with impeccable academic credentials. The list goes on and on.

The Tradition of Research

J. B. Rhine and William McDougall introduced the word *parapsychology* to the English language as the translation of a German word coined in 1889 by Max Dessoir. It derives from the juxtaposition of two words: *para* ("alongside") and *psychology* ("study of the mind.") Rhine popularized the word *parapsychology* in his book *New Frontiers of the Mind* (1937). By doing so, he initiated a shift from what was previously called "psychical research", which was qualitative and impressionistic, to the discipline of parapsychology, which is quantitative and based on research, academic discipline, and experimental design.

Rhine was a pioneer in parapsychology. He founded the Parapsychology Lab at Duke University, the Parapsychology Association, and the *Journal of Parapsychology*. In addition to *New Frontiers of The Mind*, his books included *Extrasensory Perception* (1934) and *Parapsychology: Frontier Science of the Mind* (1957). When he left Duke University, he started the Foundation for Research on the Nature of Man, which evolved into the Rhine Research Center (also known as the Rhine Center).

In 1911, Stanford University became the first American university to study ESP and psychokinesis in a laboratory setting. Parapsychology has been studied and researched at the university level for more than one hundred years. It has become, for the most part, a respectable field for scientific study, even though critics continue to challenge its respectability.

There was a parapsychology research lab at Princeton University from 1979 to 2007. Utrecht University in the Netherlands and Edinburgh University in Scotland have established chairs in parapsychology. The latter, the Koestler Parapsychology Unit (KPU), was established in 1985, in compliance with a £1-million bequest from the will of Arthur Koestler, Hungarian-British author of many popular books, including *The Roots of Coincidence* (1974) and *Darkness at Noon* (1940). It offers online undergraduate and postgraduate courses.

Peer-reviewed scientific journals have published a great deal of parapsychology research. They include the *Journal of Parapsychology*, the *Journal of Consciousness Studies*, the *Journal of the Society for Psychical Research*, and the *European Journal of Parapsychology* (which ceased publication in 2010).

Even though universities as prestigious as Duke, Princeton, and Stanford have been sites for parapsychology research, the discipline of parapsychology still carries the taint of "pseudoscience," a disparaging term that seeks to exclude parapsychology researchers from the inner circle of serious scientists.

However, parapsychology gained credibility and respect and was recognized as a legitimate scientific discipline in 1969 when the Parapsychological Association, an international scientific society, was elected as an affiliate of the American Association for the Advancement of Science (AAAS), which is the largest and most prestigious general scientific society in the world.

There are many credible researchers in the field of ESP, telepathy, telekinesis, NDE, OBE, reincarnation, and psychic abilities. This is the type of situation where you have experts on both sides of an issue and you have to make up your own mind. Many people who call themselves rationalists elevate reason and logic to an absurd degree, even above sworn testimony and personal experience. Both believers and skeptics need to keep an open mind. As Albert Einstein said, "The important thing is to not stop questioning."

Even so, I think we would be remiss if we did not acknowledge that the fields of spirituality in general, and death and dying in particular, are fraught with many opportunities for con artists to take advantage of the sick and the dying, as well as the recently bereaved, who are often vulnerable individuals.

Although she helped popularize the concept of near-death experience and was renowned for her work with dying patients and their families, even Elisabeth Kübler-Ross was taken in by a charlatan. Jay Barham was a self-ordained minister who claimed to have the ability to heal the sick and conjure up spirits of the dead. Kübler-Ross believed in him, much to her regret. She was not the only person to be taken in by a fake psychic. Many unscrupulous people who claim to be psychic are simply out to make a buck. They deserve the scorn with which most people view them, especially when they prey on vulnerable people, such as elderly widows and widowers, or parents who have lost their children and want desperately to believe that the soul abides.

Edgar Mitchell referred to people with psychic abilities as "psychoactive." He said these people are neither divine nor satanic. They are just like any other group of people. Some are dishonest. Some are honest. He said it wouldn't be fair to paint them all with the same brush, yet fake psychics have been used to discredit the whole field of parapsychology.

How does one know if a self-proclaimed psychic is genuine? Starting with a healthy dose of skepticism, one should try to assess the person's track record, as well as his or her motives and demeanor. It has been my experience that someone who is genuine will be humble and will not charge a large sum of money for a reading. A spiritual teacher who owns a fleet of Rolls Royces is not a good bet. As a general rule, the best advice is *caveat emptor*.

A lot of the hostility that is directed towards psychic and paranormal phenomena is based on fear of the unknown. We have a fear/fascination relationship with the psychic. Even aside from the fear of fake psychics, that is, the fear of being made a sucker or being taken advantage of, there is often a tendency to dismiss or ridicule any belief in paranormal or psychic phenomena as nothing but ignorance and superstition, which is viewed by educated people as a malevolent force in society.

Doctors, nurses, psychologists, scientists, and other professionals may be worried about damaging their reputations and their credibility with their colleagues if they show an interest in the paranormal, or if they decide to share their own personal, weird experiences. They are afraid of being ostracized, ridiculed, marginalized, and humiliated by being labelled superstitious or believers in pseudoscience. Nobody wants that.

Many years ago, the Greek Stoic philosopher Epictetus (55–135 CE) said, "Those who pursue the higher life of wisdom, who seek to live by spiritual principles, must be prepared to be laughed at and condemned." One needs to be brave, or possibly foolhardy, to disregard popular opinion.

In his review of the book *Debunked! ESP, Telekinesis and Other Pseudoscience* by Georges Charpak and Henri Broch, eminent theoretical physicist Freeman Dyson revealed that his grandmother was a successful faith healer, and his cousin was for many years the editor of the *Journal of the Society for Psychical Research.* He wrote that they were both "well-educated, highly intelligent, and fervent believers in paranormal phenomena.... Their beliefs were based on personal experience and careful scrutiny of evidence. Nothing they believed was incompatible with science." Dyson worked at the Institute for Advanced Studies in Princeton, where Einstein spent two decades.

Dyson cited a vast amount of evidence for the existence of paranormal phenomena, compiled by the Society for Psychical Research. He made the important point that, by its very nature, the paranormal is not always subject to scientific scrutiny. He wrote:

> The members of the society took great trouble to interview first-hand witnesses as soon as possible after the events and to document the stories carefully. One fact that emerges clearly from all the stories is that paranormal events occur, if they occur at all, only when people are under stress and experiencing strong emotion. This fact would immediately explain why paranormal phenomena are not observable or repeatable under the conditions of a well-controlled scientific experiment.

I am in agreement with Dyson's observation that paranormal events occur when people are under severe stress and are experiencing strong emotions, since the handful of paranormal events that I experienced all occurred under very trying, stressful, emotional conditions.

Many people have trod the path from skeptic to believer based on personal experience. Joel Martin was a New York radio talk show host who invited the medium George Anderson on his show in order to expose him as a fraud. Martin was formerly a schoolteacher, a college instructor, and a TV and radio producer, who was highly skeptical of anything psychic or paranormal. After Anderson told Martin personal things about himself that he could not possibly know, Martin became a believer in communication with the spirit world.

A similar thing happened to Brian Weiss, a respected academic psychiatrist and Chairman of the Department of Psychiatry at Mt. Sinai Hospital at the University of Miami. He came to a belief in the spirit world when he was told very personal details of his life by one of his patients after he used hypnotic regression to treat her phobias.

Brian Weiss, Joel Martin, and Freeman Dyson's grandmother and cousin were all highly intelligent, well-educated people. Studies have shown that the more educated segment of the population is more likely to believe in paranormal phenomena. In fact, some of the greatest minds of the twentieth century, including Albert Einstein, Nikola Tesla, Sigmund Freud, Carl Jung, and computer science pioneer Alan Turing, who helped crack the German "enigma" code in World War II, all believed in telepathy, ESP, and other paranormal phenomena.

British geneticist and evolutionary biologist J. B. S. Haldane suggested that the Universe is not only stranger than we imagine, it is stranger than we *can* imagine. I must say that I agree with Haldane. As I go through life, I often tell myself that there are certain things in life which are simply beyond my powers of comprehension. Some things are unknowable. Other things will be known in time. The great inventor Nikola Tesla once said, "The day science begins to study non-physical phenomena, it will make more progress in one decade than in all the previous centuries of its existence."

It is important to add that, when it comes to skepticism and belief, we need to be specific about each of these. One can be a religious skeptic, for example, but not a paranormal skeptic, and vice versa. If at all possible, we need to show respect for people who don't share our beliefs or, conversely, don't share our skepticism. But the respect only goes so far. As long as there is such a thing as objective reality, we have to admit that there are certain established facts which are not matters of opinion. So, for example, if someone says they don't believe in evolution or they don't believe in climate change, those people should not be called skeptics, they should be called deniers or rejectionists because these issues are not matters of belief.

My own position on paranormal phenomena, as stated throughout this book, is that it's good to keep an open mind, and it's good to be skeptical, but neither one of these attitudes can be an end in itself, and neither one should be taken to an extreme. While lived experience is no doubt the best teacher, and the wisdom of our elders should also be taken into account, we all have to decide for ourselves what we believe or disbelieve. This is how free will operates (if we believe in free will!). As William James said, "My first act of free will is to believe in free will."

Chapter 4: Information Transfer: ESP, Telepathy, Precognitive Dreams, Premonitions, Predestination

Recently I attended an international conference in Montréal. One of the attendees seemed quite distraught. My friend, who was sitting beside me, said he was afraid of her because she was so aggressive. At the break, we talked about her. I told my friend that my first impulse was to approach her and talk to her, but I didn't want to get involved in a long conversation, so I decided not to. Then I heard two words in my head: Be generous. They struck me like a lightning bolt. I immediately walked over to the woman and asked if we could talk. We had a good conversation, and I learned quite a lot by talking to her.

We are very familiar with the phrase "the mind's eye." I think we should consider a parallel concept: the mind's ear. When I "heard" the words "be generous" in my mind's ear, it wasn't at all like hearing a voice out loud. Still, I had to question whether those words were my own thoughts or whether they were a message from some unknown source, which some people may call Spirit. Others may call it conscience, spirit guide, guardian angel, higher self, or higher consciousness.

If I have the thought that I should call my cousin, the words do not form themselves in my mind as a command or an exhortation. They are not addressed to me as if by another person. It's easy to identify my own thoughts, in my own mind, which arise from my own volition. The words "Be generous" had an entirely different feel to them. They did not convey what I was going to do anyway, or what I wanted to do. It was just the opposite. The other factor that made me wonder if the words were a message was the milieu in which I found myself. Since I was attending a conference on science and spirituality, the idea of receiving messages was very much the common parlance.

I think it's worth noting that when one receives a message, its resonance is not limited to a particular time or place or person. Although the context for the "Be Generous" message was a conference, its applicability was much wider than that. It assumed a cloak of inevitability, as one of those "Rules to Live By." I think of those words often, in a variety of contexts.

I referred in Chapter 1 to my experience with thought transfer when I described my vision of the Hermit. When we have a thought, how do we know if it is our own? Even asking the question sounds suspicious. That way madness lies. Still, let's not be afraid to ask the question.

Thought transfer as described in the esoteric literature is quite different from the kind of thought intrusion or thought extraction experienced in psychosis. If a person with schizophrenia believes that thoughts are being inserted into or taken out of his or her brain, those beliefs are usually accompanied by paranoid thoughts of being controlled by outside forces and those thoughts are very disturbing and frightening. If someone has an experience of telepathy or ESP, on the other hand, that person maintains the locus of control and, in most cases, the accompanying affect is not dysphoric.

There are many different types of thought transfer. In this chapter, we will explore four different kinds: extra-sensory perception (ESP), telepathy, precognitive dreams, and premonitions. As with all things, we need to be precise with our definitions; however, definitions of the various terms used in this field cannot always be clear and precise because there is often some overlap between one term and another. Hunches, gut feelings, premonitions, pre-cognition and prescience are all similar in meaning although each word may have a precise definition.

The psychics in Steven Spielberg's *Minority Report* (which was based on a Philip K. Dick short story) are called pre-cogs. We know what pre-cogs are. They know the future in advance. They are psychic and prescient; they have precognition, hunches, and premonitions. These terms all relate to the future. ESP and telepathy, however, generally deal with the present, not the future. As discussed earlier, if you are thinking about a person and that person phones, you could say you are psychic or you have ESP or telepathy. In that context, the terms "ESP" and "telepathy" would appear to be interchangeable.

Telepathy can be defined as the mental process of sending or receiving thoughts without the use of our physical senses, so in a sense, it is a type of ESP. In another context, ESP and telepathy may have different meanings. Extra-sensory perception clearly refers to perception. It is also called "second sight." Since vision is a form of perception, this definition seems internally consistent. Telepathy, on the other hand, has the same root as the words *sympathy* or *empathy* – the Greek word *pathos*, so it refers to feeling (literally, it means *"feeling at a distance."*)

There is a distinction to be made between ESP and telepathy – one refers to perception, the other refers to feeling. Feelings and perceptions are not the same thing, although they affect each other and interact with each other. Also, telepathy is not the same as thought transfer, although it includes thought transfer because telepathy can also involve transfer of images, feelings, perceptions, and sensations, not just thoughts.

Another distinction between ESP and telepathy is that ESP occurs while we are awake; telepathy can occur while we are awake but it can also occur while we are asleep, as shown by the dream telepathy studies conducted at Maimonides Medical Center, discussed later in this chapter.

So we can see that, in the world of paranormal information transfer, thoughts, feelings, perceptions, and physical sensations are all intertwined in an endless feedback loop, somewhat akin to a Möbius strip. For the purposes of this chapter, I treat ESP, telepathy, precognitive dreams, and premonitions separately, with the understanding that the categories are indistinct and that there is often some overlap among them.

Extra-Sensory Perception

Extra-sensory perception or ESP refers to perception that occurs without the use of the five senses. ESP is the most researched of all the anomalous or paranormal phenomena, probably because it is the easiest to quantify and to design experiments for, using cards and dice.

Between 1880 and 1940, 145 experimental ESP studies were published. Most of these were conducted by scientists and psychologists. In 106 of the 145 studies, the results exceeded chance expectations. The studies that received the most publicity were conducted by Dr. Joseph Banks Rhine. His monograph, *Extra-Sensory Perception,* was published in 1934. The American Institute of Statistical Mathematics issued a statement in 1937 to affirm that Rhine's statistical methods were sound.

In 1940, J. Gaither Pratt, J. B. Rhine, and associates published *Extra-Sensory Perception after Sixty Years,* in which they met 35 different objections to their studies that had been published in the scientific and popular press. Scientists who had published criticism of ESP research were sent advance copies of the draft report. Only one of the skeptics maintained his criticism after reviewing the material.

This book was recognized as the first meta-analysis in the history of science. Meta-analysis is a powerful tool, as it combines results from different studies in order to provide a larger effect size and, therefore, greater evidence and more convincing conclusions than can be drawn from a single study.

After 90,000 trials, Rhine concluded that ESP was "an actual and demonstrable occurrence." Nowadays, ESP is widely acknowledged to be a valid phenomenon. It does not seem overly strange. It is more easily accepted than the other paranormal phenomena, like visions, apparitions, near-death experiences, or spirit communication. Why is that? Probably because so many people have experienced it and know about it so it is familiar.

In his 1997 book *The Conscious Universe*, Dean Radin wrote, "The reality of psychic phenomena is now no longer based solely upon faith, or wishful thinking, or absorbing anecdotes. It is not even based upon the results of a few scientific experiments. Instead, we know that these phenomena exist because of new ways of evaluating massive amounts of scientific evidence collected over a century by scores of researchers." Radin wrote that incontrovertible evidence is based on analysis of more than a thousand experiments.

Carl Sagan was a lifetime skeptic and implacable foe of pseudoscience. Yet even Sagan conceded that there was some validity to the research on ESP. He noted several claims that he thought deserved serious study, including: "(1) that by thought alone humans can (barely) affect random number generators in computers; (2) that people under mild sensory deprivation can receive thoughts or images 'projected' at them."

British psychologist Susan Blackmore, who was mentioned earlier, used the terms "sheep" and "goats" to distinguish people who accepted the existence of ESP (sheep: more easily led) from those who didn't (goats: less easily led). These terms were originally introduced by another psychologist, Gertrude Schmeidler, who hypothesized that people who believed in ESP were likely to perform better on ESP tests than those who didn't believe in ESP. Her initial pilot study was conducted in 1942 at Harvard University. Using ESP cards (also known as Zener cards) she did a double-blind study in which her subjects were individually tested. Her hypothesis was confirmed, namely, that belief in ESP had a strong effect on her subjects' performance. This study was replicated by many researchers.

Blackmore found that paranormal believers shared certain personality traits. The believers (sheep) were more intuitive, more open to new experience, and more likely to be sensation-seekers and risk-takers than the goats. She also found that sheep did less critical thinking than goats. Other factors found to affect performance on ESP tests were mood, physical well-being, fatigue, boredom, and distraction.

The Zener cards Schmeidler used in her ESP experiments were named for Karl Zener, the perceptual psychologist who designed the cards in the 1930s for the ESP experiments he conducted with his colleague, J. B. Rhine. There were five different designs (circle, cross, square, star, and three wavy lines) and 25 cards in each deck, with five cards of each design. The experimenter showed the reverse side of each card in the deck to the subject. If the subject had no psychic ability, the probability was that he or she would correctly guess the design 20 percent of the time, i.e., five times out of 25. If the reader's success rate was consistently above 20 percent, this would be seen as evidence of psychic ability (ESP). There was so much criticism of this methodology that Zener cards (ESP cards) are no longer used in parapsychology experiments. They have been replaced by dice or random number generators.

Zener Cards (ESP Cards), designed by Karl Zener

Another form of ESP is remote viewing. The term was coined in the 1970s by Russell Targ and Harold Putoff, parapsychologists at the Stanford Research Institute in Palo Alto. Remote viewing is defined as the practice of seeing impressions of distant targets with the use of ESP. The term was popularized in the 1990s when the U.S. government declassified documents from a U.S. military remote viewing project known as "Stargate."

Joseph McMoneagle was known as "Remote Viewer No. 1" when he worked at the U.S. Army's psychic intelligence unit at Ft. Meade, Maryland. Using remote viewing techniques, he correctly predicted the existence and location of the Soviet Typhoon-class submarine in 1979; his predictions were confirmed by satellite photos in 1980. In spite of his great success with remote viewing, the Stargate program was closed because of stigma. McMoneagle did not want his successes to be used as validation by others who claimed to have psychic abilities. He cautioned that 98 percent of all psychics are fake.

The Princeton Engineering Anomalies Research (PEAR) laboratory was in existence for 28 years, from 1979 to 2007. The principal investigator, Robert Jahn, studied remote perception, mind-machine interaction, and other consciousness-related phenomena. His *Margins of Reality* became the definitive textbook in the field. The PEAR lab morphed into the International Consciousness Research Laboratories (ICRL), which studied telekinesis (or psychokinesis) and ESP.

Telekinesis is the ability to move objects with one's mind. The word "telekinesis" was first used by Russian psychical researcher Alexander N. Asakof in 1890. It means movement at a distance. The word "psychokinesis" was coined in 1914 by American author Henry Holt, who first used it in his book *On the Cosmic Relations*. The word is a portmanteau formed from two Greek words: *psyche* (mind) and *kinesis* (motion, movement).

There have been claims of psychokinetic abilities throughout history, but most claimants were exposed as frauds. Israeli illusionist Uri Geller became quite well-known for his frequent television appearances in which he demonstrated his ability to bend spoons with his mind; however, his telekinetic claims were debunked by James Randi, Martin Gardner, and Nobel Prize-winning physicist and amateur magician Richard Feynman, among others.

Edgar Mitchell, the sixth man to walk on the moon, was a NASA astronaut and Lunar Module Pilot of Apollo 14. On his journey back to Earth, seeing Earth from space, Mitchell had an epiphany or Samadhi (enlightenment) experience concerning the oneness of all things. He performed ESP experiments in his spaceship on his way back to Earth. His results were published in the *Journal of Parapsychology* in 1971. On his return to Earth, Mitchell founded the Institute of Noetic Sciences (IONS) near Petaluma, California. It is a non-profit parapsychology research institute devoted to studies of consciousness and the mind. Its stated goal was to create a worldwide shift in consciousness.

In *The Way of the Explorer*, Mitchell wrote, "Laboratory subjects have been beating the odds selecting cards since J. B. Rhine began studies in the 1930s. And long before then, gamblers in Las Vegas were well aware of this mysterious and elusive sense." This "elusive sense" Mitchell referred to was ESP, also called nonlocal intuition. The word "nonlocal" was popularized by CERN physicist John Bell. In physics, action at a distance is the concept that an object can be moved without being physically touched by another object. It is the nonlocal interaction of objects that are separate in space.

Einstein famously called quantum mechanics "spooky action at a distance." To be more specific, he used the phrase to illustrate his dislike of the concept of wave-function collapse. Quantum mechanics states that "particle" and "wave" fail to fully describe the behavior of quantum-scale objects. Physical objects at the quantum level possess both local particle and nonlocal wave properties that become manifest depending on whether the position or wavelength is being measured. This is what Danish physicist Niels Bohr (1885 – 1962) called "the duality principle." Measurement of one quantity will affect the value of the other quantity in a future measurement. When a measurement is made and a particle's position is then known with greater accuracy, the wave-function is said to "collapse."

Einstein never liked the concept of wave-particle collapse because it would mean that a signal had the potential to be propagated at infinite speed throughout the universe, but he thought no signal could move faster than the speed of light. It was not until Bell's theorem of 1964 that the argument about the nature of this "spooky action" was resolved.

The basic idea in Bell's theorem was about the transfer of information. Through a process known as "entanglement," one particle is able to influence another particle instantaneously. In entanglement, measuring the state of one particle immediately affects the state of its entangled particle, regardless of the distance between them.

In quantum teleportation, the quantum state of one particle can be transferred to another distant particle without anything physical travelling between them. Deepak Chopra and other New Age writers have used theories from quantum physics to explain telepathy and other paranormal phenomena.

American particle physicist, philosopher, author, and religious skeptic Victor Stenger dismissed these attempts, calling them "quantum quackery" and referring to these writers as "quantum mystics." He wrote:

> The current fad of mystical physics began in earnest with the publication in 1975 of Fritjof Capra's *The Tao of Physics*. In this book, Capra asserted that quantum theory confirmed the traditional teaching of Eastern mystics: that human consciousness and the universe form an interconnected irreducible whole.

Stenger cited Amit Goswami's book *The Self-Aware Universe: How Consciousness Creates the Material World* as an example of how the existence of paranormal phenomena are explained with analogies from quantum mechanics. Goswami called distant viewing and out-of-body experiences examples of nonlocal operations of consciousness.

Edgar Mitchell, the astronaut referred to earlier, did not base his views on ESP strictly on intuition. He stressed the importance of intention. He wrote, "Robert Jahn at Princeton, physicist Helmut Schmidt, and several others have for more than two decades confirmed Rhine's early work. As their statistics show, intention can influence random processes in mechanical devices." Mitchell's views on the importance of intention in ESP experiments would seem to jive with Schmeidler's hypothesis that people who believed in ESP were more likely to do well on tests of ESP prowess.

In ordinary life, outside the laboratory, I don't think that people intentionally set out to have ESP. They just have it. The key ingredient in one's appreciation of ESP has more to do with paying attention. One can intend to pay attention to ESP and one can intend to consider ESP worthy of attention, rather than intend to have ESP.

Dean Radin explored the concept of intention as it relates to ESP and mind-machine interaction in his 1997 book *The Conscious Universe: The*

Scientific Truth of Psychic Phenomena. His team conducted a meta-analysis of mind-matter interaction studies using random-number generators (RNGs). They reviewed 832 studies conducted by 68 different investigators. There were 597 experimental studies and 235 control studies. Of these, the PEAR laboratory reported 258 experimental studies and 127 control studies. According to Radin, the results of his meta-analysis produced odds against chance which were highly statistically significant.

Radin appeared to have a convincing argument in favor of the scientific validity of paranormal phenomena such as ESP, but his analysis was challenged by Victor Stenger in a 2002 article in the *Skeptical Inquirer*. In his criticism of the research reported by Radin, Stenger invoked a well-known phenomenon in scientific research known as the file-drawer effect, which states that if only positive results get reported and negative results are left in the filing cabinet, this will greatly bias the results.

This long-standing practice no doubt was a response to the "publish or perish" imperative in the academic community, since scientific journals would tend not to publish the results of studies with negative results. Meta-analysis, discussed earlier, combines the results of many experiments with statistically insignificant results. So the file-drawer effect needs to be taken into account. Radin claimed to have taken the file-drawer effect into account, but his critics said he grossly minimized its importance.

The results of the random number generator studies were very similar to the dice study results. Radin noted the same mind-matter interaction effects were observed in nearly 500 dice and RNG experiments over a period of more than 50 years. He concluded that the human mind has a small but measurable influence on RNGs. He was in concurrence with Carl Sagan. Radin found plentiful, concrete evidence of mind-machine interaction.

Telepathy

Just like ESP, telepathy is a common, everyday occurrence, which most people can relate to because they are familiar with it. Our thoughts, feelings, perceptions, and sensations are inextricably linked and intertwined.

The basic premise of cognitive therapy is that if you change your thoughts you can change your feelings. Thoughts and feelings are not the same, but they affect and interact with each other. Thoughts affect feelings, which affect perceptions, which affect thoughts, so there is an endless feedback loop.

A personal story demonstrates some of this overlap. One day, while sitting in the parlor with her sisters in her home in Council Bluffs, Iowa, my great-aunt nodded off in her chair. After a short while, she awoke with a start and proclaimed that her brother in Romania had died. Within the hour, there was a knock on the door. There stood a young man with a telegram in his hand informing the family that my great-aunt's brother had indeed passed away in Romania.

How did she know that? Was it ESP? Was it telepathy? Did she receive a message in her dream? Or was it all three? We can say her "knowing" about her brother's death was not a premonition or a precognitive dream because those two forms of knowing are time-sensitive. They take place before the event. My aunt's dream occurred after her brother's death, not before; therefore, this would be considered telepathy, not ESP, since she was asleep and her senses were blunted.

Other cases are easier to classify. Twin tennis players, Mike and Bob Bryan, won Wimbledon in 2011. They were able to anticipate each other's moves so precisely that their opponents accused them of having an unfair advantage because they were so obviously telepathic.

Os Gemeos (Portuguese for "the twins") are the graffiti artists Otavio and Gustavo Pandolfo, identical twins born in Sao Paolo, Brazil, in 1974. They recently had a show at Boston's prestigious Institute of Contemporary Art. They are known all over the world for their huge, colorful murals painted on the outsides of buildings. They started to communicate with each other through their drawings at a very young age, around four or five, and they became addicted to drawing as a means of communication. Their work features yellow-skinned characters they have both seen in their dreams.

One study showed that 30 percent of twins are able to communicate through telepathy. But not only twins are telepathic. Telepathy can occur between other closely bonded pairs as well, including siblings who aren't twins, lovers, long-term couples, parents and children, and even close friends.

Once when I was living in Toronto and my brother was living in Winnipeg, I saw a poem by Mark Strand in the *New Yorker* which I thought he would like. I cut it out of the magazine and mailed it to him – this was pre-Internet. As it happened, my brother saw the same poem, thought I would like it, and mailed it to me. The two letters crossed in the mail. The poem is called "The Story Of Our Lives." This episode is an example of telepathic communication between closely bonded siblings. While the incident could be dismissed as coincidence, in essence it involved two people who were over 1500 km apart thinking the same thing at the same time, which, for me, is what telepathy is all about.

Many pet owners claim to have telepathic communication with their pets. The skeptics consider this assertion ridiculous. Skeptic, magician, and psychologist Richard Wiseman described his investigation of the so-called "psychic dog." This dog was always sitting in the window when his owner returned home from work, as if the dog knew when to expect its owner home. Wiseman's investigators videotaped the dog and they discovered that the dog went to the window numerous times during the day. Voila! Case solved. The dog was clearly not telepathic.

Not so fast! My mother used to tell me that when she was a child, the family dog, Trixie, went to school every day at 3:30 p.m. to wait for my mother's sister, my aunt, and walk her home from school. Did the dog go to the school at other times throughout the day? Not according to my grandmother, who said the dog seemed to know the exact time when my aunt was getting out of school. We could say the dog had a good sense of time and was not in telepathic communication with my aunt; even so, it is well known that dogs have close, emotional bonds with their human companions. It is not for nothing that the dog is known as "man's best friend."

Another theory has been advanced to explain the well-known phenomenon of dogs waiting at the door to greet their owners at the appropriate time. In her book *Being A Dog*, Alexandra Horowitz suggests that this behavior is related to the dog's finely tuned sense of smell and how long the owner's smell lingers. Once the smell starts to fade, the dog knows it is time for the owner to return.

In her short story "Nero," Native American writer Louise Erdrich described a young girl's interaction with her dog this way: "It is probably impossible for our two species, interdependent since the dim beginning of our ascendancy on this earth, not to communicate. Staring at each other, we were exchanging some signal."

Carol Buckley, co-founder of the Elephant Sanctuary in Tennessee, demonstrated that humans can communicate telepathically with elephants, and that elephants can communicate telepathically with each other.

Neurosurgeon Allan J. Hamilton described how he used *chi* (the life energy or life force in Traditional Chinese Medicine) to communicate with horses. Many other books about human–animal interaction have also documented telepathic communication between humans and animals.

In dream telepathy studies conducted between 1966 and 1972 at Maimonides Medical Center in New York, a "sender" and a "receiver" spent the night in a sleep lab. Receivers' EEGs and eye movements were monitored as they slept. Since rapid eye movement (REM) sleep is associated with dreaming, senders were told to concentrate on randomly generated images when receivers entered REM sleep, in an attempt to influence the receivers' dreams. The receivers' dream reports were rated by outside judges who compared them to several pictures, including the target image that was sent telepathically. The research, done by Montague Ullman and Stanley Krippner, showed the dreamers had a heightened susceptibility to receiving telepathic images from outside sources while in REM sleep.

This dream telepathy research was consistent with other studies that showed hypnotized subjects to be more open to telepathy and other psychic phenomena. A meta-analysis of 25 experiments between 1945 and 1981 demonstrated that hypnosis may facilitate psychic phenomena.

Although meta-analysis has been critiqued as a methodology, as discussed above, it is still widely used in scientific research.

Dream telepathy research helps us to highlight the differences between dream telepathy and precognitive dreams. In the former, images and/or thoughts can be transmitted (transferred) in the present while the latter holds information about the future. Dream telepathy can also be distinguished from "messages" we receive in dreams. In dream telepathy, as in waking telepathy, there is a sender and a receiver. With messages we receive in our dreams, there is a receiver but no identified sender. Whether the message is internally or externally generated can be a matter for discussion and speculation.

Precognitive Dreams

Precognitive or visionary dreams are dreams in which the dreamer is shown a future event that comes to pass. These dreams may convey messages from the spirit world or from the deep, dark recesses of the brain (the unconscious).

Everybody dreams. Birds dream. Animals dream. We have daydreams during the day and night dreams at night. Mostly, dreams are poorly understood. They often need to be interpreted. Most dreams that predict future events do not come true. Many are anxiety dreams; others represent wish-fulfilment.

Some people insist that they don't dream. What they should say is that they don't remember their dreams. The typical person has between three and five dreams per night, but some people dream more often. If you spend eight hours sleeping, that will usually include two hours of dreaming. We used to think that dreams occurred exclusively during REM sleep. We now know that dreams can also occur in non-REM sleep, but non-REM dreams are different. They are the dreams where you review the day's events, try to learn lessons from them, and prepare for the next day.

Dreams that occur during REM-sleep are chaotic. They are more likely to be symbolic, non-linear, creative, and predictive of future events. We are more in touch with our unconscious, as well as the collective unconscious, during REM sleep. Sleep researchers have been able to discern the difference between REM dreams and non-REM dreams by waking up the dreamers in the sleep lab while they were dreaming and asking them what they were dreaming.

I have had a few precognitive dreams myself. When I was 19, in second-year medical school, I dreamt the respirology exam the night before the exam. As I awoke, the dream was fading, as dreams do, and all I could remember was the first question. I got up and studied that particular question. When I went to take the exam, sure enough, there it was, the same question, and it was the first question on the exam, just like in my dream. Respirology was my worst subject and the ability to answer that particular question allowed me to pass the exam, which, without my dream, I probably would have failed.

I once recounted this dream to a woman who told me that she had had a similar experience, seeing the exam in her dream the night before the exam. My feeling upon hearing her story was similar to the feeling I had after I met the woman who told me she had also felt an immaterial hand on her shoulder while lying in bed. I can't emphasize strongly enough how reassuring it is to know that you are not alone and not the only one who has had the experience. In fact, that is one of the motivating factors that prompted me to write this book. The more people know that other people have had similar paranormal experiences, the more they will accept their own experiences, and the more they will accept themselves.

If I have a precognitive dream that helps me pass my exam, I know such things are possible, simply by virtue of having had the experience. Does there need to be a belief system in place to allow for the possibility of such phenomena and for them to be believed and not dismissed? Not really. If someone had told me that story before it happened to me, I probably wouldn't have believed it.

Someone could say, well, what about all those other exam dreams you had that didn't come true? But I never had any other dreams where I saw the exam the night before the exam. Another person might say that the subject in question was probably one that I hadn't studied, so my unconscious mind was telling me to get up and study it before I went to the exam. While that is a plausible explanation, it cannot account for the fact that the precise first question in my dream exam was also the very first question on my real exam. Nor does it allow for the possibility that there were also other topics I hadn't studied. Coincidence? Help from a spirit guide? It's open for conjecture. But the effect on me was striking. It was uncanny.

Another precognitive dream involved a family member. My uncle was in Palm Springs visiting family when he had a stroke. As he lay in a coma, his family was gathered around his bedside, hoping for him to regain consciousness. That night, he appeared to me in a dream. He said that he was fine, and I didn't need to worry about him, but that he was not in this world, he was in the next world. The next morning, I heard that he had died.

Yet another precognitive dream: One night I received a message in my dream. When I say "message," that's not quite the right word. It's not a voice. It's more like a form of knowing. The "message" was: "I'm aware. I'm awake. I'm alive."

I remember waking up and thinking, what an odd dream – AAA, triple A. It was very curious. It was almost funny, in a way, to have a dream, while I'm asleep, telling me that I'm awake. Later that day, I found myself in the Emergency Room with my mother who had a ruptured abdominal aortic aneurysm (AAA). As she was elderly and frail, I had to make a decision on her behalf whether or not to give permission for surgery, knowing she might not survive. She was in so much pain that I said to go ahead. The surgery not only relieved the pain, it was life-saving. She survived the surgery with flying colors. I am not in any way suggesting that my decision to give permission for surgery was influenced by my dream. In fact, I was not thinking about my dream at all while in the hospital. I only remembered it later.

My dream was precognitive in terms of the following day's events, but it was also precognitive in another way. Many years later, I was stunned, while watching a movie on TV called *The Trotsky*, to hear Jay Baruchel, playing the role of a student leader, telling his fellow students, "We are alive, we are awake, we are aware." His words were similar to the message I had received in my dream many years earlier, except he used *we* instead of *I*, and the order was reversed. Regardless, I thought it was a powerful message that stood on its own as a statement about awareness. When we are awake, we take it for granted that we are awake and we are alive. Awareness is a different kettle of fish. One can have so many different levels of awareness. "AAA" seemed to me to be a message to be more aware, more awake, and more alive.

Precognitive dreams are surprisingly common. One survey of college students reported the incidence was 8.8 percent. A well-known precognitive dream occurred in 2011 to New York Giants place-kicker Lawrence Tynes. The night before the NFC championship, he dreamt he kicked a game-winning field goal. He did kick the game-winning field goal the next day, sending the Giants to Super Bowl XLVI, which they won. In an interview after the game, Tynes said, "It's amazing. I had dreams about this last night. It was from 42, not 31, but I was so nervous today before the game, just anticipating this kind of game." Tynes dreamt his game-winning field goal was from the 42-yard-line, not the 31-yard-line, so his dream was not completely accurate. It was accurate in terms of the outcome, but not accurate in one particular detail.

Not all precognitive dreams are completely accurate. The same is probably true for most premonitions, intuitions, or hunches. If a hunch, premonition, or dream is not 100 percent accurate, it is not completely worthless. That would be like throwing out the baby with the bathwater. Don't throw out the baby! Sometimes the whole is greater than the sum of its parts. At the same time, it is important to remember that not all dreams about the future are going to come to pass.

Throughout history, both physicians and philosophers have struggled with the meaning of dreams. The Babylonians and ancient Egyptians believed that divine messages were conveyed in dreams. They saw dreams as part of the supernatural world. In *The Iliad*, Homer said Agamemnon received a message from Zeus in a dream. Plato wrote in the *Phaedo* that Socrates studied music and the arts because he was instructed to do so in a dream.

Aristotle (384–322 BCE) dismissed precognitive dreams as coincidence. He said that messages in dreams could not come from the gods because these experiences occurred in common people, and gods do not speak to common people. His argument would appear specious and classist to a modern audience.

Hippocrates (460–377 BCE), the father of Western medicine, tried to place medicine on a scientific basis by removing the influence of religion and superstition. Yet he still believed in the power of dreams.

Galen (129–c.210 CE), the Greek physician and philosopher whose medical theories were accepted for fifteen centuries, wrote a treatise called *The Best Physician Is Also A Philosopher* He said when he was 16, the god Asclepius appeared to his father in a dream and commanded him to send his son to study Medicine. Galen's father, Nikon, had wanted his son to be a philosopher, but he believed in his dream so he sent the boy to study medicine.

Both Galen and Hippocrates used their patients' own dreams to design their patients' treatments. Dreams have captured our imagination since Biblical times. Joseph's prophetic dreams were both his downfall, causing his brothers to sell him into slavery, and his salvation, causing the Pharaoh to release him from prison. Jacob's dream of the ladder going between heaven and earth is one of the best known dreams in the Western canon. "Jacob's Ladder" remains a popular cultural trope in art, music, dance, and literature.

According to Plutarch, the assassination of Julius Caesar in 44 BCE was foretold by a seer. In Shakespeare's *Julius Caesar*, a soothsayer tells Caesar, "Beware the Ides of March." His wife dreamt about his death and begged him not to go to the Senate. He went anyway and was murdered.

Many famous people have reported precognitive dreams. Charles Dickens dreamt about a woman in a red shawl who introduced herself to him with four words: "I am Miss Napier." He thought the dream very odd because he didn't know anyone by that name. What stood out for him about the dream was that it was very vivid. Later that day, after one of his public readings, a group of people came up to him to talk. The group included a woman in a red shawl. She was introduced to him as Miss Napier.

Abraham Lincoln dreamt about his assassination. Mark Twain saw his brother's corpse two weeks before his brother was killed in an explosion. There are many other examples, too numerous to recount.

Freud famously called dreams the "royal road to the unconscious." In his popular 1900 book *The Interpretation of Dreams*, he theorized that dreams represented a wish fulfilment. He talked about the *manifest* content of the dream, derived mostly from the events of the day ("the day residue") and the *latent* content of the dream which bubbled up from the unconscious, using symbolism, conflation, and condensation to disguise the meaning of the dream so as to allow it to enter into consciousness. In modern-day terminology, we link manifest content to non-REM dreams and latent content to REM dreams.

Freud dealt mostly with the psychology of dreams, not with parapsychology; however, he considered dreams to be a means of telepathic communication. In his monograph *Psychoanalysis and Telepathy,* written in 1921 but published posthumously, he wrote that it is an "incontestable fact that sleep creates favorable conditions for telepathy." American psychoanalyst Elizabeth Lloyd Mayer suggested that just as forbidden sexual and aggressive content can be disguised in dreams, so can anomalous (paranormal) material.

Dr. Melvin Morse wrote about the amazing case of James Chaffin, who died in North Carolina in 1921. At the time of his death, a will surfaced which had been written 16 years earlier. In his will, he bequeathed his entire estate to his youngest son. His wife and two older sons were not even mentioned in the will. No one could understand why he would favor his youngest son over the others. Four years after his father's death, the second son had a dream in which his father told him, "My will is in my overcoat pocket." He told his dream to his older brother, who helped him search their father's old clothing. Sewn into the lining of the father's overcoat they found a note which said, "Read the twenty-seventh chapter of Genesis in Daddy's old Bible." They rushed to the Bible and in the presence of witnesses they found a handwritten will, dated 1919, just where the dream said it would be, in the 27th chapter of Genesis. Since the other will was dated 1905, the newly found will superseded the older will. The new will called for the estate to be divided equally among all four surviving family members. This case was investigated by the court for fraud and none was found. The new will was honored by the court and the previous will was set aside.

Out of curiosity, I looked up the 27th chapter of Genesis, which was referred to in the note sewn into the lining of the father's overcoat. This chapter tells the story of Esau and his twin brother, Jacob. Although they were twins, Esau was the older son because he was born first. As the first-born son, Esau was entitled to his father's blessing; however, at the instigation of his mother (Rebekah), Jacob disguised himself as Esau and tricked his father (Isaac), who was blind, into giving him his blessing.

The story of the younger son (Jacob), who deprived the older son (Esau) of his rightful patrimony, was somewhat analogous to the Chaffin case. The father's direction in the dream to this passage in the Bible suggested that the late Mr. Chaffin had been tricked into leaving everything to the youngest son (with the collusion and possibly instigation of the mother).

Many people make fun of the very idea of precognitive dreams. I once heard the noted physicist and author Lawrence Krauss (*A Universe from Nothing*) on *Real Time with Bill Maher* saying that you might have a hundred dreams and then you have one in which you break your arm. The next day you fall and break your leg and you start to think that you must be psychic. He was laughing the whole time he was telling the story, as if to pity the poor sap who would believe it is even possible to have a precognitive dream. It is easy to ridicule and laugh at people. It is much harder to try to understand them.

Premonitions, Hunches, and Prescience

A premonition is a forewarning. It is often associated with anxiety. One speaks of a premonition of danger. A hunch is an idea based on intuition, not on proven fact. Someone might have a hunch to bet on a certain horse at the track. Prescience, on the other hand, is defined as foreknowledge. A deity who is omniscient would also be prescient. As with ESP and telepathy, each word has a distinct definition, but they are often used interchangeably.

Premonitions can occur in our sleep, but they also occur when we are awake. ESP occurs when one is wide awake. Visions may occur during the twilight hour, when one is falling asleep, or they may occur in the early morning hours, when one is waking up. They also occur during periods of clear consciousness, when one is wide awake.

In 1898, Morgan Robertson published a novella called *Futility, or The Wreck of the Titan* about a luxury ocean liner called the Titan, which sank in the North Atlantic after hitting an iceberg. Fourteen years later, the Titanic, a real-life luxury ocean liner, sank in the North Atlantic after hitting an iceberg. Both the Titan and the Titanic had been called "unsinkable"; both had less than half the number of lifeboats needed to rescue the passengers; both hit icebergs on the starboard side, in the month of April. The author of *Futility* denied he was clairvoyant.

Edgar Allan Poe's only novel, *The Narrative of Arthur Gordon Pym of Nantucket*, was published in 1838. It foreshadowed an actual event that took place in 1884. Both the novel and the event involved a ship in distress, a tortoise, and a crewman named Richard Parker. It was not for nothing that Yann Martel's award-winning shipwreck novel, *Life of Pi*, which was made into an award-winning movie, featured a character called Richard Parker. Once again, Life imitates Art. Did Robertson and Poe have premonitions?

Many people have premonitions. Andrew Cohen, award-winning jour-nalist and bestselling author, said he was a great admirer of the Kennedy family. He was devastated when President Kennedy was assassinated, but he was even more affected when Bobby Kennedy was murdered. On

June 5, 1968, he fell asleep after midnight. At 3:30 a.m. he sat bolt upright. Minutes later, once he was fully conscious, Bobby Kennedy's shooting was announced on the radio that Cohen had inadvertently left on.

Peri Lyons is a Tarot card reader in New York. Early in the 2008 presidential election campaign, before John McCain selected a running mate, she correctly predicted that McCain would "be undone by a crazy woman." Her prediction occurred long before anyone outside of Alaska had even heard of Sarah Palin.

As of this writing, Tom Hanks is the highest-grossing leading actor in the world, with worldwide box-office of more than $9.07 billion (Box Office Mojo). Hanks came from humble origins. His parents were divorced, and by the time he was ten, he had lived in ten different houses, with three different stepmoms. When he was in college, while watching *Saturday Night Live*, he turned to his friends and said, "I'm going to host that show someday." To date, Hanks has hosted SNL nine times. Did Hanks have a hunch or was it just preternatural self-confidence? Whatever it was, that kind of thing makes one sit up and take notice. The skeptic will no doubt say, what about all those other people who said they would one day host *SNL* and never did? Good point. And yet…

Melvin Morse studied premonition in parents whose babies died from SIDS (Sudden Infant Death Syndrome). Twenty-one percent of the parents reported sensing that something bad was going to happen to their babies. Many of these parents wrote in their journals, had recurring dreams, or told other people about their premonitions before the baby died. Although any new parent would have anxiety about an infant, only 3 percent of the control group (parents whose babies didn't die) reported ominous premonitions. The difference was statistically significant.

In response to criticism from his colleagues that his research on premonitions was not scientific, Dr. Morse replied that in his role as a physician it was necessary for him to understand the whole person, including the spiritual side of his patients' lives. He said that there was no deeper expression of humanity than spiritual experience, and he was not willing to neglect or ignore his patients' experiences. He noted a growing confluence of opinion in the medical and scientific communities about the importance of belief in the human spirit as it related to the quality of life.

Dr. Larry Dossey has written extensively about premonitions. He said that the warnings we are given through our dreams and premonitions should be taken seriously. He related the story of a woman who woke up with a start and told her husband she had had a dream in which the chandelier above her baby's crib came crashing down and the baby was seriously injured or killed. In her dream, she went to the nursery, glanced at the clock, saw it was 4:30 a.m., looked outside and saw a raging storm. When she woke up from her dream, she looked out her bedroom window and saw that it was perfectly calm. Her bedroom clock said it was 2:00 a.m. She was very shaken up by her dream, which she told her husband. Her husband told her, "It's just a dream, go back to sleep." She ignored his advice and brought the baby into her bed.

After a while, she and her husband were wakened by a loud crash. She ran into the baby's room and, sure enough, the chandelier had become unmoored and had crashed into the baby's crib and destroyed it. The clock in the nursery said 4:30, as in her dream. Outside the window, the storm was raging. Thanks to her dream and her decision to heed its warning, she saved her baby's life.

Dossey was asked how we would know if a dream is in fact a premonition or if it is just worry and anxiety. For example, in the above dream, the mother may have been worried about her baby. This dream was unusual because the raging storm and the time on the clock could be confirmed after the fact. He said he thinks we should pay particular attention to warnings in dreams if the dream is recurrent, if it is particularly vivid, or if it involves death.

Morse tells the story of one of his friends, a profound skeptic, who denied he had any hunches or premonitions. This man said that one time he was stopped at a red light. When the light turned green, he had an overwhelming feeling of nausea, and was unable to proceed. As he sat in his car, another driver went speeding through the red light. A policeman at the scene told him that he would have been killed instantly if he had proceeded through the intersection when the light turned green.

Predestination

Precognition and premonitions raise the question of predestination. If we are able to predict certain events, does that mean that these events were inevitable, that they were bound to happen or meant to happen? A common example of predestination is love at first sight. I have two cousins who told me independently that the first time they saw their future partners they knew right away that they would marry them one day. Even William Shakespeare acknowledged the validity of this sentiment when he wrote, "Whoever loved that loved not at first sight?" (*As You Like It*, Act III, scene 5).

My grandparents were Russian immigrants living in London, England, in the early 1900s. One evening my grandfather went with his friend to the theatre. Across a crowded room, he saw a beautiful young woman, pointed her out to his friend, and said, "One day that woman is going to be my wife." He didn't know who she was or how to contact her. After the crowd dispersed she was nowhere to be seen. Shortly afterwards, another friend asked him if he would be willing to go on a blind date. When he went to meet his date, sure enough she was the woman from the theatre. They subsequently married and moved to Canada. If it weren't for their meeting, I wouldn't be here.

The idea that the future is knowable leads to the concept of predestination, also known as fate or destiny. I was surprised to read in Walter Isaacson's biography of Albert Einstein that even the great man himself believed in predestination. Is there a role for fate, destiny, or predestination in our lives?

The idea of Fate has been with us throughout recorded history. In Greek mythology, Clotho, Lachesis and Atropos were the Three Fates. Clotho (the Spinner) spun the thread of life. She decided who would be born. Lachesis (the Disposer of Lots) measured the thread. She determined how long each person would live. She assigned to every mortal his or her destiny. Atropos (She Who Could Not Be Turned) cut the thread. She chose how each person would die. She ended the lives of mortals. The three sisters were called "daughters of the night." It was said that the sisters would appear within three days of a baby's birth, to decide the baby's fate. Their father was Zeus, King of the Gods. Their mother was Themis, the embodiment of divine law.

Synchronicity is linked to Fate. Some people think that synchronicity is a sign that one is on the right path or in tune with the Universe. Carl Jung coined the term "synchronicity", which he defined as the simultaneous occurrence of events that appear to be related significantly but have no *discernible* causal connection (italics mine). Synchronicity is also called meaningful chance or coincidence. There are those who think all coincidences are meaningful and there are no accidents, while others don't attribute any significance to coincidences, either because they don't notice them or because they are not interested.

I think coincidences are interesting and often startling, but we shouldn't overemphasize their importance. While they are no doubt meaningful on some occasions, their meaning is determined by the person who notices them. Still, even minor coincidences can be considered noteworthy for no other reason than to give people who notice them reassurance that they are on the right path, in the right place, at the right time, in the swing of things, or in tune with the Universe, if that is their belief. Some will go so far as to take even a minor coincidence as a sign that they are aligned with their life purpose. Thus, synchronicity may be equated with fate or destiny.

While I do pay attention to coincidences, I still believe in the law of cause and effect. "You reap what you sow" is a law of nature and we are part of nature. Swami Sivananda said, "You are the architect of your own fate" and "Destiny is your own creation." If we give too much credence to the idea of fate or destiny, we run the risk of shirking our own personal responsibility and denying the possibility of free will.

Having said that, I have to admit some coincidences are more startling than others. I was once asked by my friend, who is a choreographer, to prepare a series of drawings of Charles Dickens and his famous *Christmas Carol* characters, like Tiny Tim and Ebenezer Scrooge, for a dance production that she was putting on for the Christmas season. She wanted my drawings to hang in the lobby of the theatre the night of the performance. Soon after the request was made, I travelled to London to visit my daughter. I told her about my friend's request and asked her where we could find some information about Dickens. As we stood there on Marylebone High Street, talking about possibly visiting the Dickens Museum, I looked up and, to my amazement, saw that we were standing directly under a mural of Charles Dickens, Ebenezer Scrooge, Tiny Tim, and most of the characters from *A Christmas Carol*. I didn't need to go anywhere to find the images I was looking for. They were right there.

2012 was the 23rd anniversary of the Tiananmen Square massacre. Tens of thousands of protestors held a candlelight vigil in Hong Kong to commemorate the event, which occurred on June 4, 1989. In order to prevent similar attempts on mainland China, Chinese authorities blocked internet searches for the numbers 6 (the month), 4 (the date) and 89 (the year). On that day, the benchmark Shanghai Composite Index fell exactly 64.89 points. Shortly after the markets closed, a blogger from Shanghai wrote, "The Shanghai Composite Index is crying. Everybody understands it."

Prophecy

In ancient Rome, a religious official known as a haruspex inspected the entrails of sacrificed animals to interpret omens. They favored the livers of sacrificed sheep and poultry. It was a form of divination.

The ancient Greeks believed that the god Apollo spoke through the Delphic Oracle. The sibyl or priestess at Delphi delivered messages from Apollo which were often confusing or ambiguous so they were open to interpretation. People came from all over Greece with their questions about the future. This tradition began around 1400 BCE and lasted to the 4th century CE when newly Christian Rome banned pagan prophecy.

In 1555, Michel de Notredame ("our lady"), known today as Nostradamus, published a book of prophecies that has seldom been out of print. He was a physician, apothecary, and astrologer, whose predictions were written in rhyming quatrains. He was credited with predicting cataclysmic world events, although most academic sources claim any relationship between his predictions and world events is likely due to mistranslation or misinterpretation.

One famous example is his prophesy about the rise of "Hister." Many people saw a similarity between "Hister" and "Hitler" and thought Nostradamus had predicted the rise of Hitler. However, researchers discovered that "Hister" was actually the name of the lower Danube in the 16th century. Nostradamus was in fact talking about the flooding of the Danube. Nevertheless, Nostradamus remains very popular. He is still familiar to readers of the *National Enquirer* where we read about his predictions for the end of time as revealed by the Mayan calendar as we wait in the checkout line at the grocery store.

Prophets are often not believed and there are many false prophets. There are references to false prophets in the Bible. We also have them in our own time. Often, the word *prophecy* does not just mean the ability to predict the future, but also suggests that the prophet is a divine messenger. Modern-day cult leaders like Jim Jones (Jonestown), David Koresh (Branch Davidians), and Warren Jeffs (FLDS), have been called prophets by their followers.

The Fundamentalist Church of Jesus Christ of Latter-Day Saints (FLDS) is a breakaway sect of the Mormon Church that continues to practice polygamy, including child brides. Even though Jeffs is in jail for child sexual assault, his followers still call him "The Prophet." Even after his incarceration, he continued to control 10,000 of his followers from behind his jail bars.

Just as there are "prophets" whose prophecies are false, there are also prophets whose prophecies turn out to be true but are not believed. This is known as the Cassandra Complex. In Greek mythology, Cassandra, daughter of King Priam and Queen Hecuba of Troy, had the gift of prophecy. After she was cursed by Apollo for refusing his seduction, no one believed her prophecies. She foresaw the destruction of Troy and tried to warn her fellow Trojans about the Greeks hiding inside the Trojans' wooden horse, but to no avail. Thus her gift became a curse and she eventually went mad.

Nemo propheta in patria ("no one is a prophet in his own country") is a Latin proverb attributed to Pliny the Elder (23–79 CE), Roman author and philosopher. Similar sentiments are found in the Bible: "A prophet has no honor in his own country" (John 4:44). Familiarity breeds disbelief?

Greek mythology, Pliny the Elder, and the Bible all show that premonitions, predictions, and prophecies have been around for a long time. As is the case with Nostradamus, fortune-tellers remain popular even after their predictions turn out to be wrong. There is a human need to know the future, even if it is unknowable. Even if we accept premonitions, ESP, and telepathy as valid phenomena, we are still puzzled by the mechanisms involved.

Many writers, philosophers, psychologists, physicists, physicians, biologists, and theologians have written about the "collective unconscious", a term that was coined by Carl Jung. He said the personal unconscious is based on personal experience but the collective unconscious is impersonal, universal, inherited, and identical in all individuals. The personal unconscious interacts with the collective unconscious, which encompasses all of humanity. The basic idea is that at some level, through the collective unconscious, we are all connected and we are all one. The physicist David Bohm (1917–1992) wrote, "Deep down, the consciousness of mankind is one."

Bohm developed the concept of holo-movement in which consciousness is continually folding and unfolding. He said that reality is a "coherent whole, which is never static or complete, but which is an unending process of movement and unfoldment." A friend recently told me a story that illustrates this principle. He said he was thinking about dinosaurs while taking a shower, about how our ideas about dinosaurs has changed over the years as new fossils were discovered. As he dried himself off, he turned on the radio to listen to *This American Life* and found they were discussing the exact same topic. He wondered how this could happen, being the rational, skeptical person that he is. His wife turned to him and said, "It's simple. You are tuned into the universal hologram."

Dean Radin looked to quantum biology to explain telepathy, which he likened to quantum entanglement, in which things can be connected at a distance without an exchange of energy. Radin concluded that the evidence for these basic phenomena (ESP, telepathy, precognition) is so well-established that researchers today no longer try to prove that these phenomena exist; rather, they have turned their attention to trying to figure out how these things work.

Personal anecdotes may or may not be interesting (they are usually much more interesting to the person who is telling the story than to the person who is listening), but tens of thousands of scientific experiments performed since the late 19th century, as well as our own experiences, thoughts, dreams, and perceptions, suggest that telepathy, ESP, premonitions, and precognitive dreams are all valid, and valuable phenomena, as they make our lives so much richer. They extend the boundaries of what is possible and they make us question the accepted verities.

Why so much fascination with prophecy, predictions, and prognostication? I think our interest in these phenomena speaks to our attempt to alleviate our anxiety about the future. We must think if we have some inkling about what lies ahead we can prepare ourselves for the future. A vain hope, indeed. Probably the best way to prepare yourself for the future is with your thoughts, words, and deeds in the present.

Chapter 5: Limitless Mind, Limited Body, and the Rule of Four

The human mind will not be confined to any limits.

—Johann Wolfgang von Goethe (1749–1832)

Historically, one of the arguments central to both medicine and philosophy has been whether the mind is located in the brain or is separate from the brain and has a life of its own. This question is relevant to our discussion, since many paranormal phenomena, including thought transfer, telepathy, ESP, out-of-body and near-death experiences, deathbed visions, visitations, and messages would be somewhat more comprehensible if the mind were, at least in part, at least at times of severe stress, able to operate independently, outside of the brain and outside the body. The counterargument put forward by materialists, rationalists, and reductionists is that the mind is solely and at all times a function of the brain, and the brain, as it has been indelicately described, is nothing more than a piece of meat.

As an alternative to the either/or approach (either the mind is in the body or it isn't), I will adopt a multi-faceted approach in which the person is at all times considered on four different levels: the physical, which includes the brain and the body; the emotional, which affects and interacts with all the other levels; the mental, which subsumes intellect and cognition; and the spiritual, which connects us to all living things.

I will call this approach the Rule of Four. Since we are all part of nature, we must conform to the laws of nature. Just as a map has four directions, and a map wouldn't be a map without all four directions; just as the year has four seasons and the year would not be complete without all four seasons; similarly, any contemplation of the nature of mankind must acknowledge all four levels of existence. These four levels manifest in each person, in many different cultural, psychological, philosophical, and cosmological traditions.

I have tabulated some of these correspondences below.

THE FOUR PLANES OF EXISTENCE	THE FOUR ELEMENTS	THE FOUR HUMORS WITH CORRESPONDING TEMPERAMENTS	KABBALAH THE FOUR WORLDS	CARL JUNG THE FOUR FUNCTIONS
Spiritual	Fire	Blood – Sanguine (hopeful, confident)	Atzilut (world of emanation)	Intuition
Mental	Air	Phlegm – Phlegmatic (sluggish, indifferent)	Beriah (world of creation; universal mind)	Thinking
Emotional	Water	Black Bile – Melancholy (sad)	Yetzirah (world of formation)	Feeling
Physical	Earth	Yellow Bile – Choleric (angry)	Asiyah (world of action)	Sensation

The four levels or planes of existence – spiritual, mental, emotional and physical – correspond with the four elements found in nature – fire, air, water, and earth. The ancient Greeks believed these four elements comprised everything in the universe. This concept dates back to about 450 BCE. It held sway in science, medicine, and philosophy for almost 2,000 years. Hippocrates aligned the four elements in the universe with the four humors in the human body. He proposed that the humors needed to be in balance in order for there to be health in the body. Similar correspondences appeared in the Kabbalistic tradition and more recently in the work of Carl Jung and his followers.

To appreciate the merits of the Rule of Four approach, it is useful to understand some of the questions that have arisen historically around the relationship between mind, body, and spirit.

Where Is the Mind Located?

At first sight it might seem obvious that the mind and its moods, thoughts, and memories all originate in various brain structures and functions. But what about the expressions "gut feelings" or "gut instincts" or "gut reaction?" Are they just metaphors? How can feelings or instincts arise in the gut?

Michael Gershon, Chairman of the Department of Anatomy and Cell Biology at New York Presbyterian Hospital/Columbia University Medical Center, wrote in his 1998 book *The Second Brain* that the gut contains about 100 million neurons, more than the either the spinal cord or the peripheral nervous system. Embedded in the gut wall, the "second brain," also called the enteric nervous system, has sheaths of neurons filled with more than thirty different neurotransmitters, including 95 percent of the body's serotonin, a chemical which is responsible for keeping our mood in balance. A deficit of serotonin can lead to clinical depression. Neural tissue in the gut does more than just aid in digestion and excretion. The gut's "second brain" also influences mood and a sense of well-being.

Of course, we only have one brain, but if there are mental functions embedded in the gut wall, we may also have a "second mind." Electrical stimulation of the vagus nerve, which runs from the brain to the gut, has been used to treat depression and epilepsy. Although neurotransmitters in the gut can affect our mood – we are all familiar with the sensation of "butterflies" in the stomach – Gershon allows that the "second brain" is not responsible for cognition, logic, poetry, or philosophy.

Biologists at Tufts University showed that trained planarian flatworms retained their memories after they were decapitated. Surprisingly, flatworms have many of the same organs as humans, including a brain and a nervous system, as well as many of the same neurotransmitters. They are capable of remembering complex tasks. The decapitation experiments showed that flatworms were able to store memories outside of their brains.

In epigenetics, "cellular memory" refers to the idea that non-genetic information can be passed on from one generation to the next. This has been shown to be the case with post-traumatic stress disorder (PTSD) survivors. Epigenetics studies genetic effects not encoded in the DNA of the organism. Since memory is generally considered a mental function, we can say that, just like the mind, memory has also expanded its boundaries. Research is starting to catch up with both folk wisdom and the practical experience of holistic health practitioners when it comes to "gut feelings" and "cellular memory."

For decades, the idea that traumatic memories can be held in the body's musculature has informed modes of therapy known as "bodywork." Some of its major proponents have been Wilhelm Reich (orgone therapy); Ida Rolf (rolfing); Alexander Lowen (bioenergetics); Bennet Wong and Jock McKeen (Haven bodywork); F. M. Alexander (the Alexander technique); and Moshe Feldenkrais (the Feldenkrais method).

The mind, with its memories and its emotions, is not just in the brain and in the gut. It is also in the muscles, the immune system, and possibly other systems and organs. Jon Kabat-Zinn, in his CD *Mindfulness for Beginners*, says that in Asian languages the word for "mind" and the word for "heart" is the same word. American neuroscientist David Felton, co-founder and co-editor of *Brain, Behavior and Immunity* and co-editor of *Psychoneuroimmunology*, made the bold statement, "Your mind is in every cell in your body."

Cartesian Mind-Body Dualism

There are clear differences between the mind and the brain, as reflected in our language. If I said I was losing my mind, no one would think I was losing my brain. If I said my mind was wandering, I don't think anyone would send out a search party for my brain. The separation of mind and body is called Cartesian dualism in honor of the 17th-century French philosopher René Descartes, father of modern philosophy, who famously proclaimed, *Cogito ergo sum* (*I think, therefore I am*). He was saying that the mind ("I think") was distinct from the body ("I am"). The famous phrase first appeared in 1637 in French (*Je pense, donc je suis*) in his *Discourse on the Method*. It later appeared in Latin in his *Principles of Philosophy* (1644) where he wrote, *dubito, ergo cogito, ergo sum* (*I doubt, therefore I think, therefore I am*).

Descartes devised a thought experiment in which he tried to imagine that he didn't have a body. This task was relatively easy, as he was able to see himself flitting around as a ghost or a spirit. Next, he tried to imagine that he didn't have a mind. This he was unable to do, for imagination is a function of the mind. He concluded, therefore, that the mind was separate from the body.

Thousands of reports of near-death and out-of-body experiences have raised an obvious question: If the mind can exist outside the body, where exactly *does* the mind reside? Does the mind reside in the brain or outside the brain? Could it be both? Could the mind be in the body at certain times and outside the body at other times, for example, if there is a great deal of stress and emotional upheaval?

The idea that the mind resided in the body was called the materialist philosophy; the idea that the mind resided outside the body was known as the idealist philosophy. Idealism suggested that consciousness was the only reality, and matter was an illusion created by our minds. Materialism suggested that consciousness could only exist in the world of objects, the physical world. Modern research has offered some insight into these propositions.

Walter B. Cannon and Hans Selye were pioneers in the field of stress research. Cannon was Professor and Chairman of the Department of Physiology at Harvard Medical School. His book *The Wisdom of the Body*, published in 1932, was very influential. Cannon coined the term "fight or flight response."

Hans Selye, a Hungarian-Canadian endocrinologist, was the first to demonstrate the effects of biological stress in a lab. He worked mostly at the University of Montréal, where he had 40 research assistants and 15,000 lab animals. He published 1,700 research papers, 15 monographs, and seven popular books. His book, *The Stress of Life*, was published in 1956.

Selye described how the brain and immune system can communicate with each other through a feedback loop, the hypothalamic-pituitary-adrenal (HPA) axis and the sympathetic nervous system. The hypothalamus and the pituitary gland are located in the brain. The adrenal glands sit atop the kidneys. They release stress hormones (cortisol and adrenaline) when stimulated. Selye was the first person to describe the HPA axis, the system by which the body copes with stress. Back in the 1920s, Cannon discovered that cortisol was released into the blood stream during stress.

Psychobiological, neuroendocrine models exist for many stress-related disorders. The links between emotions and health are well-established. There is now widespread acceptance of the role of stress in causing disease, even mortality. Studies of bereavement, for example, have shown a large increase in the mortality rate from all causes in the first month following the death of a long-term spouse. The mechanism is the massive release of stress hormones, such as cortisol, which can affect heart function. There is, in fact, a well-known syndrome known as "broken-heart syndrome." When Debbie Reynolds died one day after Carrie Fisher, her beloved daughter, had died, many people said that Debbie Reynolds had died of a broken heart. Her son, Todd Fisher, said that 15 minutes before his mother died, she said, "I want to be with Carrie."

We can all relate examples of how the mind affects the body. It's easy enough to recall times when we felt nervous and noticed that we had a dry mouth, rapid heartbeat, shallow breathing, fine tremor, and so on. These are all symptoms of autonomic arousal. This is the classic fight or flight response, brought on by fear or anxiety, which prepares us to flee or to fight some perceived enemy. Public speakers often experience a dry mouth before they begin to speak, so they learn to carry a water bottle with them. The dry mouth is simply a manifestation of anxiety.

It is more surprising to think that even our hair and skin can be affected. If someone gets bad news, they may go pale. If they get angry, they could get red in the face. Pale skin is due to the constriction of blood vessels; looking flushed would be the opposite, dilation of blood vessels. Blushing, caused by embarrassment, is also due to dilation of blood vessels in the face.

The skin can also be raised, so-called goose bumps, in response to a threat, whether physical (cold temperature) or emotional (anger, fear, or some other strong emotion). Goose bumps can also be due to positive emotions. I might have goose bumps if I am listening to an especially beautiful piece of music or watching a very dramatic, emotional film.

Hair turning white can be due to aging, but it can also be due to strong emotions. My beautiful grandmother had long, white hair as long as I knew her. I was told that her hair turned white overnight when she was in her twenties, after she received a sudden shock. Hair can stand on end, if one is anxious or fearful. The same phenomenon is found in animals. The raised hair makes the animal look larger, and therefore, more formidable to an enemy. This is particularly noticeable in porcupines.

Perhaps the most dramatic example of how the mind affects the body is the "placebo effect." Double-blind drug studies are those in which neither the researcher nor the research subjects know which pill contains the active ingredient and which pill contains a placebo (sugar pill). A certain percentage of patients will show clinical improvement even though they are on a placebo.

In his book *It's The Thought That Counts: Why Mind Over Matter Really Works,* David R. Hamilton cited numerous studies in which patients got better while taking a placebo. In one remarkable study of 80 patients with Irritable Bowel Syndrome (IBS), the researchers found that there was significant, clinical, symptomatic improvement in patients taking a placebo even when they knew they were taking a placebo.

Ted Kaptchuk is the Director of the Program in Placebo Studies and the Therapeutic Encounter, based at the Beth Deaconess Medical Center, which is a Harvard Medical School teaching hospital. His groundbreaking placebo studies were listed by the *New Yorker* as "The Most Notable Medical Findings of 2015."

The effectiveness of placebos have been attributed to beliefs, expectations, anticipation, and suggestion, all of which are reasonable explanations; however, there may also be a physiological mechanism. An injection of saline (salt water), which was described as a drug, was shown to reduce the symptoms of Parkinson's disease by increasing the brain's production of a neurotransmitter, dopamine, which is lacking in Parkinson's disease.

It is worth noting that when patients are warned about possible side effects, even patients on placebos will develop side effects. It seems counter-intuitive that patients receiving placebos can develop side effects but it does happen.

Mind-Body Unity

Cartesian dualism has been challenged by philosophers for centuries. It was rejected by many in favor of the unity of mind and body. Mind-body unity or mind-body identity was the theory favored by the Dutch-Jewish philosopher Baruch Spinoza (1632–1677). For many generations, philosophy students debated Descartes vs. Spinoza. Currently, materialist philosophers such as Daniel C. Dennett continue to promote Spinoza's belief in mind-body unity.

The word "psychosomatic" is derived from two Greek words – *psyche* (mind) and *soma* (body). Psychosomatic medicine was a new discipline in the late 1930s and early 1940s. The journal *Psychosomatic Medicine*, which is the official journal of the American Psychosomatic Society, began publication in 1939. Although the term "psychosomatic" is nowhere to be found in DSM-5 (*Diagnostic and Statistical Medicine – 5th Edition*), the official list of psychiatric disorders of the American Psychiatric Association, the term "psychosomatic" continues to be used in everyday language, and the journal *Psychosomatic Medicine* is still being published.

Franz Alexander (1891–1964), Hungarian-American physician and psychoanalyst, is considered one of the founders of psychosomatic medicine. His 1943 article "Fundamental Concepts of Psychosomatic Research" explored how our emotions affect our health. His work was very much in line with that of Cannon and Selye.

Peptic ulcer disease, ulcerative colitis, and rheumatoid arthritis were all considered "psychosomatic" at one time because they were thought to be associated with specific personality types or particular neurotic conflicts.

We now have a more scientific explanation for what causes these diseases. For example, instead of attributing peptic ulcer disease to repressed anger, the list of known causes now includes infection by a bacterium, *H. pylori*, and regular use or overuse of painkillers like aspirin or non-steroidal anti-inflammatory agents (NSAIDs), such as ibuprofen or naproxen.

Still, we cannot disregard the notion that illness and disease often follow stressful situations. Separation and loss have been identified as precipitating factors in a number of illnesses, including ulcerative colitis.

In the 1940s, studies of psychiatric patients showed impaired immune response in patients with schizophrenia, including a reduction in the number of white blood cells called lymphocytes and diminished antibody response to pertussis vaccination compared to a non-psychotic control group.

There is a well-known correlation between depression and heart disease. Patients with heart attacks or heart failure are more likely to suffer from depression; conversely, patients with depression are more likely to incur heart disease. Major Depressive Disorder is three times more common in post-heart attack patients than it is in the general population.

In 1964, UCLA psychiatrist George Solomon investigated the effects of emotion on inflammation and the immune system after he observed that people with rheumatoid arthritis reported a worsening of their symptoms when they were depressed. Solomon coined the term *psychoimmunology*.

Dr. Solomon and Dr. George Engel, a psychiatrist from the University of Rochester, were pioneers in the field of psychosomatic medicine. Engel was known for his *biopsychosocial* model, which was the prevailing model in psychiatry at the time I did my training at McGill University. We were taught that for every illness we need to identify predisposing, precipitating, and perpetuating factors and to look at each of these from a biological, psychological, and social perspective.

In the 1960s, Herbert Benson, a cardiologist, demonstrated that meditation could lower blood pressure, heart rate, and respiratory rate. He coined the term "relaxation response" as a scientific term for meditation. He said the relaxation response was the opposite of the "fight or flight" response. He became the founder and president of the Mind/Body Medical Institute at the Massachusetts General Hospital in Boston and a professor of mind-body medicine at Harvard Medical School. Today's explosion of interest in all kinds of meditation, including mindfulness meditation, is no doubt linked to its proven benefits for overall physical and mental health and wellbeing.

In 1975, Robert Ader, a research psychologist, and Nicholas Cohen, an immunologist, showed that the nervous system could affect the immune system in an experiment they designed that used classical conditioning to suppress the immune system in rats. They found that stress could have just as powerful an effect on the immune system as immunosuppressant medication. Ader subsequently coined the word *psychoneuroimmunology* (PNI) to describe the study of the link between psychology, neurology, and immunology. He subsequently went on to launch the journal *Brain, Behavior and Immunity*. Ader and Cohen are considered the co-founders of psychoneuroimmunlogy for their work demonstrating the link between the mind and the body's immune system.

Candace Pert, the neuroscientist and molecular biologist who played a key role in the discovery of endorphin, has been referred to as the "mother of psychoneuroimmunology" for showing that stress and emotions affect immunity in humans as well as in rats. Her research at the National Institutes of Health showed that neuropeptides and neurotransmitters act directly on the immune system, thereby establishing a direct link between the immune system and the limbic system, a collection of brain structures involved with emotion, memory, behavior, and motivation.

Neuropeptides are small, protein-like molecules used by neurons to communicate with each other. They are involved in many different brain functions. Pert published more than 250 articles on neuropeptides and their role in the immune system, as well as several books, including the bestselling *Molecules of Emotion: The Science behind Mind-Body Medicine*. In his review of *Molecules of Emotion* for the *Smithsonian Magazine*, Paul Trachtman said Pert and her colleagues joined together what Descartes had put asunder.

Can the Mind Exist Outside the Body?

The term Universal Mind is used in spiritual and esoteric literature to represent universal higher consciousness or source of being. Each individual mind is part of Universal Mind, in the same way that the personal unconscious is related to the collective unconscious in Jungian psychology. Universal Mind has been conceptualized as a form of non-local consciousness. It encompasses the idea that, in essence, we are all one, one with nature, one with the source of being, and one with the universe. Meaning that, if you harm another person, you harm yourself, and if you harm Nature, you harm yourself.

If I can say that I am not my body (I am more than my body); and I am not my mind (I am more than my mind); and I am not my role, my function, my story, or my personality, then what am I? What's left? Eckhart Tolle, Deepak Chopra, Ram Dass, and others would say that what is left is pure being, pure spirit, or pure consciousness. As discussed earlier, when Ram Dass had a stroke, he said that *he* didn't have a stroke, his body had a stroke. He was just fine. In fact, he was perfect in every way. He didn't identify with his body. He saw himself as a spiritual being, pure consciousness, with no beginning and no end. One is reminded of the words of the French idealist philosopher and Jesuit priest Pierre Teilhard de Chardin:

"We are not human beings having a spiritual experience; we are spiritual beings having a human experience."

In his 2012 book *Brain Wars: The Scientific Battle over the Existence of the Mind and the Irrefutable Proof that Will Change the Way We Live Our Lives*, University of Montréal neuroscientist Mario Beauregard presented evidence that the mind, which he also calls "consciousness," can exist outside the brain. He says that the mind is filtered and transmitted by the brain but is not generated by it. Beauregard calls himself a nonmaterial neuroscientist. He is in the minority.

More typical is Kevin Nelson, a neurologist, researcher, and professor whose book *The Spiritual Doorway to the Brain: A Neurologist's Search for the God Experience* attempted to demystify spiritual experiences by linking them to neuroanatomical structures and neurotransmitters. Nelson wrote, "I have faith in molecules." He did, however, invoke William James's dictum about spiritual experiences: "Ye shall know them by their fruits, not by their roots." In other words, whatever the cause of the spiritual experience, the most important feature is the effect, not the cause.

Prior to his near-death experience, neurosurgeon Eben Alexander said he was Christian but not religious. He did not think it was possible for his mind to leave his body. After his near-death experience, he thought otherwise. He said that, although his brain was offline when he was in a coma, his mind continued to function. As a result, he started to see his mind as expansive and non-local, and he concluded that his mind was not permanently located in his brain.

Qualia and P-Zombies

Qualia represent the subjective aspect of experience. They have been called the heart of the mind-body problem. They are the states that philosophers use in thought experiments to show that there is a distinctive mental state for each individual which influences how he or she experiences perceptions, sensations, and feelings. Common examples of subjective experience would be smelling a rose, feeling pain, or seeing the color red. Daniel C. Dennett called qualia "the way things seem to us."

According to a thought experiment proposed by Australian philosopher David Chalmers, the status of qualia is essential to a proper understanding of the nature of consciousness. In the philosophy of mind, philosophical zombies – or p-zombies – are physical duplicates of people, without any qualia. A p-zombie is a hypothetical being that is identical in every respect to a normal human being except in one regard; it lacks consciousness. The p-zombie can mimic pain behavior. It can say that it is in pain; it can say, "Ouch," and it can recoil from the painful stimulus, but it cannot feel pain.

Chalmers argued that if p-zombies are physiologically equivalent to human beings, even as a logical possibility, they would be a sound refutation of physicalism, which is the idea that all of human nature can be explained by physical means. The idea that p-zombies are even possible suggests that consciousness cannot be purely physical.

Thomas Nagel is Professor of Law and Professor of Philosophy at New York University. He has written many important, influential books, including the 2012 book *Mind and Cosmos: Why the Materialist Neo-Darwinian Conception of Nature is Almost Certainly False.* He is well known for his critique of materialism and reductionism, the proposition that all mental processes can be reduced to neuroanatomy, neurochemistry, and neurophysiology.

Nagel developed the concept of qualia in his widely-read paper "What is it like to be a bat?" He wrote, "Consciousness is what makes the mind-body problem really intractable." His paper is considered one of the most influential papers on consciousness of the past century. He said that reductionists tend to use analogies from modern science because they try to explain what is incomprehensible in terms of what is comprehensible, but they are essentially comparing apples to oranges. He went on to say that we have no plausible explanation for the physical nature of mental phenomena, since our own experience provides the basis for our imagination, which is limited. One cannot know what it is like to be a bat because one isn't a bat and one does not have the consciousness of a bat. He concluded that there are facts that are not expressible in human language, but that we can recognize the validity of these facts without being able to comprehend them.

The British philosopher of mind Colin McGinn agreed with Nagel that consciousness was basically unknowable. In his famous paper "Can We Solve the Mind-Body Problem?" he wrote that somehow we feel "the water of the physical brain is turned into the wine of consciousness" but we don't know how. He calls the whole process mysterious, magical, and miraculous.

These philosophical musings about p-zombies and qualia contribute to our discussion and understanding of paranormal phenomena, which may be at some level incomprehensible. In fact, all these questions – Where is the mind? What is the mind? What is consciousness? – are relevant for an exploration of paranormal phenomena.

Future Directions

Dr. Adrian Owen, at the University of Western Ontario's Brain and Mind Institute, has devised ways to determine responsiveness in comatose patients who were previously thought to be in a brain-dead, vegetative state. Using functional MRIs, Owen showed that when he asked non-responsive patients to imagine they were playing tennis, the patients' brains lit up in the areas responsible for the movement. He could detect a response where previously none was apparent. His research has profound implications for end-of-life decision-making, since people who were previously thought to be brain-dead and would, therefore, be disconnected from their life supports were shown to be still responsive at some level which required cognition.

Another mind-blowing experiment (not a brain-blowing experiment!) was carried out at the Institute for Brain Science at Brown University in Providence, Rhode Island. Researchers wired up a mute, paralyzed woman to a robotic arm. When they instructed her to think about drinking a cup of coffee, she was able to raise a coffee cup to her lips with the use of the robotic arm. Her thoughts triggered electrical activity in the part of the brain that was responsible for the action and the electrical impulse travelled down the wire to the arm. The researchers are now working on a wireless version of their experiment. Can we say that her thoughts created a new reality for her?

Mind-Body Reality

It seems there are three options: the mind resides in the brain; the mind is both in the brain and outside the brain but it remains in the body; the mind can exist in the brain or outside the brain and even, at times, outside the body.

Literally hundreds of books and thousands of articles have been published in the scientific literature and the popular press on the topic of mind-body medicine, how our emotions affect our health, and the effects of stress on the body, written by scientists, psychologists, physicians, psychiatrists, and philosophers. We can only hope to scratch the surface of this huge field. Our purpose here is not to be exhaustive but to show how the mind-body problem is relevant to our discussion of the paranormal.

With the exponential growth of the OBE and NDE literature in recent years, as well as the explosion of interest in past-life regression therapy and induced or spontaneous after-death communication, it seems evident that the mind can be separate from the body, at least at certain times, such as after death or during out-of-body experiences. Therefore, the mind must have an independent function.

Melvin Morse said that certain aspects of consciousness are independent of brain function. Pioneering neurologist Wilder Penfield said the mind is independent of the brain. He likened the brain to a computer which is programmed and conditioned by something outside of itself – the mind. In this model of mind-brain, the brain is the hardware and the mind is the software. Deepak Chopra took it one step further when he compared the brain to a radio receiver that is able to pick up signals from anywhere in the universe.

My cousin told me her father left his body during surgery and that afterwards he was able to report everything he had seen and heard while out of his body. He did not associate the experience with religious ideas like soul or spirit. We can say that his mind (or consciousness) left his body; his brain did not leave his body. For him, any discussion of soul, spirit, or religion was irrelevant.

I don't have any problem with the idea that the mind and the body are one, but I conceptualize the mind as so much more than that – not only the idea that the individual mind relates to the universal mind, but also the idea that the mind relates to society.

Austrian-British philosopher Ludwig Wittgenstein, one of the most influential philosophers of the 20th century, noted that private experience is embodied in the public sphere and not only in the brain, since the subject's behavior occurs in his or her social context. Anthropologist Gregory Bateson agreed with Wittgenstein when he wrote, "The mental world – the mind – the process of information processing – is not limited by the skin."

Dr. Denis Noble, Emeritus Professor of Cardiovascular Physiology at Oxford University said that the mind has nothing to do with genes, nerve cells, or molecules. He seemed to be in agreement with Wittgenstein when he said, "I think we'll find that the mind lies outside the body, in the neural networks of social and cultural life." He preferred to think of the mind as a process, not as an object located in space. In his view, the mind is non-local.

Robert Jahn, the aerospace engineer who headed the Princeton parapsychology research lab, suggested that consciousness can exist in two states at once, both local and nonlocal. Just as a photon can be both a particle and a wave, the mind can be like a particle, localized in space and time, during ordinary states of awareness, or like a wave, leading to subjective feelings of timelessness and mystical oneness with all things, during extraordinary states. Dean Radin said that we can be more particle-like or more wave-like depending on what we wish to be, or what is suitable to be at the time, or what we are motivated to become. This statement sounds pretty outlandish, at first glance, but I prefer to think of it as a metaphor.

Dr. Roderick McInnes, one of the world's leading medical geneticists, said, "We're probably never going to understand the brain at the level of individual neurons. We'll probably have to look at it the way astrophysicists approach understanding a billion stars." Both Drs. Noble and McInnes take us from the micro to the macro level, from the individual to the relational and the cosmic or universal.

The brain's weight (3 lbs. or 1,400 grams) represents about 2 percent of our total body weight. It has 100 billion neurons. The spinal cord also has about 100 billion neurons. Each neuron can connect with up to ten thousand other neurons so the total number of synapses in the brain is at least 100 trillion. There are more synapses in the central nervous system than there are stars in the Milky Way.

A hundred billion neurons and a hundred trillion synapses in our brain. A hundred billion stars in our galaxy. Scientists using the Hubble Space Telescope have estimated that there are roughly two trillion galaxies in our universe, which is 14 billion years old. These numbers are beyond our powers of comprehension.

Our understanding of brain function is still rudimentary. Dr. David Kaplan, Canada Research Chair in cancer and neuroscience at the University of Toronto and the Hospital for Sick Children, said, "Almost everything we know about the brain we know from the last 10 or 15 years, a time of exponential learning." He said what we need most at this juncture is not more money for research; rather, what we need most for a better understanding of the brain are fresh ideas.

At one time, we thought that the brain was a static organ, incapable of any kind of change, other than degeneration. We now know that the brain's neuroplasticity means that it can reorganize itself by making new neural connections throughout life. Environmental factors, such as diet, exercise, and cognitive training can alter brain structure and function.

Studies have shown that meditation is associated with increased thickness of the cerebral cortex and increased density of the grey matter. The continuing, longitudinal Nun Study on Aging and Alzheimer's Disease emphasized the importance of community, faith, and attitude for healthy aging (as well as the absence of drug and alcohol abuse, tension, stress, and turmoil).

Although mind/body/spirit is a continuum, there has been a lot of discussion of the mind/body problem with very little attention paid to the spiritual side. The real-world consequences are devastating. Strange as it seems, 30 percent of American health-care dollars are spent keeping patients alive in the last few months of life. In spite of this massive outpouring of scarce health care resources, patients' lives are not any better. End-stage quality of life for most hospitalized patients remains abysmal, except for those hospitals that provide palliative care. Doctors will often order unnecessary tests just to make sure they haven't missed anything or, in some cases, to reduce liability.

So much time, money, and effort are spent prolonging the patient's life or to be more accurate, prolonging the patient's suffering. To what end? Most of us would rather die at home, surrounded by loving family and friends, than hooked up to machines in hospital. Dying with dignity should be more important than squeezing every single last little drop out of life.

Stanislav Grof wrote, "[We are] fighting for the mechanical prolongation of life [but] the quality of the patient's last days and his psychic and spiritual longings do not receive enough attention." That's putting it mildly.

The paltry funding for consciousness research pales in comparison to the huge amounts of money spent on brain research. As a society, we prioritize the physical level of existence over any other. The body is king in our hospitals and nursing homes. Mind, emotion, and spirit are the serfs and vassals.

One day, in the not-too-distant future, I predict that this trend will be reversed. Individuals who have had near-death and out-of-body experiences, who have learned to overcome their fear of death, will lead the way. We will, in time, re-order our priorities as we re-direct our energy to quality of life rather than quantity of life.

We should remember the Rule of Four and not neglect the role of emotional and spiritual factors in our daily lives, as they are constantly interacting with each other as well as with the mind and the body. The important thing to remember is the need for balance and harmony amongst all four elements.

The emotions can clearly affect the mental function. Someone with depression, for example, will often find that their thinking is slowed down. Similarly, emotions can also affect the physical function, as clearly shown by Candace Pert and a long line of researchers before her.

Spirituality, or its dearth, can affect the emotional function, leading to joy or despair, alienation or a sense of belonging. All four planes of existence can affect all the other levels. There is constant interplay and interaction. Just as it is essential that we take good care of our bodies, it is equally important for us to pay attention to and take good care of our mental, emotional, and spiritual lives. The need to balance the four planes of existence is nothing new. In his description of the four humors, Hippocrates said essentially the same thing over two thousand years ago. The Rule of Four is a timely reminder of this wisdom, which is both ancient and modern.

Rules are meant to be broken. The so-called Rule of Four is not really a rule. It's more like a guideline or a suggestion. In our society, we tend to over-value the mental world (thinking and over-thinking) and the physical world (materialism, consumerism, bodily health and bodily functions). We tend to undervalue, or disregard, the emotional and spiritual side of life. Many people are either not aware of their feelings or, if they are, they choose not to express them. We swallow our feelings. Similarly, the spiritual world goes begging. The central issue is not the dominance or prominence of one world or another. What is needed is balance, equilibrium, harmony, and awareness.

Across the four seas, all men are brothers.

—Confucius

Is this a rule? Is it a guideline? Is it a belief?

I prefer to think of it as an idea whose time has come.

Chapter 6: *All experience is an arch*: Empiricism vs. Rationalism

I am a part of all that I have met;
Yet all experience is an arch wherethrough
Gleams that untraveled world whose margin fade
For ever and for ever when I move.

—Alfred, Lord Tennyson, "Ulysses"

I always loved the poem "Ulysses", from the time I first read it when I was in high school. Everything that happens to us becomes a part of us. Reading this poem, I was enriched, and the poem became a part of me.

As Tennyson so beautifully said, "All experience is an arch." Experience points us in a certain direction, the direction of further experience and further learning ("that untraveled world"). Once we learn a lesson, we cannot unlearn it. We can only move onto the next lesson. We can't move backwards in life. We can only move forward. Experience provides us with an arch, a window, an unseen world that we long for and move towards. That's why our reach should exceed our grasp.

> *Ah, but man's reach should exceed his grasp,*
> *or what's a heaven for?*

— Robert Browning, "Andrea del Sarto"

Empiricism and rationalism are opposing philosophical theories about how we know what we know. Empiricism states that we gain knowledge through our senses, through experience, experiment, and observation.

Sensory perception is paramount. The nub of empiricism is expressed in the maxim "seeing is believing." One of the best-known empiricists is the British physician, diplomat, and philosopher John Locke (1632–1704). Other important empiricists were Francis Bacon (1561–1626), George Berkeley (1685–1753), and David Hume (1711–1776).

Rationalism regards reason (the mind) as the chief source of knowledge; it claims we gain knowledge independent of experience and the five senses (the body). Rationalist philosophers in the ancient world included Pythagoras, Plato, and Aristotle. Enlightenment rationalist philosophers included René Descartes (1596 –1650), Baruch Spinoza (1632 –1677), and Gottfried Liebniz (1646 –1716). Spinoza was opposed to the mind-body dualism of Descartes, but they were both rationalists.

In his review of Anthony Gottlieb's book, *The Dream of Enlightenment*, Adam Kirsch points out an odd fact: almost all of important Western philosophy that in still relevant in the 21st century is the product of two eras: Athens in the 4th and 5th centuries BCE and Western Europe in the 17th and 18th centuries.

Michael Shermer is a rationalist. He related interest in the paranormal to pattern-seeking behavior. He postulated, in *The Believing Brain,* that the brain looks for patterns and infuses these patterns with beliefs. Once the beliefs are established, the brain looks for and finds confirmatory evidence. Some people think seeing is believing (empiricists); others think the reverse, that believing is seeing (rationalists). Shermer is clearly in the latter camp. He thinks belief comes first and explanations follow.

I tend to favor the former position (seeing is believing) based on my own personal experience. I knew nothing about out-of-body experiences until I had one. The same thing applies to precognitive dreams. I hadn't been reading about them or talking about them. I didn't even know they existed. I didn't have a belief in out-of-body experience or precognitive dreams. I needed to have the experience before I could believe it was possible. Experience led me to reading, learning, and attempts at understanding anomalous phenomena. But the experience came first. In fact, I could say it was essential.

In general terms, I think it is safe to say that paranormal believers tend to be empiricists; paranormal skeptics tend to be rationalists, also known as materialists, physicalists, or reductionists.

This dynamic fits in with Jung's theory of personality types that distinguishes introversion from extroversion. He said introverts are more involved in their inner world of thoughts and feelings, while extroverts are more interested in the outer world of people and objects. We would expect introverts to be more open to the paranormal, while extroverts would be more prone to skepticism.

As outlined in the table on The Rule of Four, Jung described four mental functions: thinking, feeling, sensation, and intuition. Each of us has strengths and challenges in each of the mental functions. So, for example, someone whose strength is thinking, who favors the life of the mind, would tend towards rationalism. Another person, whose strength is sensation, who relishes the life of the senses, would tend to favor empiricism.

Just as we should have a healthy balance between skepticism and belief, we should acknowledge the contributions of both rationalism and empiricism. While I have emphasized, for the most part, the empirical approach, as I discussed some of my paranormal experiences, I would not want to disparage rationalism in any way. There is more than one way of learning about the world we live in. My endorsement of the empirical approach, with its emphasis on learning through experience and observation, does not in any way deny the importance of the rationalist approach. As a man of science, I can hardly deny the value of rationalism, although my comments about scientism included a word of caution against over-zealousness and exclusiveness. Once again, we need to strive for balance and harmony.

Immanuel Kant (1724–1804), the central figure in modern philosophy, wished to reconcile the rationalist approach with the empiricist approach. He said that experience not processed by reason was purely subjective, while reason not applied to experience led to "theoretical illusions." Many people believed that the conflict between empiricism and rationalism was resolved by Kant when he said that both sides were correct because our perceptions are filtered through mental categories.

Be that as it may, these contrasting belief systems about the source of knowledge continue to play out in our popular culture. In the movie *A Late Quartet*, for example, an ageing cellist has to stop playing when he gets Parkinson's disease. In one scene, he is telling a group of his students about the time he met with one of the greatest cellists of all time, Pablo Casals, when he himself was a student. He was so nervous that he couldn't speak. Casals could see that the young student was tongue-tied, so he asked him to play something. He was so nervous that he made many mistakes. He hung his head in shame. Casals said, "That's wonderful. That's splendid." But he walked away terribly disappointed in himself and embarrassed by his performance.

Years later, he met Casals at a social function. By that time, he was in a famous string quartet that played in concert halls around the world. After a couple of drinks, he said to Casals, "Why weren't you honest with me when you heard me play as a student?" Casals picked up a cello that was in the room. He played a few notes. He said, "You did this." He played a few more notes. He said, "You did that." Then he said, "For me, it was novel. Let the morons talk about what they don't like. I can be grateful for a moment of transcendence."

I, too, can be grateful for a moment of transcendence. For me, it's the experience that counts. It's like the song says:

How you gonna keep 'em down on the farm after they've seen Paree?

Paris is the City of Light, *la ville lumière*, the city of the Enlightenment. Once you have seen the light, you can't pretend that you haven't seen it. A single moment of light, an insight, an epiphany, can change your life forever.

Gestalt therapists Erving and Miriam Polster emphasized the importance of the experience itself, rather than the interpretation of the experience. They believed that this practice would guard against authoritarianism. The person who has the experience is the one who has credibility. The person who attempts to explain or interpret the experience assumes an attitude of superiority without necessarily knowing what he or she is talking about.

Gestalt therapists are closely aligned with existential philosophers such as Jean-Paul Sartre, who famously declared "existence precedes essence." In *Existentialism is a Humanism*, Sartre wrote: "Man first of all exists, encounters himself, surges up in the world – and defines himself afterwards." Existentialists say there is no such thing as human nature, but all humans share the human condition. The essence of a person is not innate; rather, it is shaped by experience (the empirical approach).

Danish existentialist philosopher Søren Kierkegaard wrote, "Life is not a problem to be solved, but a reality to be experienced." He also said, "The highest and most beautiful things in life are not to be heard about, nor read about, nor seen but, if one will, are to be lived." There is no short cut. There is nothing like living to learn about life.

Some people say we learn from our mistakes, but why call them mistakes if we learn from them? Why not call them lessons or experiences that we can learn from? Hopefully, we can learn from everything that we attract into our lives. Just as we have to review our lessons in school over and over until we finally learn them, so do we keep repeating lessons that present themselves as experiences until the lesson is truly incorporated into our essence. Then we can move on to the next lesson, or the next level of learning (the next grade).

Wayne Dyer says we attract into our lives not what we want but who we are. We can shift gears with our thinking, based on our experience. Consequently, life can be more interesting and meaningful, not just a series of random events.

As mentioned previously, I have had a series of experiences that could be described as psychic, paranormal, or anomalous. I like to think I have learned about the real nature of life from these experiences, which include near-death and out-of-body experiences, as well as prophetic dreams, apparitions, angels, and all sorts of otherworldly phenomena. While I would have been willing to overlook one or two strange events that couldn't be explained by logic or reason, when the paranormal events started to pile up, they demanded attention. I was not able to overlook them or pretend they didn't happen. For me, it has also become important to share my experiences with other people.

In his essay "Why I Write: Making No Become Yes," Elie Wiesel (1928-2016), Nobel Laureate, Holocaust survivor, professor, political activist, and author of 57 books, including *Night,* which was based on his experiences as a prisoner at Auschwitz and Buchenwald, said that he had to write in order to give meaning to his experience. He wrote that the only role he sought was that of witness.

> I believed that, having survived by chance, I was duty-bound to give meaning to my survival, to justify each moment of my life. I knew the story had to be told. *Not to transmit an experience is to betray it.* (Italics mine)

While I am not comparing my experiences in any way to the horrific events suffered by Wiesel, I agree with him about the need to report and document experience because not to do so would be a betrayal of the experience.

Memento Mori

Although I did not have the typical near-death experience, in the sense that I did not see a bright light or a tunnel, nor did I meet a spiritual being or any of my dead relatives, I did have what might be called an atypical near-death experience. Once, I had a dream in which I found myself in the most beautiful, lush, green garden. Everything was green. It was just like how I imagined the Garden of Eden. It reminded me of one of Henri Rousseau's jungle paintings which, oddly enough, is called *Il Sogno* (*The Dream.*)

Henri Rousseau, Il Sogno (The Dream)

The feeling that accompanied the image was one of pure joy. It catapulted me into a different realm of existence, which bleeds through from time to time. This "heavenly" experience occurred when I was very ill. I will never forget it. I was forever changed by my experience. My dream was spontaneous and it occurred in an oppressive context. But some people manufacture experiences to remind themselves of their own mortality, the shortness of life, and the imminence of death. Not just risk takers, but many others as well. Even if we have not been close to death ourselves, we have all known family and friends who have died. Death is a central part of every human life. We all know we are going to die, but we usually put that thought out of our minds. Freud called death "the worm at the core of our happiness." It is impossible to go through life without being touched by separation, loss, and death.

Encounters with death tend to focus the mind. Medieval scholars used to keep a skull on their desk to remind them that life is short. The skull was called a *memento mori*. It was a constant reminder of death. *Memento mori* is Latin for "Remember you will die." Dutch and Flemish artists in the 17th century often used images of skulls as a reminder that life is short. A good example is *Self Portrait with Skull*, c. 1661, by Flemish painter Michiel Sweerts. The skull, faded flowers, and rotten food were known as *vanitas* (vanity) symbols. "Vanity of vanities, all is vanity" (Ecclesiastes 1:2). This tradition was carried into the 20th century by Paul Cézanne in his famous 1910 painting *Pyramid of Skulls.*

Michiel Sweerts, Self Portrait with Skull

We are surrounded by reminders of death but, for the most part, we tend to ignore them.

> *Better to smile on all that smile,*
> *and show there is a comfortable kind of old scarecrow.*

—William Butler Yeats, "Among School Children"

Impact of Near-Death Experience

The dramatic impact of a near-death experience was described by Dr. Yvonne Kason, a Toronto family physician. Her near-death experience changed her life. She developed psychic abilities after she survived a plane crash when she was a 26-year-old medical resident assigned to Sioux Lookout, Ontario. Her plane went down in a blizzard in Northern Ontario as she accompanied a patient to hospital. After the crash, she found herself in the Lake of the Woods. She felt panicky at first, but her fears soon gave way to bliss when she saw a white light surrounded by a loving intelligence. With the shoreline 100 meters away, she thought that, with her parka and heavy boots, it would be too hard for her to swim to shore. In the icy water, she was sure she would drown.

But a voice in her head told her to swim. As she started to swim, she felt her consciousness leave her body. She was watching herself from a vantage point fifteen meters above her head when she saw her body go under twice. Still she kept swimming. Once she was close to shore, she reached out and grabbed a tree trunk and pulled herself to shore. Afterwards, she described the episode as the most beautiful, most blissful experience of her life.

Two months later, as she was driving to see a friend, she had a psychic flash that her friend had meningitis. When she arrived at her friend's house, the friend had a bad headache, but no other symptoms. She told her friend about her vision and what to watch for. When symptoms of meningitis subsequently started to appear, her friend headed straight to the hospital. Kason thought her vision – of a brain surrounded by pus – probably saved her friend's life.

Spurred on by her experience, Kason began to study the literature on paranormal phenomena. As a result of informing her medical colleagues of her experiences and her interest in the paranormal, she had many patients referred to her who had similar experiences. She found that most of them were afraid to talk about their experiences for fear of being labelled crazy.

After a great deal of research and reflection, she decided that her psychic abilities and those of her patients were not pathological. Her extensive reading convinced her that her psychic experiences were quite normal, and furthermore, they were universal. She discovered that transformative, spiritual experiences have been found in every culture throughout history. She learned that many philosophers, great thinkers, and scholars had been writing about paranormal and psychic experiences for centuries.

The experiences may vary in frequency or profundity, but they are present in every society. She understood that some individuals with psychic abilities could develop a psychotic illness if they started to think that they were special or that they had a direct line to God. Some of the patients referred to her became grandiose and went on to develop mania. When her patients started to believe they were being controlled by outside forces, they developed an illness that resembled paranoid schizophrenia. In most cases, the psychotic episodes were transitory and responded well to conventional treatments. She found that there was a greater likelihood of a psychotic break if there was a family history of mental illness, because of genetic predisposition.

David Lukoff, a psychologist in California, proposed a new diagnostic category for persons who became psychotic after a mystical/spiritual experience: *transient psychosis with mystical features.* He wanted the psychiatric community to acknowledge that mystical experiences were a normal part of consciousness but that they may occasionally lead to brief, psychotic episodes. Like Kason, he found that these episodes were most often temporary and they tended to resolve spontaneously. The individual undergoing such an episode needed supportive care and counseling but, in most cases, would not need to be admitted to a psychiatric ward.

Many people who have psychic or paranormal experiences feel excited, intrigued, or fascinated by them; they feel curious and challenged. Others feel overwhelmed, disturbed, and frightened, especially if the experience contradicts their view of reality. While the former group is able to turn a major challenge into an opportunity for learning and growth, the latter group found that they could not cope; their defenses were overwhelmed, and they felt out of control and unable to distinguish inner reality from outer reality.

Kason came to the conclusion that she was changed in a good way by her near-death experience which led her to psychic abilities. She could not deny her own reality, based on her own experience. She came to believe that everyone has psychic abilities, whether they acknowledge them or not.

Everyone Is Psychic

The idea that everyone is psychic, to a greater or lesser extent, is a common theme throughout the paranormal and psychic literature. Some people choose to develop their psychic abilities; others do not. Some people are fascinated by their paranormal experiences; others are scared by them or indifferent.

Dean Radin noted that, just as some people are gifted musically while others are more athletic, there is a certain segment of the population that is good at extended perception, ESP, telepathy, and clairvoyance.

Kason cited a Gallup poll that showed that one in ten Americans has had a spiritual or mystical experience. Another poll showed that 30 percent of people believed in ghosts, and 15 percent claimed to have actually seen a ghost or an apparition. These numbers may seem high for the simple reason that most people don't talk about their paranormal experiences for fear of being ridiculed or called crazy. They might tell an anonymous caller doing a telephone survey but not close family or friends.

Jack Canfield, co-creator of the *Chicken Soup for the Soul* series, said in an interview that he sees "bank presidents, corporate leaders, military people and policemen who have had near-death experiences, visitations from angels, intercessions from higher powers, and awakenings. But they're afraid to talk about it because they don't want to be seen as 'woo woo.' "

I have been surprised by how many people that I have shared some of my anomalous experiences with will respond by telling me strange and unusual experiences of their own. By sharing our own experiences we give permission for others to do the same. We may open the floodgates.

Abraham Maslow, Carl Jung, Sigmund Freud, William James

In her research into mystical experiences, Kason discovered an extensive literature on the subject, written by the some of the most distinguished names in the field of psychology.

Psychologist Abraham Maslow coined the term "peak experience" to describe mystical experiences, which he considered the apex of one's personal growth, the high point of one's life. He wrote that these experiences lead to a feeling of wholeness or self-actualization. For Maslow, self-actualization was the ultimate goal in life.

Carl Jung wrote about his own mystical experiences, which he called "numinous." He saw the mystical experience as a very positive force in his own personal growth. He postulated that these experiences led to individuation of the self.

According to Jung, Freud's views of parapsychology evolved over the years. He said Freud initially rejected parapsychology as nonsense because of his materialist philosophy but in his later years, "[he] recognized the seriousness of parapsychology and the factuality of 'occult' phenomena."

Freud wrote a paper called "Psycho-Analysis and Telepathy" (1921), which was published posthumously. His monographs "Dreams and Telepathy" and "Dreams and Occultism" were included in his *New Introductory Lectures on Psychoanalysis* (1933).

William James (1842–1910) was born into a wealthy, prominent family in New York City. His father, Henry James, Sr., was a Swedenborgian theologian (i.e., he was a follower of the Swedish mystic Emanuel Swedenborg.) William's brother, Henry James, was the author of many well-known novels, including *The Golden Bowl, Portrait of a Lady,* and *The Bostonians.* William's sister, Alice James, was known as a diarist. William attended Harvard Medical School but never practiced medicine; instead, he became a psychologist, philosopher, educator, and author. As an educator, James offered the first course on psychology in the United States. William James said repeatedly that he accepted spirituality and mysticism as an important part of his life. His widely-read book *The Varieties of Religious Experience* has been in print continuously since it was first published in 1902 and it is still influential.

The generally conservative American Psychological Association (APA) published a collection of papers in 2000 that reviewed and assessed claims of paranormal activities including mystical experiences, alien abduction, auditory and visual hallucinations, out-of-body experience, lucid dreaming, past lives, anomalous healing, and other paranormal phenomena. The authors agreed these experiences could not be dismissed as signs of psychopathology. Their report was called *Varieties of Anomalous Experience: Examining the Scientific Evidence.* The title of the APA report echoed and paid homage to William James's *The Varieties of Religious Experience.* Substituting *anomalous* for *religious,* the authors made a connection between what we call psychic, paranormal, or anomalous phenomena and experiences that in another era were called religious, mystical, or spiritual. By stating that paranormal experiences were not signs of psychopathology, even an august body like the APA was affirming that these events are essentially "normal."

Yet most people still can't accept them. Maybe it's not just the fear of being labelled crazy or being rejected or ridiculed by one's peers. Maybe it's that we don't like to be shaken out of our rigid, codified belief systems. The fear of being called crazy for discussing one's paranormal experiences is a variation of worrying about what other people think about you. An old friend of mine once quoted the popular saying: "When I was twenty, I used to worry about what other people were thinking about me. When I turned forty, I decided I was going to stop worrying about what other people were thinking about me. When I turned sixty, I realized that other people weren't thinking about me. They were thinking about themselves." How true. As another popular saying goes, "We get too soon old and too late smart."

William James was not religious in the conventional sense. He was not interested in the church, its rites and rituals, or even its religious ideas; his main concern was religious feelings. The subtitle of *Varieties* is *A Study in Human Nature*. James was interested in human nature, not divine nature. His fascination with spiritualism and mysticism was directly related to their benefits for human psychology.

James's views about religion and mysticism were based on the idea that awareness of a different type of consciousness can make people happy and make it easier for them to cope with their lives. His idea of truth was related to a concept's utility. He knew that his religious visions were not in one sense true because they were drug-induced (by his use of nitrous oxide); but they nevertheless revealed a higher truth.

He was convinced of the benefit of positive illusions. In his final essay, which he completed just before his death, he affirmed his belief that nitrous oxide had a lasting benefit on his philosophy and his life. He believed that religion could help people, even if it was an illusion. Freud, we recall, similarly wrote about religion in a monograph called "The Future of an Illusion."

Optimistic people generally are happier than people who think of themselves as realists. Beliefs are an individual choice. The idea that religion can provide comfort and help people cope with death was expressed by King David in the 23rd psalm, which is often recited at funerals:

> *Yea, though I walk through the valley of the shadow of death,*
> *I will fear no evil,*
> *For Thou art with me;*
> *Thy rod and Thy staff, they comfort me.*

James thought that beliefs, for humans, were adaptive survival mechanisms, like a giraffe's long neck or a tiger's claws. He said we help to create the "truths" that we believe in.

Thomas Jefferson (1743–1826), the third president of the United States, was one of the chief drafters of the Declaration of Independence. He wrote, "We hold these truths to be self-evident: that all men are created equal; that they are endowed by their Creator with certain unalienable rights; that among these are life, liberty, and the pursuit of happiness." Yet Jefferson was a slave owner. He owned hundreds of African-American slaves. When he said these truths are self-evident, he was talking about truths that were evident to him. His statements were in accordance with William James's assertions that a philosopher's theories are a reflection of the philosopher's personality. But they may not be in accordance with the facts.

Just as beauty is in the eye of the beholder, it seems that truth is also in the eyes, ears, and mind of the beholder. One man's meat is another man's poison. One man's truth is another man's delusion.

Jung's four different mental functions – thinking, feeling, sensation and intuition – in different combinations will produce different personality types. In each individual, there is a dominant function and, according to Jung, each function has an extroverted or introverted attitude. Based on my experiences, if my dominant mental function is intuitive and my attitude is introverted, one might speculate I am more prone to pay attention to paranormal experiences, with their accompanying "truths."

I was touched by some of my formative experiences in my early years, but these experiences – sleep paralysis, sleepwalking, and imaginary companions – are by no means uncommon. On the contrary, sleep paralysis is quite common in young children, as are the other phenomena. Similarly, serious accidents and close calls with death are also way too common. These experiences were ordinary; they were not extraordinary. Their effects were cumulative and subliminal. The inner knowing gained through these lived experiences was invaluable.

Manuel Matas, M.D.

There's nothing you can know that isn't known
nothing you can see that isn't shown
there's nowhere you can be that isn't where
you're meant to be
It's easy

—John Lennon and Paul McCartney, "All You Need Is Love"

Chapter 7: Psychedelics: Expanding the Mind

Reflecting on his adventures with amphetamines, chloral hydrate, and morphine, Oliver Sacks had this to say about recreational drug use:

> Humans share much with other animals – the basic needs of food and drink or sleep, for example – but there are additional mental and emotional needs and desires which perhaps are unique to us. To live on a day-to-day basis is insufficient for human beings; we need to transcend, transport, escape; we need meaning, understanding and explanation; we need to see overall patterns in our lives.

All of these basic human needs – the need to transcend, the need to find meaning, and the need to see patterns – lead many of us on a spiritual quest. Whether that search is fueled by longing, inner vision, meditation, prayer, hallucinogenic drugs, or any combination of these is a personal choice.

Many of the paranormal phenomena we have discussed, such as out-of-body experiences, second sight, inner vision, moments of bliss and transcendence, and "oceanic" feelings of oneness with the universe, can occur spontaneously but they can also be induced by mind-altering drugs, whose proponents are legion. The 40-year gap in scientific research that started with President Nixon's "War on Drugs" is now coming to an end as research on the benefits and risks of psychedelic drugs is being carried out at teaching hospitals and universities throughout North America and Europe.

Drugs that cross the blood-brain barrier and act primarily on the central nervous system (the brain and the spinal cord) are called *psychoactive*.

These drugs affect brain function. They cause changes in mood, perception, cognition, behavior, and consciousness. They can be used for medicinal or recreational purposes or both. Psychedelic or hallucinogenic drugs are a subcategory of psychoactive drugs.

The word *psychedelic* ("manifesting a clear mind") was coined in 1956 by British psychiatrist Dr. Humphry Osmond in a letter he wrote to Aldous Huxley. Dr. Osmond was working at the Weyburn Mental Hospital in Saskatchewan when he started doing experiments with LSD. He is credited with introducing Aldous Huxley to LSD. Huxley, whose essay "The Doors of Perception" described his experiences with mescaline, asked to be given 100 micrograms of LSD on his deathbed. Huxley was prescient, in a sense, because psychedelic drugs are now being given, on an experimental basis, to terminally ill cancer patients, to help them overcome their fear of death.

Although many drug users – especially users of heroin, fentanyl, crack, cocaine, and methamphetamine – need drugs to get high or to feed their addictions, psychedelic drug users are more likely to be interested in using altered states of consciousness to achieve other goals, for these drugs can increase psychological introspection and spiritual growth. Users say that plant-based drugs can evoke feelings of oneness with the universe, the unity of all things, beautiful visions of the divine, and higher levels of consciousness.

The term "spiritual experience" may seem vague and open to interpretation, but I think that, generally, it relates to the issues outlined earlier by Sacks – the need for meaning, transcendence, and patterns, all three of which are related to what might be called the higher self.

Many substances found in plants or fungi have been used in traditional spiritual ceremonies for millennia. They include ergot from Eurasia, morning glory and peyote cactus (mescaline) from Central and North America, and ayahuasca from the Amazon. Other plant-derived psychedelic drugs, like psilocybin ("magic mushrooms") and ibogaine have been used for traditional and sacramental purposes by native-American cultures, as well as by many other groups, for a very long time. Revered as a sacred medicine by members of the Native American Church, peyote was legalized for church members in 1994, under an amendment to the American Indian Religious Freedom Act.

Ayahuasca, known as the sacred vine of the Amazon, is used as a sacrament in Santo Daime churches in Brazil. It has also been used throughout North America and Europe. Dr. Gabor Maté used ayahuasca to treat addictions in Canada until he was told by the authorities to stop as the drug was not legal. The U.S. Supreme Court, on the other hand, ruled in 2006 that ayahuasca is legal for religious purposes. Many North Americans go to Peru to drink ayahuasca tea in the presence of a shaman, who guides spiritual seekers. Ayahuasca has been called an "entheogen," which means "the divine within."

It is important to point out that these drugs can be dangerous if not used properly. There have been deaths reported in ayahuasca tourists in Peru.

Ibogaine, a hallucinogen that comes from the roots of a shrub found in West African, has been called an "oneirogen" because of a dream-like state which it induces. It has been used to interrupt the cycle of addiction by blocking opiate receptors in the brain. The Toronto Ibogaine Centre emphasizes that ibogaine interrupts but does not cure drug addiction. Although used in dozens of alternative medicine clinics around the world, ibogaine can be dangerous as it has a propensity to cause cardiac arrhythmia and sudden death.

Psilocybin, the active ingredient in "magic mushrooms," was traditionally used in Mexico by aboriginal tribes for its divinatory and healing properties. Although its use for terminally ill cancer patients is now being studied in various research settings, its use for inducing spiritual experiences is well established. Psilocybin is found in more than 200 species of mushrooms. These mushrooms are found on every continent, but the majority are in subtropical humid forests. Archeological digs have uncovered rock paintings in modern-day Spain and Algeria that show psilocybin mushrooms were used in spiritual ceremonies thousands of years ago.

Psilocybin was identified as the active ingredient in hallucinogenic mushrooms by Albert Hofmann (1906–2008), a Swiss chemist who was also the first person to synthesize, ingest, and describe the effects of LSD (lysergic acid diethylamide), which he called "medicine of the soul." During his lifetime, he saw an explosion of interest in psychedelic drugs. In 2007, Hofmann tied for first place on *The Telegraph*'s list of "The 100 Greatest Living Geniuses." He was tied with Sir Tim Berners-Lee, who is generally acknowledged to be the inventor of the World Wide Web.

There is a famous study with psilocybin called the Good Friday Experiment, also known as the Marsh Chapel experiment, in which psilocybin was administered to volunteer graduate divinity students at Boston University's Marsh Chapel. In a placebo-controlled study designed by Walter Pahnke, who was a graduate student at Harvard Divinity School, almost all of the students who received psilocybin reported profound spiritual experiences. In a 2002 follow-up study by Roland R. Griffiths at Johns Hopkins University, more than half of the divinity students rated the psilocybin experience as one of the top five spiritual experiences of their lives.

Prague-born psychiatrist Stanislav Grof used LSD therapy back in the sixties, but he eventually discovered that he could get the same effects using highly specialized breathing techniques. It is well-documented that altered states of consciousness can be induced by a variety of means, including music, dance, literature, art, drumming, sensory deprivation, meditation, and chanting.

Another word used to describe psychedelic drugs is "psychotomimetic" because they can produce a state that mimics psychosis. Drug-induced (toxic) psychosis differs from a true psychotic disorder, however, as it is most often short-lived, and there is usually full recovery. Toxic psychosis will usually clear within 24–48 hours, with the proper treatment.

Psychedelic drugs are often called hallucinogens because they can produce hallucinations, but the hallucinations produced are often more like illusions or distortions. Psychedelic drug users may object to the word "hallucination" when it is applied to drug-induced visions. Grinspoon and Bakalar (1979) wrote that "hallucination" was far too crude a word to describe "the estheticized perception or fascination effect, enhanced sense of meaningfulness in familiar objects, vivid closed-eye imagery, visions in subjective space or visual and kinesthetic distortions induced by drugs like LSD." They thought that the word "hallucination" should be reserved for a failure of reality testing, which is the hallmark of psychosis. They said that these drugs are rarely hallucinogenic, and they suggested that drug-induced visions should be called visions or visual distortions, not hallucinations.

The blurring of boundaries that can be part of these drug-induced experiences was expressed by John Lennon in his song "I Am the Walrus".

I am he as you are he as you are me and we are all together.

Lennon said he wrote "I Am the Walrus" after taking LSD. He was in good company. Many artists, writers, poets, and musicians used mind-altering drugs to enhance creativity. The British romantic poets, including John Keats, Lord Byron, and Percy Bysshe Shelley used opium. Samuel Taylor Coleridge said his poem *Kubla Khan* came to him unbidden, in an opium-induced dream. He had been reading a book about Kubla Khan before going to sleep.

He wrote,

> *In Xanadu did Kubla Khan*
> *A stately pleasure-dome decree*
> *Where Alph, the sacred river, ran*
> *Through caverns measureless to man*
> *Down to a sunless sea.*

Psychedelics were heavily praised in 20th century pop music. John Lennon famously sang, "I'd love to turn you on" in "A Day in the Life". The Beatles' "Strawberry Fields Forever" was a leading example of the psychedelic rock genre. Psychedelic rock groups included the Grateful Dead, Cream, Pink Floyd, Jefferson Airplane, and The Jimi Hendrix Experience. In the 21st century, songs with drug references continued to show up on the pop charts, songs like "Rehab" by Amy Winehouse, "High by the Beach" by Lana Del Ray, and "Can't Feel My Face", The Weeknd's ode to his love affair with cocaine.

Rather than using the catch-all term "psychedelic" to describe drugs and music, Russell Smith has broken down various musical genres and listed their associated drugs:

> Reggae has its herb, punk its heroin, heavy metal its speed, techno its ecstasy. Each of these drugs matches the music's mood. Dubstep's drug might well have been ketamine, the dissociative hallucinogenic anesthetic that makes you alternately comatose and completely insane.

He might have added that acid rock has its acid (LSD).

As well as poets, writers and musicians, there were celebrated psychologists and philosophers who extolled the benefits of mind-altering drugs. Timothy Leary, a psychologist, was one of the leading figures of the 1960s counter-culture movement known as "flower power" which developed in the U.S. in opposition to the Vietnam War. With his popular catchphrase, "Turn on, tune in, drop out," Leary was a colorful character, known for his eccentric personality. He conducted experiments at Harvard University with psilocybin.

Because of his advocacy of psychedelic drugs, President Nixon called Leary "the most dangerous man in America." After Leary was fired from Harvard, he started a new religion, The League for Spiritual Discovery (LSD), which, as the name implies, extolled the benefits of using LSD for spiritual and sacramental purposes. The Beatles' song "Lucy in the Sky with Diamonds" was also seen as a thinly disguised reference to LSD.

Another proponent of the beneficial effects of LSD was the late Steve Jobs, who credited LSD, along with his study of Zen Buddhism, for making him "enlightened." One of his friends described Jobs as "enlightened but cruel." People who are enlightened are not usually cruel, and they don't usually say they are enlightened. Whether Jobs *was* "enlightened" or not remains a matter of opinion.

In his biography of Steve Jobs, Walter Isaacson quoted Jobs as saying that taking LSD was one of the most important things he ever did in his life.

Jobs said, "[LSD] reinforced my sense of what is important, creating great things instead of making money." This sentiment is frequently voiced by advocates of mind-altering drugs. The proposed benefits of LSD – more creativity and less materialism – echo the personality changes seen in near-death experience survivors, who tend to become more altruistic, more spiritual, less judgmental, and less materialistic.

Timothy Leary was not an aberration in the history of psychology. As discussed earlier, the father of American psychology, William James, was also enamored with psychedelics. In his case, it was nitrous oxide, an anesthetic known as "laughing gas." James was greatly influenced by his experiences with nitrous oxide. He became known as "the nitrous oxide philosopher."

If not for laughing gas, James would have been a very different philosopher. James first wrote about his nitrous oxide-induced metaphysical insights in an essay published in the *Atlantic Monthly* in 1882. In 1874, at the age of 32, he reviewed an anonymous pamphlet called "The Anesthetic Revelation and The Gist of Philosophy." He was very much influenced by this pamphlet in which the author described how he found the secrets of religion and philosophy in nitrous oxide intoxication. He eventually discovered the author's name was Benjamin Paul Blood. He was a poorly educated farmer/philosopher/inventor who lived in a small town called Amsterdam in upstate New York.

James called Blood "the perfect picture of the half-baked American eccentric." Blood's writings consisted mostly of letters to the editor of the local newspapers (something to which I can relate, as I am an inveterate writer of letters to the editor of the *Globe and Mail*). Some of Blood's letters were compiled for publication in the *Journal of Speculative Philosophy*. He also published a few poems and wrote a book called *Pluriverse: An Essay in the Philosophy of Pluralism*.

In his 1882 essay, James wrote:

> I myself made some observations on nitrous oxide intoxication and reported them. . . One conclusion was forced upon my mind at that time, and my impression of its truth

has ever since remained unshaken. It is that our waking consciousness, as we call it, is but one special type of consciousness, whilst all about it, parted from it by the flimsiest of screens, there lie potential forms of consciousness entirely different.

He allowed that it was possible for some people to achieve these other states of consciousness without drugs. James also wrote glowingly about the mystical properties of alcohol but later called it poison after his brother, Robertson, died from alcoholism.

Oliver Sacks said he started his successful writing career with an all-night amphetamine binge. He may have been just as productive without amphetamines, but we will never know.

Risks and Benefits

At a concert, Tom Shipley once called "One Toke over the Line", his signature song, "our cannabis spiritual." Of course, not all songs with drug references would be considered "spiritual." There are many songs about the ravages of drug and alcohol abuse, but they often have a romantic or sentimental quality.

In his profile of Leonard Cohen for the *New Yorker*, David Remnick wrote that when Cohen was living on the Greek island of Hydra, he used fasting to concentrate his mind, and pot, speed, and acid to expand it. He quoted Cohen who said, "I took trip after trip, sitting on my terrace in Greece, waiting to see God. Generally, I ended up with a bad hangover."

Although psychedelics are often glamorized, they are not entirely without risk. In spite of ringing endorsements from cultural icons like Steve Jobs, there are potential problems with psychedelic drugs, which, like any substance, can be misused. Psychedelics can precipitate psychosis in vulnerable individuals with a genetic predisposition to psychosis, or if the drugs are taken in massive doses or in combination with other drugs or alcohol. Psychedelic drugs may lead to mystical visions and feelings of oneness with the universe, but they may also lead to brain damage or acute psychotic episodes.

Phenylcyclidine (PCP, angel dust, wet, embalming fluid, rocket fuel) is classified as a recreational dissociative drug. It has both hallucinogenic and neurotoxic effects. Other drugs in this category include ketamine (K or Special K), dextromethorphan (cough syrup) and nitrous oxide (laughing gas). Ketamine is also known as "horse tranquilizer" because it is used as a general anesthetic in veterinary medicine.

"Bath salts" can lead to severe psychosis. It is a so-called designer drug, a potent combination of synthetic stimulants. Its major ingredient is a powerful stimulant called MDPV – a dopamine and norepinephrine reuptake inhibitor. "Bath salts" was banned in the U.S. in 2011 and in Canada in 2012.

Stimulants like meth (methamphetamine), coke (cocaine) and crack (crack cocaine, rock) can similarly lead to psychosis if consumed in high doses or over a long period. As discussed earlier, chronic cocaine use can lead to "formication," a condition in which the cocaine user feels like he or she has bugs crawling under the skin. Cocaine use can also lead to sudden death, due to cardiac arrest or respiratory arrest following seizures. Amphetamine psychosis is characterized by paranoid delusions and auditory hallucinations.

Any of these drugs can also cause delirium with visual hallucinations. Some of these drugs are called hallucinogenic because they produce hallucinations, but not all hallucinogens are considered psychedelic. Opium is classified as a narcotic; cocaine, crack, and methamphetamine are stimulants. These drugs are not technically psychedelics, but there is often an overlap of symptoms with psychedelic drugs; they can be called mind-altering (not in a good way).

Between 1948 and 1970, the U.S. Army conducted classified research at the Edgewood Arsenal in Maryland. A small portion of the research was devoted to psychochemical warfare. About 7,000 soldiers were exposed to more than 250 chemicals, including sarin, mustard gas, and psychoactive agents such as LSD, PCP, cannabinoids, and BZ. When the Edgewood Arsenal human subject research became public, there were Senate hearings, scandal, recrimination, and multiple lawsuits.

Psychedelics also featured prominently in CIA-financed brainwashing experiments in the 1950s and early 1960s known as *MK-Ultra*, conducted by Dr. Ewen Cameron in Montréal at the Allan Memorial Institute, which was part of the Royal Victoria Hospital, a McGill University teaching hospital. Cameron gave massive doses of LSD to his patients without their knowledge or consent. Many of his hapless patients were left brain-damaged or severely impaired. Class-action suits were successfully launched against the CIA and the Canadian government as a result of Cameron's experiments, which are now viewed as barbaric.

Current studies of psychedelic substances in patient populations are miles away from the egregious mistreatment of research subjects that took place in the CIA-financed brainwashing experiments in Montréal or the Edgewood Arsenal experiments in Maryland. Fully informed consent is now obtained from patients, who are screened to exclude those with a past history or family history of psychosis, and the study protocols must be approved by university and hospital ethics review boards. Clinical protocols are designed to minimize risk and to maximize benefits.

Research in Therapeutic Applications

There was a great deal of research on the benefits of psychedelic drug therapy in the 1950s and 1960s. Thousands of papers were published on the therapeutic benefits of psychedelic drugs. In 1970, LSD and other psychedelic drugs were reclassified as Schedule 1 drugs, thus prohibiting their medical use. As a result, President Nixon's "war on drugs" effectively put a chill on psychedelic drug research for 40 years.

In 1971, Nixon called drug abuse "public enemy number one." His drug control policies led to mandatory minimum sentencing and massive incarceration of minorities. By 2009, the Director of the Office of National Drug Control Policy stated that drug addiction was a disease that could be prevented and treated, and that the Obama administration would no longer use the term "war on drugs." The self-appointed Global Commission on Drug Policy issued a report in 2011 stating that the war on drugs had failed. The global community started moving towards a policy of legalization and decriminalization of psychoactive drugs; the emphasis would be shifted from punishment to prevention, rehabilitation, and research.

There is now a revival of interest in the therapeutic use of psychedelic drugs such as LSD and psilocybin. They are being used or studied for the treatment of depression, anxiety disorders, cluster headaches, post-traumatic stress disorder, obsessive-compulsive disorder, smoking cessation, and addiction to opiates and alcohol. There is ongoing research at many institutions, including UCLA, New York University, the Psychiatric University Hospital in Zurich, and Imperial College London. Many studies have established the safety and efficacy of "psychedelic medicines" (as these substances are now sometimes called) as well as their long-term benefits.

In a review article of contemporary psychedelic medicine research, Kenneth Tupper described a typical scenario:

> After obtaining fully informed consent from the patient, clinical sessions take place in healthcare facilities, in quiet treatment rooms with pleasant and comfortable décor. Headphones deliver music, hospital and laboratory equipment are minimal and discreetly placed, and a two-person co-therapist team is in attendance throughout the drug's action. During a session, interaction between patients and therapists is kept to a minimum, with the patient encouraged to spend much of the time engaging in self-reflection while listening to carefully selected music. Follow-up sessions that are non-drug assisted provide opportunities to integrate the insights gleaned from the experimental sessions.

It is important to note that psychedelic drugs given to patient populations are used as adjuncts to psychotherapy; they are not given by themselves without any follow-up.

There is a plethora of new research showing benefits of psychedelic drugs, especially in the treatment of addictions. Peyote, ayahuasca, and ketamine have all been shown to be effective in the treatment of alcoholism. Alcoholics are often able to abstain while in rehab but frequently relapse post-discharge. Dr. Ravi Das and his colleagues at University College London studied single-dose ketamine to block NMDA (N-methyl-D-aspartame), a glutamate receptor, in order to destabilize memories temporarily following retrieval, so as to block triggers which often cause alcoholics to relapse.

Evgeny Krupitsky, a psychiatrist at the St. Petersburg Scientific Research Centre of Addictions and Psychopharmacology, also used ketamine in low (sub-anaesthetic) doses to treat alcoholics and heroin addicts. In one study with alcoholics using ketamine psychedelic therapy (KPT), he found 65.8 percent of alcoholics achieved total abstinence for one year in the KPT group compared to 24 percent in the group that received conventional treatment.

Ketamine has also been used to treat depression in patients with treatment-resistant bipolar disorder. In a study by Anita Autry and colleagues, a single, sub-psychotomimetic dose of ketamine relieved depressive symptoms within a few hours, as opposed to the several weeks or months it takes to treat depression with selective serotonin reuptake inhibitors.

British psychiatrist James Nutt, at Imperial College London, published a study finding that psilocybin may be effective in treating severe depression. Deborah Mash, a neurologist at the University of Miami, College of Medicine, used ibogaine to treat opiate and cocaine addicts. Philippe Lucas, a researcher with British Columbia's Centre for Addictions Research, found that using ayahuasca to treat alcohol and drug addictions in a coastal aboriginal band was very successful. At six-month follow-up, he found significant reductions in cocaine, alcohol, and tobacco use. He determined that the plant-based substances – ayahuasca, peyote, and ibogaine – were not habit-forming, that is, there was no physical dependence and no withdrawal symptoms upon cessation, but any substance can foster psychological dependence.

Psychedelics have also been used to help terminally ill patients overcome their fear of death. Dr. Charles Grob, a research psychiatrist at Harbor-UCLA Medical Center in Torrance, California, gave psilocybin to end-stage cancer patients. He found that it lessened their pain, anxiety, and depression about their impending deaths.

Dr. John Halpern used MDMA (ecstasy) with terminal cancer patients at McLean Hospital, a psychiatric training hospital for Harvard Medical School. He also studied the use of peyote by Navajo Indians in New Mexico, Arizona, and Utah. Psychoactive drugs such as psilocybin and ecstasy mimic one of the major aftereffects of a near-death experience, namely, reduced fear of death, hence their effectiveness with terminally ill patients.

There are many other applications for psychedelic drugs. Francisco Moreno, a psychiatrist at the University of Arizona, College of Medicine, gave psilocybin to patients with obsessive-compulsive disorder. Another psychiatrist, Pedro Sopelana Rodriguez, who works at the Psychiatric Hospital of Madrid, used ecstasy to treat 29 women suffering from post-traumatic stress disorder.

There has been a lot of speculation about the mechanism whereby psychedelic drugs can lessen the fear of death. Dr. Grob noticed that the reduction in death anxiety in his cancer patients lasted for weeks and months after ingestion of psilocybin. He said that his patients had a transformative spiritual experience, which altered their view of themselves and their world. Many of the patients came to see death not as an end but as a transition. He called taking psilocybin in a supportive, therapeutic environment "existential medicine." Grob also emphasized the importance of a controlled environment for his patients and the distinction between controlled psychedelic drug treatments and casual, recreational drug use.

One of the foremost benefits of psychedelic medicine is to provide spiritual insight and healing. Bill W., founder of Alcoholics Anonymous, talked about the role of a "higher power" in the healing journey of alcoholics. As it happens, many alcoholics have no use for religion, and they are put off by the idea of a higher power. They often use their objection to this concept as a reason to reject AA in its entirety. For those alcoholics who reject the philosophy of AA because religiosity is anathema to them, I suggest they use the term "higher self" instead of "higher power." This would apply to other 12-Step programs as well.

Ongoing research and the enduring popularity of mind-altering drugs through the ages and in various cultures is a testament to humanity's search for enlightenment and higher consciousness. The need to explore altered states or alternative realities and a longing to create heaven on earth are enduring features of human endeavor and aspiration. Psychedelic drugs and near-death experiences can reduce death anxiety and introduce people to a spiritual side of life that may have been neglected in their education and absent from their philosophy or life experience.

There is speculation that DMT (dimethyltryptamine) is released into the body at the time of death. DMT is a naturally occurring psychoactive compound that is ubiquitous in plants. Ayahuasca, for example, contains DMT. It is also found in trace amounts in mammals, including humans. DMT could activate that part of the brain, the temporal cortex, which mediates spiritual experience, whether drug-induced or associated with near-death experience. It is possible that psychedelic drugs, near-death experience, and deathbed visions have a final common pathway involving DMT.

Rick Doblin, founder and executive director of the non-profit Multidisciplinary Association for Psychedelic Studies (MAPS) is an advocate for the legalization of psychedelics. He thinks they should be available not just to treat disorders such as post-traumatic stress disorder, obsessive-compulsive disorder, depression, and substance abuse; they should also be available for personal growth, transformative spiritual experiences, and couples counseling.

Many people use psychedelic drugs solely for recreational purposes, but these compounds also have tremendous potential for therapeutic benefits. They have been used for thousands of years, in many different cultures, by spiritual seekers, for spiritual practices, introspection, and access to higher states of consciousness; psychedelic drug research, however, is still in its infancy.

We have noted the similarities between drug-induced, mind-altering, spiritual experiences and spontaneous paranormal experiences such as out-of-body and near-death experience, visions, spirit contact, and oceanic feelings of joy, bliss, and oneness with nature and the universe. All roads lead to Rome. Whether paranormal and spiritual experiences are induced or spontaneous, the net effect is the same. Whatever the cause of the experience, the person who has had the paranormal experience will be forever changed. Whether that change leads to spiritual transcendence and growth or into the gutter of clinging and despair is up to the individual. The universe presents us with certain opportunities and challenges. It is up to us to decide what we want to do with them.

Chapter 8: Paranormal Activity: Mediums, Channels, Spirit Guides, Guardian Angels, and Some Theories about Reincarnation

Art is to console those who have been broken by life.

—Vincent Van Gogh

Artistic expression is a manifestation of higher consciousness. Our fascination with the paranormal is reflected in every aspect of our popular culture, from books, movies, radio, and television to music, theatre, and dance. One can hardly turn on the TV or check out local movie listings without seeing at least one or two shows with paranormal themes.

A quick perusal of the *New York Times* bestseller list will usually reveal several books about the paranormal. Books about near-death experiences have been particularly popular. Another popular genre is channeled books, or books written by psychic mediums, many of whom have popular TV shows.

On the radio, the paranormal-themed *Coast to Coast AM* was the highest-rated talk show in its time slot. NPR's *This American Life* had several episodes with paranormal themes. Movies like *Paranormal Activity* or *The Blair Witch Project*, made on shoestring budgets, grossed hundreds of millions of dollars at the box office and spawned numerous sequels. And it's not just small indie pictures. Mainstream Hollywood movies like *Arrival, Doctor Strange, Signs, Ghostbusters, The Exorcist, Poltergeist, The Others, The Haunting, Communion, Ghost,* and *The Sixth Sense* have been extremely successful, as have TV shows like *Saving Hope, Heroes, Ghost Whisperer, The Listener, The Twilight Zone, Medium, Touched by an Angel, The X-Files,* and *Legion.* Paranormal skeptics even have their own TV shows, like *Ghost Hunters* and *Fact or Faked: Paranormal Files.* Many TV shows feature characters who are psychic and clairvoyant or who have telepathic or telekinetic powers. Mediums are particularly popular.

Movies and television shows with paranormal themes are entertainment, mostly, but they can also have an educational component. They resonate with many people because they touch a chord of recognition and there is validation of previously held beliefs about contact with spirits, the power of intuition, pre-cognition, and premonitions.

SPOILER ALERT!! For those of you who have not seen the movie Arrival and still want to see it, you can skip ahead to the next section.

Arrival is a 2016 American movie directed by Denis Villeneuve, written by Eric Heisserer, starring Amy Adams, Jeremy Renner, and Forest Whitaker. The screenplay is based on a short story by Ted Chiang called "Story of Your Life." The title of the short story was oddly familiar. It was very similar to the title of the poem by Mark Strand, "The Story of Our Lives," which was connected to the wildly synchronistic event mentioned earlier.

I had a particularly vivid, paranormal experience while watching *Arrival.* When I first read about this movie and I saw that it was about spaceships and aliens, I wasn't really that interested because I'm not a big science fiction fan. Things changed when my cousin (who is a science fiction nut!) wrote on her Facebook page that *Arrival* was "spectacular."

I checked out Rotten Tomatoes. *Arrival* had a rating of 100. I had never seen that before. After I made plans to go see the movie with my friend, I spoke to another person who said he thought the movie was so-so. I went back to Rotten Tomatoes. By then the rating had fallen to 93. I read a review by one of my favorite reviewers, and he didn't really like it. He thought it was slow and boring. I talked to my friend about whether we should go or not. She suggested we should go ahead and make up our own minds, so we did.

By the time we went to the movie theatre, my enthusiasm for the movie had already waned. As I started to watch the movie, I was thinking the reviewer was right, the movie was very dark and very slow. The actors often had their backs to the camera so it was hard for me to make out what they were saying. I started to fall asleep. Then, Boom! I woke up! And I was blown away.

The basic story line is that aliens have landed in twelve different locations around the globe. Their spaceships look like black obelisks. No one knows what they want, if they came in peace or if their intentions were aggressive. The U.S. Army enlists the help of the character played by Amy Adams because she is a professor of linguistics who had previously done some translation work for the Army. She is taken to the spaceship that has landed in Montana and tries to establish contact with the aliens. The alien she talks to looks like an octopus squirting black ink which then forms a symbol. At first, she tries to decipher one of the symbols and she thinks it means "weapon." From this one word the Army thinks the aliens are planning to attack.

The Chinese plan to launch a first strike. After much drama, Amy Adams says, "No, it doesn't mean weapon, it means gift." When I heard that my jaw dropped. I was in a state of disbelief. Her words brought me back to a message I had received more than thirty years earlier, which I never understood. In those days, I would not have called it a message. I just called it a poem. The words of the two-line poem just popped into my head. I remember telling my friend about it at the time. My poem was:

A weapon is a gift.
A gift is a weapon.

I didn't know why those words came to me. I thought it was odd, but I didn't make too much of it. Then 33 years later, there it was, on the big screen, as I was watching *Arrival*. The basic message in the movie is that time is not linear. What we think is a flashback turns out to be a flash forward. Amy Adams's daughter asks her why she named her Hannah. She replies that Hannah is a special name because it is a palindrome, the same backwards and forwards. The palindrome is a clue to the movie's concept of time.

In the movie Amy Adams is able to forestall the Chinese attack on the aliens by calling the Chinese leader on his private phone number (which she would have no way of knowing) and telling him the exact words his wife said to him on her death-bed (which, of course, she would also have no way of knowing).

There were so many mysterious elements in the movie, but the biggest one was the concept of time. To say the message resonated with me would be an understatement. I was thunderstruck. Especially because I had just been writing about the author Anita Moorjani, who had similar ideas about time. Her near-death experience and the lessons she learned about time while she was out of her body will be discussed later in this chapter.

The reason I went into such great detail about whether or not I was going to see this movie is that, although it seemed to me something momentous happened while I was there, I almost didn't go. Remembering my message from three decades earlier while watching the movie was an illustration of the theme of the movie: time isn't linear. It was also an affirmation. But I had to wrestle with myself before I was ready to receive the message.

Just a word about "messages." I realize the word may be off-putting to some readers. We could use different words, depending on the type of message we are talking about. With some messages, the meaning is readily apparent. They could be called insights or even epiphanies. Other messages are more like riddles or puzzles. What became clear to me in this instance was that even though the meaning of a message may not be clear at the time the message is received, he meaning will unfold over time.

When I received the message "Be generous," I knew right away what it meant. At the time I received the original title of this book, "Blood and the Dominion," when I was 12, I had no idea what it meant. It took me 55 years to find out. Similarly, when I heard, in my mind's ear, "A weapon is a gift," it didn't make any sense to me until 33 years later. However, 12, 33, and 55 are just numbers and pretty meaningless if time is not linear. If the meaning of the message is not immediately clear, stay tuned, stay present, and be patient. In time, the meaning will be revealed.

I was reminded of Paul McCartney's great song, "Let It Be."

There will be an answer. Let it be.

McCartney said "Let It Be" came to him in a dream. Not the way "Yesterday" did, fully-formed. It was just that his mother, whose name was Mary, and who died when he was 14, came to him in a dream when he was troubled and she said to him, "It's going to be okay. Let it be." He woke up and wrote the song.

Psychics, Mediums, and Spiritualists

The word "medium" has several different meanings. One meaning, according to *dictionary.com*, is "an intervening agency, means, or instrument by which something is conveyed or accomplished."

As we have seen in cases of bereaved spouses, many people who do not ordinarily consider themselves psychic may be able to communicate with the spirit world under special circumstances; however, under ordinary circumstances, someone wishing to contact spirits may turn to an intervening agency, namely, a medium. It is interesting in this context to remember Marshall McLuhan's famous dictum, "the medium is the message." He meant that the medium could shape or influence how the message is perceived. He was referring, of course, to traditional means of communication, such as radio, television, or newspapers, but his axiom could apply equally well to psychic mediums who claim to bring messages from the spirit world.

Mediums, also known as "intuitives" or "sensitives," have been part of society throughout history. As he was preparing for battle with the Philistines, King Saul called upon the Witch of Endor, also known as the Medium of Endor, to summon up the spirit of the prophet Samuel. Saul lived in the 11th century BCE (1080–1010 BCE). The Martha Graham

Dance Company in New York premiered "The Witch of Endor" (choreography and costumes by Martha Graham) at the 54th Street Theatre in 1954.

Mediums are also spiritualists. A "spiritualist" is someone who believes that the world is comprised of both matter and spirit and that the spirits of the dead have both the capacity and the need to communicate with the living.

The American spiritualist movement began in 1848 when two sisters, Margaret (Maggie) and Kate Fox, from Hydesville, New York, claimed they were able to communicate with spirits using a table-tapping system. Although they conducted many séances, became famous, had a stage act, and were promoted by P. T. Barnum, they eventually admitted they had perpetrated a fraud and denounced spiritualism. Maggie Fox outlined the details of the fraud she and her sister had perpetrated in her 1888 memoir *The Death Blow to Spiritualism*. Nevertheless, spiritualism remained very popular.

Maggie was 15 and Kate was 12 when they learned to make snapping, popping, and thumping noises by cracking the joints of their toes. What started out as a game the girls devised to scare their mother got out of hand when their mother told neighbors that their house was haunted. E. E. Lewis, an attorney in a nearby town, decided to investigate. He subsequently published a pamphlet, "A Report of the Mysterious Noises Heard in the House of John D. Fox." Maggie and Kate's eldest sister, Leah Fox Fish, a 33-year-old divorced woman living in Rochester, read the report and returned to Hydesville. Since she had also read the recent bestseller *The Divine Principles of Nature* by Andrew Jackson Davis, she thought the hauntings at Hydesville could be the fulfillment of spiritual prophecy, as outlined in Davis's book.

Andrew Jackson Davis (1826–1910) was a seer, medium, spiritualist, and clairvoyant. Often called "the first American prophet," he was born into a poor family. His father did odd jobs. His mother was illiterate. He had very little formal schooling. At 17, he attended a lecture on mesmerism (hypnosis). Soon after, a local tailor who was learning mesmerism put him into a trance in which he said he entered into a higher state of consciousness and was given higher spiritual knowledge.

He became clairvoyant. Many of his predictions came true. He described the afterlife in detail and said he could enter it at any time. He could read closed books; he could diagnose illnesses and prescribe treatments, which usually worked. He asserted the existence of the planets Neptune and Pluto before they were discovered. He wrote about the theory of evolution ten years before Darwin published *The Origin of Species*.

While in an altered state, Davis was given knowledge of health, psychology, education, physics, chemistry, philosophy, astronomy, and government. He spent 15 months dictating a book based on his revelations – *The Divine Principles of Nature*, published in 1847. He was 21 at the time. Although he had only five months of formal schooling, and did not read more than six books in his lifetime, he wrote and published more than 30 books in 45 editions. His stated goal was to help people advance spiritually.

Davis popularized the theories of Emanuel Swedenborg, who was mentioned earlier. He wrote that all human existence was only a reflection of a larger spiritual universe, and that the spirits of the dead were in daily contact with the living. Swedenborg (1688–1722) was a Swedish clairvoyant, scientist, inventor, theologian, philosopher, and mystic. He is best known for his book about the afterlife, *Heaven and Hell* (1758). His writing was very influential. Among his followers were Johnny Appleseed, William Blake, Ralph Waldo Emerson, Arthur Conan Doyle, Jorge Luis Borges, Carl Jung, Henry James Sr. (father of William James and Henry James), and Immanuel Kant. Swedenborg said he was commanded by the Lord to publish his writing, even though he knew it would make him look ridiculous, even insane.

Lily Dale is a spiritualist community in upstate New York which was incorporated in 1879 as a meeting place for Spiritualists and Freethinkers. The name was changed in 1903 to The City of Light and changed again in 1906 to Lily Dale Assembly. The Fox childhood home was moved there in 1916. With a year-round population of 275, Lily Dale has 22,000 registered visitors a year who attend lectures, workshops, church services, and mediumship demonstrations. Speakers have included Tibetan monks, the cast of a reality television show called *Ghost Hunters*, and many psychics and mediums.

Sorpong Peou, a 55-year-old university professor, was reunited with his father in Cambodia after 36 years. He thought his father was dead, murdered by the Khmer Rouge in 1975. However, in January 2010, he started having recurring dreams about his father. He told his brother in Ottawa about his dreams. His brother went to see a psychic, who said their father was alive and Sorpong should go to Cambodia to look for him. He did so but didn't find him. When he returned to the psychic and told her what had happened, she didn't say she was wrong. She insisted that his father was alive and she told him to return to Cambodia. He followed her advice, returned to Cambodia, and he did indeed find his father, an old man begging on the side of the road. There was a joyful reunion. I think it's safe to say that if this man, who didn't believe in psychics, had not told his brother about his dreams, and if the brother had not gone to see the psychic, this man would not have been found his long-lost father.

Psychics have been used successfully many times by police forces to find missing persons. Psychics are not always right, but sometimes their work is invaluable. In 2014, a self-described intuitive, Norm Pratt, helped police find the remains of a missing Coquitlam father. The family turned to him after extensive police search attempts had failed to locate the man. They expressed their deep gratitude to him after the body of their loved one was found.

D. J. Adams had an accident in a swimming pool when she was nine. She hit her head, was knocked unconscious, and almost drowned. She was then in a coma for a month. When she woke up, she was unable to speak or move, but she could hear, see, and feel other people, and she was able to perceive clairvoyantly events in their lives. As an adult, she used her clairvoyant skills to help police find 14 missing children, all of whom were found alive. She now writes crime fiction based on her real-life case files.

Once I met a medium. She was a friend of a friend who thought I would like to meet her. She was a psychologist who worked with autistic children. One of the first things she said to me was "Who's Harry?" (He was my father). Then she said, "He's here with Anna" (my grandmother). She said, "He says to tell you he finally understands the meaning of Jacob's ladder." This message completely blew me away. I was, of course, surprised she knew the names of my father and my grandmother, but her remark about Jacob's ladder had a special resonance for me. It wasn't the kind of thing that she could have said to just anyone. When I saw the angels at my father's funeral, one on each side of the casket, I thought of Jacob's ladder, with the angels going up and down the ladder between heaven and earth. At the time, I had the idea that the angels were helping my father make the transition from this world to the next. I thought that here was no way the medium could have known about the appearance of angels at my father's funeral or how it related to the story of Jacob's ladder. Was it telepathy or mind-reading? No, I don't think it was because I hadn't been thinking about Jacob's ladder at the time I met her; in fact, I hadn't thought about it in years.

One might ask why a psychiatrist would want to talk with a medium. It was mostly curiosity, but from a historical perspective, it should not be surprising. Over the years, many psychiatrists and psychologists have been interested in parapsychology. Both Freud and Jung showed an interest in the occult. Jung studied Kabbalah, astrology, alchemy, and Tarot. Freud wrote about the occult and telepathy in dreams. Many well-known physicians, like Deepak Chopra, Bernie Siegel, Raymond Moody, and Brian Weiss, and psychologists, like Michael Newton, David Lukoff, and David Benner, have been heavily involved in spiritual inquiry. When the Society for Psychical Research (SPR) was founded in London in 1888, many of its members were physicians, psychologists, scientists, researchers, and academics. When the Canadian Society for Psychical Research was formed in 1908, it was likewise composed mainly of medical doctors and academics.

Psychic medium, television personality, and author James Van Praagh described four different realms of existence:

1.   The physical world (Earth Plane)

2.   The astral world (where discarnate entities reside)

3. The ethereal world (Thought Plane, Universal Mind, or Pure Consciousness, where "Higher Self" resides)

4. The celestial realm (the Angelic Realm) where angels, archangels, and ascended masters dwell. This is a world of lightness, bliss, joy, love, and oneness with Spirit.

These four realms or worlds correspond to the levels or planes of existence previously described in the Rule of Four: the earth plane, the physical or material world, is the same; the astral world corresponds to the world of emotions; the ethereal world is the world of ideas and Universal Mind; and the celestial world is the spiritual realm.

The idea that we all inhabit more than one realm or level of existence at the same time is known as multidimensionality. According to Van Praagh, mediums are able to contact discarnate entities on the astral (emotional) plane. Their messages may help bereaved individuals. Channels, on the other hand, also known as trance channels, deliver messages from the ethereal plane (also known as the etheric plane, or the spiritual realm). They convey messages they believe can benefit humanity. These messages can be delivered through automatic writing or through speaking while the channel is in a trance state. Writing, music, or art of any kind may be channeled. So can scientific discoveries and inventions.

Channeled Art and Science

Wassily Kandinsky was a Russian painter and art theorist whose book *Concerning the Spiritual in Art* (1912) was highly influential. He compared human existence to a spiritual pyramid, and he asserted that it was the role of artists, through their work, to lead others to the pinnacle.

In Greek mythology, the Muses inspired everything from dance, music, literature, and philosophy to geography and mathematics. In our own day, we can say there would be no art, literature, music, or scientific discovery without inspiration, intuition, and imagination (and hard work).

Channels are mediums who, while in trance, say they receive messages from spirit guides in the higher realms. According to their authors, best-selling books such as *Conversations with God* by Neale Donald Walsh and *A Course in Miracles* by Helen Schucman were channeled via automatic writing, a dissociative phenomenon in which the subject writes words on paper without knowing what he or she has written. The phenomenon of automatic writing has been attributed to various sources, including the unconscious, plagiarism, cryptomnesia (hidden memories), or a spiritual source, with or without the author's awareness of the content. Jung wrote about cryptomnesia in his essay "On the Psychology and Pathology of the So Called Occult Phenomena" (1902).

Jane Roberts (1929–1984) was a self-proclaimed psychic who channeled more than 20 books with teachings from an entity that called himself "Seth." These books, known as the *Seth Material*, had a huge impact, selling more than 7 million copies. Roberts dictated them to her husband between 1963 and 1984 while she was in a trance, interrupted only by her daily activities. The Seth readings are considered to be the cornerstone of the New Age philosophy and the most important books of the New Age movement, along with *The Course in Miracles*, which was channeled by Helen Schucman. Roberts wrote a novel called *The Oversoul Seven Trilogy* (1995) based on the Seth material.

A Course in Miracles has sold over two million copies. Helen Schucman (1909–1981) said the books were dictated to her over a seven-year period (1965–1972) by an inner voice whom she identified as Jesus. Schucman's identity was not known until after her death. She was a psychologist who taught at Columbia University and Columbia-Presbyterian Medical Center. Sales of *A Course in Miracles* increased dramatically after it was discussed on *The Oprah Winfrey Show* by Marianne Williamson in 1992. *A Course in Miracles* has been called everything from psychobabble to the New Age Bible.

Other examples of channeled books include: *Emmanuel's Book: A manual for living comfortably in the cosmos*; *Emmanuel's Book II: The Choice for Love*; and *Emmanuel's Book III: What is an Angel Doing Here?* (Pat Rodegast and Judith Stanton). The first two books in the series have an introduction written by Ram Dass. The *Emmanuel* trilogy brought spiritual teachings and messages of hope and healing from an entity called Emmanuel.

Visualization is a technique whereby one forms or recalls mental pictures or images in order to create one's own future. The central teaching of the Seth readings was that we create our own reality with our thoughts, beliefs, and expectations. The notion of visualization was popularized by Shakti Gawain, whose 1979 book *Creative Visualization* was an international bestseller. In it, she taught her readers how to use visualization, meditation, and affirmations to connect with their higher selves.

A spectacular illustration of the benefits of visualization was provided by a well-documented lottery winner. After her brother was killed in a car accident in 1999, Cynthia Stafford was determined to provide a home for her brother's five children. In 2004, the number $112 million appeared in her mind. She wrote the number down, put it under her pillow, and went to sleep every night with the visualization that she had won the lottery. When the Quick Pick jackpot rose to $112 million in 2007, she bought a ticket. The winning ticket, announced on Mother's Day, was hers alone.

To prove this wasn't a fluke, she decided to keep going with her visualizations. After she won the lottery, she visualized a successful film production company, which was a lifelong dream. After this dream was realized, she visualized what she thought would be the perfect boyfriend for her. She found her perfect boyfriend on the film set of her production company.

When he was 14, Wayne Dyer was watching Steve Allen host *The Tonight Show*. He somehow knew that one day he would be on *The Tonight Show* talking to Steve Allen. He could see himself on the set, talking to Steve. As he wrote in his memoir *I Can See Clearly Now,* he actually became preoccupied with this image. He told his family and friends about it but later stopped when he saw how his vision was being received. Twenty-two years later, after he wrote his first book, he was indeed invited to appear as a guest on *The Tonight Show*. By that time Johnny Carson was the host. Nevertheless, when Dyer went to the studio, he learned that Steve Allen was one of the guests that evening. So, in the end, he did in fact talk with

Steve Allen on the set of *The Tonight Show* just as his vision (visualization) had shown him so many years earlier.

A similar thing happened to the actor Jim Carrey. He came from a poor family. At one time, he was homeless. He worked as a janitor. His dream was to be a famous, wealthy actor. He started to visualize his success every day. In his mind's eye, he would visualize people in the movie industry coming up to him and telling him they liked his work. He wrote himself a post-dated check for $10-million and on the bottom of the check he wrote, "For acting services rendered." He subsequently moved to L.A. and started getting small acting roles. He carried the check around with him in his wallet for years. Near the date he had put on the check, he found out he had been hired to do a movie, *Dumb and Dumber*, for which he would be paid $10 million. When Oprah heard about his story, she called Jim Carrey one of her greatest teachers because she had not previously been aware of the power of visualization.

The power of visualization is really the power of the mind. Did Carrey's thought (the cause) create financial and artistic success (the effect)? Do we create our own reality with our thoughts? This story is amazing and certainly provocative. Carrey had a vision of great success. We cannot say with certainty that his visualization created his success or if it was due to his talent, hard work, and perseverance. Still, the fact that he had written the date and the exact amount on the check years in advance does give one pause. Even Oprah was impressed!

J. Z. Knight channeled more than 25 books from the entity known as Ramtha. There were eight books in the *Conversations with God* series by Neale Donald Walsh; eight books in the *Abraham* series, channeled by Esther Hicks; and four books in the *Michael Teachings*, channeled by Chelsea Quinn Yarbro. The first book in the *Messages from Michael* series was one of the most popular channeled books of the 1970s and 1980s. All of these channeled books were avidly read by spiritual seekers.

Automatic art and automatic writing are examples of psychic automatism, a form of dissociative state. Swedish artist and mystic Hilma af Klint (1862–1944), a pioneer in the abstract art movement, belonged to a group that called itself "The Five." They claimed to receive messages from higher spirits. Along with other well-known abstract artists, like Wassily Kandinsky and Piet Mondrian, Klint was influenced by the esoteric, spiritual philosophy known as Theosophy.

William Blake is another famous artist and writer whose work was channeled. When his dearly beloved brother, Robert, fell ill, Blake looked after him and was with him when he died. At the time of Robert's death, Blake said he saw Robert's soul leave his body and fly heavenward. Subsequently, Blake said Robert's spirit remained with him and told him how to illustrate his poems.

Canadian artist Alma Rumball was also a channeled artist. She said she did not know what she was drawing, only her hand knew; she just sat there and watched her hand move. She drew forms and figures of which she had no knowledge. When The Dalai Lama was shown her drawings in Toronto, his spokesperson said some of the figures were Tibetan deities. There is a documentary about her called *The Alma Drawings*.

I am a portrait artist. I am an Elected Member of the Portrait Society of Canada. Did I ever do channeled art? Yes, I did, on one occasion. I was not in a trance or an altered state. I was just doing a drawing. My portraits consist of the head, neck, and shoulders. I had drawn the head and neck, and I was trying to decide where to put the line for the shoulder, when the line suddenly appeared on the paper. I didn't draw it. I just saw it. Then I drew the line where I was shown it should go. It was very odd. You could say I hallucinated the line, but whatever the cause, it was very strange.

Each of my "visions" (the apparition, the angels, and the line on the paper) lasted just a few seconds. Were my eyes playing tricks on me? Possibly.

The source of channeled artwork, whether writing, drawing, or painting, is open to interpretation. Many writers, poets, and lyricists claim that their words come *through* them, not *to* them. Their claims do not generally specify whether the material is divinely inspired or a product of the unconscious (personal or collective). Many famous works of art, music, and literature have arisen from the twilight world of dreams and hallucinations.

Neil Young said he doesn't write songs, he writes them down. Vincent Van Gogh said, "I dream my paintings, and then I paint my dreams."

Harriet Beecher Stowe said that *Uncle Tom's Cabin* came to her in a vision. She didn't write it, she received it. Stowe and her husband, Calvin, believed they received communication from the spirit world, specifically through Calvin's deceased first wife. When Abraham Lincoln was introduced to Stowe, he said, "Is this the little woman who made this Great War?" thus acknowledging the importance of *Uncle Tom's Cabin* as a push for the abolition of slavery, which in turn would be a cause of the American Civil War.

But it is not just poets, artists, and literary types who say they are channeling words, images, or ideas from sources outside of conscious awareness. Inventors and scientists say the same thing.

In *The Art of Scientific Discovery*, W. I. B. Beveridge examined the role of intuition, dreaming, and imagination in scientific discovery. He saw scientific innovation as a creative art. In *Seeds of Discovery*, he described the "logic, illogic, serendipity, and sheer chance" that accounted for many scientific discoveries.

German organic chemist August Kekulé had a vision of the benzene ring, one of the most significant discoveries in organic chemistry, while staring into a fire. He saw the structure of the benzene molecule (C6H6) as a carbon atom united with a hydrogen atom at each point on a hexagon.

Descartes discovered the basic theories of analytic geometry in a dream-like state. Einstein's theory of relativity came to him while he was in an altered state. He said his famous formula $E=mc^2$, which revolutionized our view of the universe, came to him in a Eureka moment, emerging full-blown from his mind. Nikola Tesla, the Serbian-American electrical engineer and physicist who discovered the electrical alternating current (AC) and invented the first AC motor, said his inventions were revealed to him in blinding flashes of light. Tesla Motors was named in his honor. The Tesla Roadster is an electric car with an AC motor that is based on Tesla's original 1882 design.

One of the inventors of the polio vaccine, Jonas Salk, used to wake up in the night and write down messages from what he called another realm. Over the years he collected more than 12,000 pages of communication. Some of this information was used in the development of the polio vaccine.

James Watson, Nobel Laureate and co-discoverer of DNA, guessed that the DNA structure was a double helix after he had a symbolic dream of two intertwined snakes. Elias Howe, inventor of the sewing machine, said his invention came to him in a dream.

All of these discoveries, inventions, and theories can be categorized as channeled, either through dreams or fantasies that occurred while the receiver was in an altered state or in a waking state.

There have been many successful medical intuitives able to channel both diagnosis and treatment for afflicted individuals. By far the best-known is Edgar Cayce (1877–1945). Cayce was known as America's sleeping prophet for his ability to put himself into a trance and answer questions on a variety of topics while appearing to be asleep. He reluctantly answered questions on health and healing, on one condition: that he not be paid for his readings.

Cayce was considered the founder of the New Age Movement and the father of holistic medicine, but he was not without his critics. Some of his predictions did not come true, and some of his readings, such as the ones on Atlantis or on the "five different races" were quite controversial.

Edgar Cayce's son, Hugh Lynn Cayce, wrote a book about him called *Venture Inward: Edgar Cayce's Story and the Mysteries of the Unconscious Mind*, as did Thomas Sugrue, *There Is a River: The Story of Edgar Cayce.* The title is from *Psalms 46:4*.

There is a river, the streams whereof make glad the city of God.

I read Hugh Lynn Cayce's book when I was quite young. It made a big impression on me. The message in the title, "Venture Inward," was an entirely new concept for me. Although it was new, it was quite appealing.

Of course, Cayce had his detractors in the Skeptics Society. Still, as William James said, people need something to believe in. For some people, it is a kind of survival strategy, and it makes them happy. For me, it wasn't a question of survival or feeling happy. It was about a new way of looking at the world and also looking at myself. A new philosophy of life.

Towards the end of his life, Cayce became quite famous. He was receiving letters requesting help and healing from sick people around the world. He founded the Association for Research and Enlightenment (A.R.E.) in Virginia Beach, Virginia, in 1931. There are now 37 Edgar Cayce centers around the world. They offer camps, retreats, conferences, lectures, and webinars.

Modern-day medical intuitives include Adam McLeod (known as "Adam" or "Dreamhealer"). He is now a naturopath, but before he received any formal training. he was credited with healing hundreds of people by the time he was 16. I first heard about Adam after reading a newspaper article in which Ronnie Hawkins said Adam cured his pancreatic cancer with distant healing.

Mona Lisa Schulz is the author of *Awakening Intuition: Using Your Mind-Body Network for Insight and Healing*. She received her MD and PhD (Behavioral Neuroscience) from Boston University. She gives lectures and phone readings.

Guardian Angels and Spirit Guides

People often say to someone they like or to someone who has helped them, "You're an angel." They don't mean it literally, but the idea is there. Many years ago, I had an experience on an airplane that seemed otherworldly to me at the time. I had been assigned the window seat in a row with three seats. Soon after takeoff, the 300-pound man sitting in the middle seat fell asleep. As he slumped in his chair, his knees touched the seat in front of him, and I felt completely enclosed and trapped. I started to feel claustrophobic, like I had to get off the plane right away. I broke into a cold sweat, got short of breath and felt panicky. It was a full-blown panic attack. I had to climb over the sleeping man sitting next to me to get to the aisle. When I reached the aisle, I started pacing up and down. I asked the flight attendant if I could have a ginger ale. She said no and barked at me to return to my seat. At that exact moment, a young woman sitting in the aisle seat in the last row of the cabin saw my predicament and kindly offered to change seats with me. Once I was seated in the aisle seat at the back of the plane, I quickly settled down, I could breathe again, and the panicky feelings started to pass.

Since it was winter, I had left my winter coat in the overhead bin just above my original seat, about half-way up the aisle. I thought the woman who changed seats with me must have left her coat in the bin above her original seat at the back of the plane. I wanted to thank her, so I waited until the plane emptied out, thinking I would see her when she came to the back of the plane to retrieve her coat. However, she had disappeared. There was no sign of her, no evidence she had ever been there. She wouldn't have left the plane in the middle of winter without a coat. The thought occurred to me that she must have been an angel who had materialized in my hour of need to help me out. I know it sounds far-fetched, but desperate minds seek desperate solutions.

Many people report seeing angels, but the angels are not always the usual kind, the winged variety. They may just look like ordinary people, who appear, perform a service, and then leave. At times, they don't even appear, but their presence is felt. For example, it was reported that a pregnant woman lost her footing while walking up the stairs. Just as she was about to fall over backwards down the stairs, she felt a hand behind her pushing on her back and preventing her fall. When she turned around, there was no one there.

Another woman reported that just as she was about to drown, after she went under for the fourth time and her lungs were starting to fill up with water, she felt herself being lifted up. A boat appeared from out of nowhere and she was rescued. She said it was a miracle.

In his book *The Angel Effect: The Powerful Force That Ensures We Are Never Alone,* John Geiger documented many cases of people who reported that they were visited by an otherworldly presence when they were in great danger or were feeling completely desperate and lost. This phenomenon is very similar to the "third man factor," discussed earlier, in which an unseen, benevolent presence brings hope and guidance to people in extreme circumstances.

In his work with dying children, Melvin Morse reported that 50 percent of the children in his near-death studies reported seeing their "guardian angels" as part of their near-death experience. According to *Newsweek*, 13 percent of Americans reported that they saw or felt the presence of an angel during the previous year. A 2011 poll showed 75 percent of Americans believed in angels.

Angels have been reported throughout history. All the major religions include references to angels. In the Koran, the Prophet Muhammad spoke of being visited by three angels, who cleansed him. In the Old Testament, an angel intervened to save Isaac from being sacrificed by Abraham. Another angel protected Daniel in the lion's den. A third angel wrestled with Jacob in the desert. In the New Testament, Paul frequently spoke of his contact with angels. He saw angels interacting with other angels, and he observed the souls of dead men being accompanied by angels on their way to heaven.

Raphael, Sistine Madonna (detail)

Angels have frequently been represented in art, literature, music, movies and television. In fact, they have become kitsch, found on everything from coffee mugs to calendars to tee shirts. The two winged cherubs from Raphael's "Sistine Madonna" are instantly recognizable. Botticelli's famous painting "Birth of Venus" shows Venus being carried by a winged male angel who blows the breath of life into her.

Pierre Jovanovic was a reporter for *Quotidien de Paris* who believed his life was saved by a guardian angel. Driving home one day from an interview in Silicon Valley, he felt a hand push him to the side just before a bullet passed through his windshield and past his head. The police told him he would have been killed instantly if he hadn't moved. As a result of his experience, he decided to research the subject of guardian angels. He spoke with other journalists, some of whom were war-zone survivors. He learned from other reporters that such stories were not unusual. He published the results of his investigation in his book *An Inquiry into the Existence of Guardian Angels: A Journalist's Investigative Report.* He concluded that guardian angels are real and are not uncommon.

Near-death experience researcher Kenneth Ring said he did not like to use the term "guardian angel" because of its religious connotations; he preferred to talk about "spiritual guides" or "Higher Self." Many people today refer to their "spirit guides," who are seen as incorporeal helpers.

Some Evidence and Theories of Reincarnation

Reported accounts of angels, spirit guides, channels, and mediums raises the question of the immortality of the soul. Whether or not we personally believe that the soul survives the body, millions of people around the world believe in reincarnation, including Buddhists, Hindus, Jains, and Kabbalists.

The standard version of reincarnation says that the soul leaves the body at the time of death and subsequently incarnates in another body, either at the time of birth or at the moment of conception. Although believers in reincarnation are in the minority in North America, in the global community they are in the majority. Past-life therapy has turned many non-believers into believers.

Psychiatrist Brian Weiss and psychologist Michael Newton independently documented past-life and between-life reports from patients under hypnotic regression. They popularized past-life regression therapy as a way to access past-life memories, in order to deal with unfinished business and unhealed wounds in this life.

Carol Bowman started to research children's past-life memories after her own five-year-old son developed an extreme fear of loud noises during a Fourth of July celebration. His fear lasted for months, and it was so bad that his mother was frequently called to take him home from school. A family friend who was visiting at the time happened to be a hypnotherapist.

When Carol told him her son's problem, he said to the boy, "Why don't you sit on your mother's lap, close your eyes, and tell me what you see when you hear those loud noises."

Sitting on his mother's lap, with his eyes closed, the boy described in great detail a battle scene from the American Civil War. His account of the battle, in which he fought as a soldier, was later verified by an historian. After the cathartic recollection of his traumatic memories (known as an abreaction), the boy's fear of loud noises completely disappeared. His abreaction had other benefits as well. When he said he had been shot in the wrist, his nine-year-old sister, who had been listening, said, "Oh, that's where his eczema is." His eczema was so bad that he was constantly picking at it until it bled. His mother had taken him from one specialist to another without any benefit. As a result, his mother kept his wrist covered at all times. No salve, ointment, or cream would help. After his recollection of his past-life Civil War wounds, his severe eczema on his wrist cleared up completely and never returned.

Ian Stevenson is a psychiatrist who spent 40 years documenting past-life memories from children all over the world. He had more than 3,000 cases in his files, which he called the best evidence yet for reincarnation. He decided to work with children because many of the adults who contacted him claiming to have past-life memories turned out to be frauds or else their memories had been recovered under hypnosis. The children he worked with had not been hypnotized. Their memories were spontaneous, not coaxed or cajoled.

Among Stevenson's many cases were two people who started speaking languages they had never learned. The ability to speak a foreign language that the speaker cannot account for is called xenoglossia. Stevenson documented the case of a woman in Ohio called Delores whose husband, a Methodist minister, used hypnosis to alleviate her back pain. One time when he was using hypnotic regression on her, she answered his questions in German. In subsequent hypnotic sessions, she said "*Ich bin Gretchen*" and she continued to speak German. The poor minister had to use a dictionary to understand her.

The minister contacted Stevenson, who spoke German. He was able to elicit details from her about her past life in Germany in the 19th century. She named the town where she lived and her family members. There were no records for her family, but her historical details were verified. Delores grew up in West Virginia. She had not known any German speakers growing up, nor did she learn the German language in school.

Brian Weiss documented a case of xenoglossia in a Chinese surgeon who came to see him for a past-life regression. She was accompanied by a translator, as she did not speak English. During the regression she spoke about a past life in San Francisco and she started to speak English, which she had never learned.

Stevenson interviewed children between the ages of two and five because children usually learn to speak when they are two; by five they tend to forget their past-life memories. He described the case of a Turkish boy who, almost as soon as he started to speak, said, "What am I doing here? I was at the port." The child said he was a dockworker and had been killed in an accident.

Jim Tucker is a child psychiatrist who worked with Dr. Stevenson. He has documented over 2,500 cases of children's past-life memories. Although Dr. Stevenson's cases were mostly in Asia, the children Dr. Tucker interviewed were mostly in the United States. One of Dr. Tucker's investigations is featured in the documentary "The Boy Who Lived Before." It can be seen at: www.documentaryheaven.com.

Weiss, Stevenson, and Tucker are all psychiatrists with sterling academic credentials. I have no reason to doubt the veracity of their reports.

Bowman, Stevenson, and Tucker, who all worked with children, emphasized the importance of allowing children to talk about their past-life memories. Parents usually dismiss their children's past-life memories as nonsense, or else they ignore them. However, abreaction of traumatic, past-life memories, if recalled, can have a positive, healing benefit in this lifetime.

Actress and dancer Shirley MacLaine popularized the concept of past lives and reincarnation for an American audience in her 1983 bestselling memoir *Out On A Limb*, which was made into a 5-hour ABC mini-series in 1987; however, as the Stoic philosopher Epictetus said, anyone who pursues a spiritual path will be subjected to ridicule, and MacLaine certainly was.

Systems theorist Ernst Laszlo wrote that reincarnation does not mean that the soul keeps coming back to earth in different bodies. Rather, every thought, word, and deed in our lifetime is recorded as a hologram in the Akashic Field (also known as the Information Field or the Akashic Records) and people can access this information through their psychic abilities while in a trance state. According to Laszlo, when people recall past-life memories, they are accessing the Akashic Records. There has been a great deal written about the Akashic Records, including Laszlo's *Science and the Akashic Field* and Lisa Barnett's *The Infinite Wisdom of the Akashic Records*.

Indian sage Ramana Maharshi said, "The true self is continuous and unchangeable. The reincarnating ego belongs to the lower level, mainly the world of thought. It will be transcended through self-realization."

The Many-Worlds Interpretation (MWI) of quantum mechanics was first introduced by American physicist Hugh Everett III at a lecture in Dublin in 1957. He used the term "relative state formulation." His formulation was renamed "many-worlds" and popularized by Bryce Seligman DeWitt in the 1960s. The basic idea is that whatever could have happened has happened in an alternate universe.

The multiverse, championed by Britain's Astronomer Royal Sir Martin Reese, is a term used to denote that our universe is not the only universe; rather, there are a multitude of parallel universes, as suggested by string theory and the famous thought experiment known as Schrödinger's Cat, in which the cat is both dead and alive at the same time.

The parallel universes in the multiverse are sometimes called "alternate universes" or "parallel worlds." In Superstring Theory there are ten dimensions: the three dimensions with which we are familiar (length, width, and height); the fourth dimension (time); and the six other dimensions which are hidden and unobservable. It is in these hidden dimensions that the possible worlds reside.

Anita Moorjani, who survived a near-death experience and a subsequent miraculous recovery from stage-four Hodgkin's lymphoma, wrote that, according to her understanding of the information she was given while out of her body during her near-death experience, all of our lives – past, present, and future – occur simultaneously. I find this idea rather appealing, as it accords with the notion of the multiverse, parallel worlds, and parallel lives.

During her illness, Moorjani was so weak that she was unable to walk and unable to eat. Her weight had fallen to 85 lbs. Her organs had shut down, and she lapsed into a coma. Her family was notified that she was dying. Four days after she woke up from the coma, her swollen lymph nodes had shrunk to 70 percent of their original size; five weeks later, they were completely gone. This finding was confirmed by three ultrasounds which failed to detect any pathological lymph nodes. Ten years late, she was still cancer-free.

While in a coma, she saw her deceased father who told her she had to return to her body because her work was not yet done. After she woke up from her coma, she said she had been in another realm. She described her state of being while out of her body as one of great clarity and "pure consciousness."

Moorjani's near-death experience led her to new beliefs about reincarnation. Raised in a traditional Hindu family, she thought that reincarnation involved the soul's departure from the body at the time of death and subsequent embodiment after the passage of time in another body. After her near-death experience, she came to see reincarnation in a different light. She was given the understanding that all time is now and all of our reincarnations, past lives, and parallel lives are occurring in the present moment.

In *Dying to Be Me*, Moorjani wrote, "I realized that time doesn't move in a linear fashion unless we're using the filter of our physical bodies and minds. Once we're no longer limited by our earthly senses, every moment exists simultaneously. I've come to think that the concept of reincarnation is really just an interpretation, a way for our intellect to make sense of all existence happening at once."

In other words, we, as human beings, do not have the mental capacity to understand how time works in our lives. Moorjani's assertion that time is not linear is the same idea put forward by the movie *Arrival*, discussed earlier. While the idea that all time is now has long been a staple of esoteric literature, it is now reaching a mainstream audience through books like Moorjani's and movies like *Arrival*. The Amy Adams character in *Arrival* has the gift of clairvoyance. The idea that time is not linear could help explain clairvoyance. It could also have more practical applications.

People who are depressed tend to think about the past and are often filled with negative thoughts, leading to regret, remorse, and recrimination. People who are anxious about the future tend to worry about things that may never happen. Thus the admonition, as old as yesterday's newspaper, to cherish the moment, stay present, and live for today. Tomorrow will take care of itself. *Carpe diem.*

Eckhart Tolle (*The Power of Now*), Ram Dass (*Be Here Now*), and many other spiritual and psychological teachers have stressed the importance of staying present in the now. But what if the future is now? And the past is now? They are, in the sense that whether time is linear or not, by thinking about the past we bring it into the present. The same thing applies to the future. The idea that all time is now is not a new idea, but it still a heady one, almost too complex to grasp and, at the same time, difficult to ignore.

When I was ill, I bought Louise Hay's book *You Can Heal Your Life* and started saying the affirmation that she recommends for people with leukemia: *I move beyond past limitations into the freedom of the now. It is safe to be me.* I still say this affirmation at the gym from time to time as I am running around the track. I found the words "the freedom of the now" to be a good way to stay present and to feel free. When I told my hematologist/oncologist what I was doing with meditation, visualization, and affirmations, he encouraged me to keep doing it and each time he saw me he asked me if I was still doing it. He thought these techniques were helpful. He was a great believer in complementary medicine (not alternative medicine).

Almost all of the phenomena described in this chapter – including the ideas about time, spirit guides, guardian angels, channeled writing, and the rest – would likely be placed in the "woo-woo" category by some readers who have not had confirmatory experiences. Like other paranormal phenomena that might have spiritual, mystical, or supernatural dimensions, one's mind is often made up in advance about the reliability of reports or anecdotes which seem almost too weird to be true and are not borne out by personal experience. Nevertheless, as the saying goes, truth is stranger than fiction.

When it comes to credibility, as with many of the other paranormal phenomena described earlier, personal experience changes everything because it challenges our pre-conceived notions and it spurs imagination. William Blake considered his imagination to be the divine part of himself. He wrote, "The eternal body of man is the imagination."

In *Living Philosophies,* Einstein wrote, "The intuitive mind is a sacred gift and the rational mind is a faithful servant. We have created a society that honors the servant and has forgotten the gift." Einstein also said, "The most beautiful thing we can experience is the mysterious. It is the source of all true art and science." Why did Einstein call intuition "a sacred gift?" Why is it sacred? Is intuition somehow related to channeling? Are intuition, inspiration, and imagination all related to channeling in some as-yet unknown way?

As Shakespeare wrote,

> *There are more things in heaven and earth, Horatio,*
> *than are dreamt of in your philosophy.*

> *Hamlet* (Act 1, scene 5)

Now here's the kicker. I mentioned that *Arrival* was based on a short story by Ted Chiang called "Story of Your Lives" and that the title of the short story was very similar to the title of the poem by Mark Strand, "The

Story of Our Lives," that my brother and I had unwittingly exchanged decades earlier.

Shortly after seeing the movie and re-reading Mark Strand's poem, I picked up a book on my bookshelf that had been sitting there for decades but that I had never read, *Time Is an Illusion*, by Chris Griscom. It was published in 1986, so it was sitting there on my bookshelf waiting to be read for 30 years. Soon after I re-read the poem "The Story of Our Lives," which closes with the lines, "They are the book and they are/nothing else," I read the following paragraph in *Time Is an Illusion*:

> Thus, El Salvador was a challenging tool for exploration into the astral dimension and helped me to begin the vital perception of that dimension's laws of existence. I was very careful then about 'scientifically' collecting and documenting data, to 'prove' real every supernatural occurrence. Later I read through these notes and realized that they weren't important to me, as I knew experientially what was true. Upon my departure I discarded them, the way I had discarded my books in moving from one house to another in Galisteo. In both cases my Higher Self made clear to me, '*You are the book.*'(Italics mine.)

The story of our lives. Story of your lives. They are the book. You are the book. Is time an illusion? It sometimes seems that way.

There have been many challenges over the years to the idea that time is a straight arrow going forward. Physicist and astrobiologist Paul Davies, in his book *About Time: Einstein's Unfinished Revolution*, wrote that Einstein saw our perception of time divided into past/present/future as "stubbornly persistent illusion." For Einstein, time was elastic, bending, curving, and warping in response to space, gravity, mass, and motion.

I am reminded of the message I received in a dream many years ago: "This is not reality. This is a world of illusion. And the biggest illusion is time."

Chapter 9: *Stone walls do not a prison make*: A New Reality

Everything you can imagine is real.

—Pablo Picasso

Nothing is real.

—John Lennon, "Strawberry Fields Forever"

People who have never experienced paranormal phenomena, or who question their validity, often say they are not real. This, of course, raises fundamental questions about the nature of reality, which we need to address. However, as the diverse opinions quoted above suggest, there are no easy answers.

In general terms, we can say that there are two kinds of reality: subjective reality and consensus (objective) reality. Out-of-body and near-death experiences, visions, messages, ESP, telepathy, and other paranormal phenomena can be easily dismissed as unreal, illusory, hallucinatory, or delusional by people who have either never had these experiences or have never had an interest in them. Our challenge is to move the dial on the conversation in order to increase our understanding of these events and to shift them from one category (subjective) to the other category (consensual). In order to do that, we need to explore different notions of reality.

The title of this chapter is from a poem written in 1642 by Richard Lovelace, called "To Althea, from Prison." The first line of the poem is often quoted:

Stone walls do not a prison make, nor iron bars a cage.

Although the poet is in prison, as long as he has his love for Althea, in his mind he is free. That is his subjective reality. Of course, the objective, consensual reality would be that he is in prison and therefore not free.

Psychiatrists have long been concerned with the meaning of "reality" because, as part of their jobs, they are often required to do mental status examinations, one component of which includes what is called "reality testing." This process may involve a determination of whether a statement made by the patient is real or delusional. Delusions are defined as false beliefs that cannot be shaken. It is up to the examining psychiatrist to determine which of the patient's statements or beliefs are false (delusional) and which are true. In this context, reality is equated with truth. It is usually not that difficult to distinguish between true and false statements, as they relate to ideas or perceptions, but it may be more difficult to determine with accuracy the validity of a belief.

The significance of a false belief would be determined by whether or not the person was willing to act on its behalf. If someone had a false belief that the world was flat, for example, it wouldn't really matter, unless he or she tried to prove it by attempting to sail off the edge of the world.

Mark David Chapman was a delusional young man whose assassination of John Lennon in 1980 rocked the music world. Chapman was found at the scene of the murder reading *Catcher in the Rye*, which he said was his "statement." He claimed to be part Holden Caulfield (the protagonist of *Catcher*) and part devil. His false belief had tragic consequences.

Andrew Sims is a Professor of Psychiatry at the University of Leeds. Like other psychiatrists, he had to use his own experience to determine what was real and what was fantasy or delusion. In his textbook *Symptoms in the Mind*, he wrote:

> We are able in our own experience of our thinking to distinguish between reality and imagination (fantasy). I know whether I am a cricketer or just imagining myself to be. The distinction between fantasy and reality is assumed as being obvious, and it is unusual to have difficulty deciding which forms of experience we have.

According to Sims, one should be able to distinguish between fantasy and reality, and the distinction should be easy; but for anyone whose reality testing is impaired, the distinction is not at all easy.

Karl Jaspers, author of *General Psychopathology* (1913), mentioned earlier, wrote that psychotic symptoms should be diagnosed by form, not by content; that is, if patients had visual or auditory hallucinations, what they actually saw or heard was not as important as the fact that they were hallucinating.

Jasper's views were challenged by controversial Scottish psychiatrist and poet R. D. Laing. He and David Cooper, a South African psychiatrist, became identified with the anti-psychiatry movement. Laing's 1960 book *The Divided Self: An Existential Study in Sanity and Madness* was very influential.

Unlike Jaspers, Laing thought that the content of delusions was important in understanding the individual who had them. He wrote that what we label as delusional is culturally determined. Different cultures and different eras have divergent notions about what is real and what is delusional. Thus, cultural, social, historical, and developmental factors all need to be considered before diagnosing hallucinations or delusions. Similarly, although our perception of reality can be conceptualized as brain function, the brain changes. Reality can be perceived in different ways by different people, or by the same person at different stages of his or her life.

"Reality testing" is a technical term in psychiatry which hinges on the definition of "psychosis" as meaning "out of touch with reality." When the word *reality* is used in this sense, it clearly means the objective, consensual version of reality. Disorders of reality testing can be due to brain disorder, disease, or damage; consequently, there is a biomedical component to the ability to know the difference between "real" and "unreal."

Disorders of reality testing can be readily identified as pathological by virtue of their idiosyncratic nature. These disorders include functional psychoses, such as schizophrenia and bipolar disorder, as well as organic brain disorders, such as Korsakoff Syndrome or Alzheimer's disease, in which the patient constructs his or her own reality. In the majority of cases, the false nature of the patient's utterances is readily apparent, especially if there are bizarre delusions or hallucinations. In some cases, however, persons so afflicted can construct a personal narrative that sounds plausible. They might sound quite sane and reasonable, while saying things that are completely untrue.

Confabulation is defined as the falsification of memory that occurs in a clear consciousness and is associated with amnesia. It is due to organic brain disorder. An example of a condition in which one finds confabulation is Korsakoff Syndrome, which is a memory disorder caused by a severe thiamine (Vitamin B1) deficiency, usually due to chronic alcoholism. It is characterized by amnesia, lack of insight, denial of disability, and confabulation. Other symptoms include disorientation, severe impairment of learning, and loss of memory for recent events. Confabulation is also present in traumatic brain injury; carbon monoxide, arsenic, or lead poisoning; drug intoxication or withdrawal; and tertiary syphilis.

Describing a 37-year-old alcoholic writer with severe amnesia, Sergei Korsakoff (1854–1900) wrote, "He not only recalls facts, but also things said in his presence, possibly even his dreams, and all of this is now part of his consciousness; all of it presents but a chaos because, if he remembers something, he cannot decide whether it happened in reality or whether he dreamed it. The trace left by a real incident is only little different in intensity from the one left by a dream or an idea."

Armin Schnider is Professor of Neuro-rehabilitation at the University Hospital of Geneva. In *The Confabulating Mind: How the Brain Creates Reality*, he describes the case of Mrs. B., a 63-year-old psychiatrist who suffered massive damage to her brain while on vacation. She had a severe headache, the worst headache of her life, followed by loss of consciousness. The CT scan revealed a subarachnoid hemorrhage (bleeding into the space between the skull and the brain) caused by a ruptured cerebral aneurysm. After rapid neurosurgical intervention, she slowly regained consciousness. She recovered gradually and within three months her speech was coherent and her behavior seemed normal. There was only one problem. She was confabulating.

She had invented a new identity for herself. She seemed to have lost twenty years from her memory and acquired a new career. She said she was a physiotherapist in her forties. She told people her mother and her brother had come to visit her, although they were both dead. She said she was planning to take her children to the zoo, and she spoke about them as though they were still children, even though they were both in their thirties.

She had no insight into the fact that her memory was affected by her brain injury and she insisted that all her confabulations were true. She was unable to remember anything for more than ten minutes. Eventually, after 17 months, she stopped confabulating and acknowledged that her memory was bad. This is a classic example of reality distortion due to brain injury. Mrs. B. had created her own reality, which was objectively false, but true to her.

False memories are not necessarily due to brain damage or disease. They can be implanted during hypnosis, or even during psychotherapy without hypnosis if the therapist is very insistent and the client is highly suggestible and wants to please the therapist. Just as Mrs. B. was convinced that her made-up identity was real, individuals with false memories can be insistent that their memories are accurate. The unreliability of eyewitness testimony is another example of how false memories can become engrained and are often mistaken for the truth. In this case, there is no brain damage or disease, no hypnotic trance or other factor to account for the fact that memory is simply not always reliable; however, one instance of poor memory function is not the same as impaired reality testing, delusion, or confabulation.

Aside from delusions and hallucinations, other psychiatric symptoms can also be manifestations of impaired reality testing. These include unreality feelings, such as depersonalization, derealization, Capgras Syndrome, *déjà vu* and *jamais vu* phenomena. Depersonalization refers to feelings of unreality concerning oneself; derealization refers to feelings that a familiar environment is unfamiliar. An extreme form of derealization is *jamais vu* (never seen), the opposite of *déjà vu* (already seen), in which an unfamiliar environment seems familiar. Capgras Syndrome refers to a particularly insidious and bizarre delusion in which the individual thinks his or her spouse, child, or parent has been replaced by an impostor. While delusions and hallucinations usually occur in the context of psychosis, unreality feelings can occur with extreme anxiety. Psychedelic drugs can also cause unreality feelings. *Déjà vu* phenomena can be seen in temporal lobe epilepsy.

Our brief discussion of the contributions of Jaspers, Laing, and Korsakoff presented an overview of historical, psychiatric perspectives on the nature of reality. There is also another approach to the topic of reality, represented by physicists such as Neil Turok, Director of the Perimeter Institute for Theoretical Physics in Waterloo, Ontario. Poets, writers, artists, philosophers, biologists, and psychologists also have a crucial role to play in the ongoing dialectic about the true nature of reality.

As a physicist, Turok had a different perspective on the nature of reality. He said that physics was about the human mind making sense of the universe, on a scale from one-billionth the size of an atom to ten trillion times the size of the solar system. In the "concurrence model" the universe is 73 percent unknown dark energy, 22 percent unknown dark matter, and 5 percent ordinary matter and radiation. This model of reality, from one of the world's leading theoretical physicists, states that 95 percent of the universe is unknown. That is the reality of our physical universe. We might as well get used to it. 95 percent of our universe is unknown. That is the universe of which we are a part. That is our reality.

Regarding the impact of quantum physics on the way physicists think, Turok said,

We had to give up any notion of being able to picture things as they really are, or of being able (even in principle) to measure and predict everything there is to know. These ideas had to be replaced with a more abstract, all-encompassing theory which reduced our capacity to 'know' or 'visualize' reality, while giving us a powerful new means of describing and predicting nature.

Descriptions and predictions are fine, but they cannot replace knowing. Cutting-edge, theoretical physics tells us we cannot ever fully know or measure reality.

Another physicist, Albert Einstein, wrote,

A human being is part of a whole, called by us [the] 'Universe,' a part limited in time and space. He experiences himself, his thoughts and feelings, as something separated from the rest – a kind of optical delusion of his consciousness. This delusion is a kind of prison for us, restricting us to our personal desires and to affection for a few persons nearest to us. Our task must be to free ourselves from this prison by widening our circle of compassion to embrace all living creatures and the whole of nature in its beauty.

Einstein saw the "delusion" of separateness as a prison. If we were ever to escape from this prison, there would be enormous benefits for humanity. "Stone walls do not a prison make" presents the case of the lovelorn poet whose mind is free in spirit in spite of his "reality" of being in prison. Einstein says we restrict our freedom and imprison ourselves by living in the illusion of separateness.

William James, too, was convinced of the oneness of all things and all people. He challenged the illusion that we are all separate. He believed that we are all connected. James believed that the feeling of oneness with the universe was the paramount spiritual experience a human being can have. He wrote,

> We with our lives are like islands in the sea, or like trees in the forest. The maple and pine may whisper to each other with their leaves . . . but the trees also commingle their roots in the darkness underground, and the islands hang together through the ocean's bottom. Just so, there is a continuum of cosmic consciousness against which our individuality builds accidental fences.

Jung had similar ideas about the collective unconscious.

> Just as the human body shows a common anatomy over and above all racial differences, so, too, the human psyche possesses a common substratum transcending all differences in culture and consciousness. I have called this substratum the collective unconscious.

He compared human beings to rhizomes, plants with horizontal underground stems. He said that what seem to be many different plants on the surface are, in fact, all shoots from a single plant system, connected underground. The shoots wither and die each year, but they come up again in the spring.

Many writers and philosophers have expressed similar ideas about the unity of mankind. Colin Wilson wrote, "Our individuality is a kind of eddy in the sea of mind, a reflection of the total identity of the universal humanity."

When writers as diverse as Einstein, James, Jung, and Wilson speak with one voice on the nature of reality and the oneness of all humanity, I think it behooves us to take notice and seriously consider the merit of their words.

Do these words have any relevance to our discussion of paranormal phenomena? I think they do. In the light of repeated, poetic assertions that we are all the same and all one, under the skin, then ESP, telepathy, and other paranormal phenomena do not really seem that surprising. They make sense. We are all individuals, but we are also part of something much larger, just like each grain of sand on the beach or each drop of water in the ocean or each bee in the bee colony. I like to think of us as ants in an anthill, all working together, but each of us has our own identity. We are all one but at the same time not.

It is one thing to read about or philosophize about the oneness of humanity, quite another thing to experience it. The overwhelming feeling, which I have experienced in a moment of peak joy, includes a sense of oneness, the unity of all things, and what Freud called the "oceanic feeling." Freud said the source of the oceanic feeling was regression to an earlier, infantile fusion with the mother, but to me, it was more like a fusion with Mother Earth and with all things big and small. When I had this feeling, the feeling was fleeting, but its impact was enduring. In fact, its impact was lifelong.

In the *Tibetan Book of Living and Dying*, Rinpoche wrote,

> The Buddha compared the universe to a vast net woven of a countless variety of brilliant jewels, each with a countless number of facets. Each jewel reflects in itself every other jewel in the net and is, in fact, one with every other jewel.

Teilhard de Chardin wrote,

> The farther and more deeply we penetrate into matter, by means of increasingly powerful methods, the more we are confounded by the independence of its parts. Each element of the cosmos is positively woven from all the others.

Whether physics, philosophy, psychology, or spirituality, there is a general consensus towards a connection, a lack of separation, between and among all phenomena, people, and things in the universe and in the cosmos. We think we are separate individuals, but that idea is an illusion. Only in moments of great clarity, peak experience, trance, or deep meditation, do we perceive the unity of all humanity, and the oneness of all things. Then boundaries melt away, and we are left with a new reality, the idea that the world we see with our eyes is not the real world. This idea seems strange to us because it makes us question the nature of reality. But that's a good thing. It's important to question reality if human knowledge is to move forward.

In his 1997 novel *Illusions: The Adventures of a Reluctant Messiah*, Richard Bach said reality is based on perspective, not on perception. He wrote, "What the caterpillar calls the end of the world, the master calls a butterfly." Or to look at it another way, what the caterpillar calls the end, the butterfly calls the beginning.

Buddhists, Sikhs, and Hindus share a belief in the concept of *maya*, a Sanskrit word that is usually translated as "illusion." They believe that the world we see with our eyes is not the real world; it is a world of illusion. There is a famous story in Sikhism about a rope and a snake. On a moonless night, a man saw a snake on the floor. When the sun rose, he saw that the snake was in reality a rope. When one is enlightened ("the sun rose") one sees the true nature of reality (the snake is really a rope); until then, one lives in illusion, darkness or *maya* (the snake).

Sikhism believes that people are trapped in this world because of five vices: lust, anger, greed, attachment, and ego. *Maya* enables these five vices. Alan Watts wrote, "The *maya* doctrine points out, firstly, the impossibility of grasping the actual world in the mind's net of words and concepts, and secondly, the fluid character of those very forms which thought attempts to define."

In his allegory of the cave, Plato says that those who only use their eyes to see the world are blind to the true nature of reality. In *The Republic*, he describes prisoners who spend their whole lives chained to the wall of a cave, unable to move. There is a big bonfire behind them and they watch shadows projected on the wall by people passing in front of the fire. The prisoners think the shadows are reality. He says the philosopher is like a prisoner, freed from the cave, who comes to understand that the shadows are not reality. When he returns to the cave and tries to explain the true nature of reality to the prisoners, they don't believe him. They say his vision was corrupted by the light. The prisoners take the shadows to be real things, not just a reflection of reality, and they think the sounds they hear are real sounds, not just an echo. Plato's Theory of Forms (or "Ideas") states that forms or ideas are the highest kind of reality, and that that they are more real and more substantial that the fleeting, ephemeral, material world of change that we perceive with our senses.

Joseph Chilton Pearce wrote in *The Crack in the Cosmic Egg: New Constructs of Mind and Reality* that "all things are possible to him who believes – that is, to him that believes in the possibility." He said, "Man's mind is a mirror of the universe that mirrors man's mind, though the mirroring is subtle, random and unfathomable." It's like saying that art imitates life, which imitates art (which imitates life, which imitates art). The wheel goes round and round.

For Pearce, there is no such thing as "supernatural," but instead, there are an infinite number of natures. He suggests a new construct is neither true nor false, it is simply a choice. We choose what to believe and what to think about the nature of reality. He wrote about the farmer who went to a zoo and saw a giraffe for the first time. The farmer looked at the giraffe, snorted, spat on the ground, and said, "There is no such animal."

The farmer's unwillingness to perceive the giraffe leads to a discussion about the nature of reality. To quote Sidney Cohen, a physician who warned about the dangers of LSD and the author of *The Beyond Within: The LSD Story,* "We can only perceive what we can conceive." The farmer was not able to conceive that there could be such a creature as a giraffe, as the giraffe was beyond his imagination and his conceptual (therefore perceptual) capacity.

When the Indian mystic Gopi Krishna was asked to describe the best way for an ordinary person to achieve a state of higher consciousness, he said,

> The surest way should be to voluntarily develop the characteristics of higher consciousness. For instance, to always keep in mind that there is no barrier, no distinction, no wall between man and man…. This would be, perhaps, the most effective way to melt the barriers which are created by the ego – to always put oneself in the shoes of another.

This admonition is very much in keeping with The Golden Rule. "Do unto others as you would have them do unto you" and "Love thy neighbor as thyself" are principles to live by, for many people. One interpretation of this idea is that when you love your neighbor as yourself, you are, in effect, loving yourself, because you and your neighbor are really one and the same.

When the great philosophers, writers, poets, and artists discuss the illusions of reality, it seems to me that, for the most part, they are talking about the illusion of separateness, as it pertains to reality. Depending on your belief system, you could say the illusion is that we are separate from the Universe, separate from each other, separate from Nature, or separate from God. They are all illusions of separateness.

Sometimes, as an exercise, when I see a person walking towards me, especially a beggar or a homeless person, whether male or female, young or old, I will try to picture myself walking towards myself. If I see a homeless person sleeping on the sidewalk or on a park bench, I don't say to myself that could be me. Rather, I say to myself, that *is* me. I try to see myself through his or her eyes. If we are all, in essence, a seething, roiling mass of humanity, then we are like ants in an anthill, drops of water in the ocean, or grains of sand on the beach. In other words, the whole is greater than the sum of its parts. We all have our own individual, small identities, but we are also part of something much larger than ourselves, much bigger than we can imagine.

The Dalai Lama said,

> In the course of rebirths, which must be infinite in number, every being has been included within your sphere of existence and has had a relationship with you just like the one you enjoy with your mother in this life. You must make this your strong conviction. And on the basis of this understanding, you will gradually begin to consider all beings as friends.

He also said that "the qualities of love and compassion are utterly fundamental."

In an interview promoting her book *Time Warped*, Claudia Hammond said, "Physicists may argue about whether time is simply an illusion, but what definitely exists is our perception of time." The same thing could be said about reality. We have all had the experience of being in rush hour, in heavy traffic, waiting at a red light, and a minute seems like an hour. Conversely, when we are engaged in an activity about which we are passionate, time disappears.

Time flies when you're having fun. Time flies. *Tempus fugit.* Many older people complain that that as we get older, the days seem long, but the years fly by. Time can be plastic and elastic. So can reality. Whether one is alive for three days, three years, 30 years, or 90 years, it's all over in a flash, in the context of infinity and eternity. One can snap one's fingers, and it's over. It is totally a matter of perception.

In his 2011 Man Booker Prize-winning novel *The Sense of an Ending*, British author Julian Barnes captured a common notion about reality, the idea that only weirdos, philosophers, university professors, and adolescents question the nature of reality.

> Hunt gave a brief nod to Colin's attempt to undermine everything, as if morbid disbelief was a natural by-product of adolescence, something to be grown out of. Masters and parents used to remind us irritatingly that they too had once been young, and so could speak with authority. It's just a phase, they would insist. You'll grow out of it; life will teach you reality and realism.

Life will teach you reality. It's called "the school of hard knocks." This is the developmental aspect. "What we called realism turned out to be a way of avoiding things rather than facing them," Barnes wrote. He said that his characters thought they were being realistic, but in retrospect, they weren't. They just used the idea of what's "realistic" as an excuse for inaction or cowardice.

In the movie *On the Waterfront*, when Eva Marie Saint tells Marlon Brando that she thinks that we are all one, he looks at her quizzically and says, "Do you believe in that drool?" She replies that she does, and she asks him what he believes in. He responds by showing her his fist. He says, "My philosophy of life is, do it to them before they do it to you." Here we have, in stark contrast, two competing philosophies about the nature of reality.

Just before the ball is dropped in Times Square to herald the New Year, it has become a tradition to sing John Lennon's "Imagine."

> *You may say that I'm a dreamer,*
> *but I'm not the only one.*
> *We hope one day you'll join us*
> *and the world will live as one.*

Epilogue: Blood and the Dominion

When I was twelve, I had the idea that when I grew up I would write a book called *Blood and the Dominion*. Just the title of the book came to me. I had no idea what it meant or what the book would be about. In my city, as I was growing up, there was a chain of grocery stores called "Dominion." The word *blood* brought to mind the meat section of the Dominion. Initially, I thought the book could be a murder mystery set in a grocery store. As I got older, I entertained the idea that "blood" might refer to bloodlines, ancestry, or even "bad blood."

I never told anyone about my book, but it was always in the back of my mind. Time went on and time went on. I went to medical school, received my Diploma in Psychiatry from McGill, got married, had kids, moved to different cities, got divorced (twice), and all the while maintained the idea that one day I would write this book.

It wasn't an obsession, by any means. Most of the time I didn't even think about it; however, when I was in my early fifties I was diagnosed with leukemia. At the time, I was not thinking about my book at all, but afterwards, it struck me as odd that forty years prior to being diagnosed with a blood disorder, I had the idea that one day I would write a book with the word *blood* in the title. There was no particular reason I could think of why this title came into my mind. There wasn't a history of blood disorders in my family. I didn't know anyone who had leukemia. It was just one of those strange things.

I lived with leukemia for sixteen years, with a series of remissions and relapses, many rounds of chemotherapy, hospitalizations, and blood transfusions. Although I continued my work as a psychiatrist, I had to admit that my quality of life was compromised.

Eventually my hematologist asked me to consider a treatment that would not just improve my condition but had the potential to cure it completely. He was talking about a stem cell transplant. He said I couldn't keep getting more and more rounds of chemotherapy because it was doing too much damage to my body. He told me the five-year mortality rate post-transplant was 50 percent. When I asked him what he estimated the 5-year mortality rate for my condition would be without a transplant, he said 100 percent.

I agreed to the transplant.

The next step was to find a donor. Both of my brothers kindly offered to be donors. Each one had a 25 percent chance of being a suitable donor. As it turned out, neither one was compatible. When we turned to the worldwide donor bank, I was very fortunate to find a donor who was a perfect match for me, based on ten out of ten parameters that were being used at the time to determine compatibility.

The chances of finding a suitable match depend very much on one's ancestry (bloodlines). Because my grandparents were European immigrants, I had a 60 percent chance of finding a suitable match. If my ancestry had been aboriginal, Asian, or African, my chances of finding a compatible donor would have been much lower, around 20 percent, because of a smaller pool of potential donors.

Everything went smoothly with my transplant, in fact, better than expected. I was told that I would be in the hospital for four to six weeks. In the event, my hospital stay lasted just over three weeks. My recovery, for the most part, was uneventful, and there was no rejection of the transplant. It has been more than five years since the transplant. I have done remarkably well.

While I was recovering from my transplant, I started to write my long-delayed book. After all my travails with blood disorders, blood transfusions, and ultimately a cure of my leukemia with a transplant of bone marrow stem cells harvested from the blood of an anonymous donor, my decades-long riddle was half solved. The meaning of the word *blood* in my proposed title, *Blood and the Dominion*, seemed clear. I still didn't know what *dominion* meant.

I had various theories. I thought that since *blood* probably referred to my blood disorder, it could be a synecdoche, by which a part represents the whole. Thus, *blood* could represent the body or, in a broader sense, the physical or material world. My association with the word *dominion* took me in a more spiritual direction.

I thought of the passage from *Genesis* which describes the sixth day of Creation:

> *And God said: 'Let us make man in our image, after our likeness; and let them have dominion over the fish of the sea, and over the fowl of the air, and over the cattle, and over all the earth, and over every creeping thing that creep- eth upon the earth'* (Genesis 1:26).

This passage, especially the beginning ("Let us make man in our image"), resonated with me because it suggested that we create our reality with our thoughts, in the sense that the Creator created us in his/her image. This idea appealed to me because it brought the Creator and the Creation together in a universal, divine intelligence. We become the creator and the creation. The idea is similar to the one expressed by W. B. Yeats in his great poem "Among School Children",

> *How can we know the dancer from the dance?*

Dominion is an old-fashioned word. We seldom hear it anymore, but there is another word that can be considered its modern-day equivalent – *domain*. *Domain* is similar to *dominion* in that it signifies power or control. Once you register your domain name, you own it. You control it. Domain, like dominion, can also mean home, realm, or sphere of influence. The twin concepts of dominion and domain raised interesting questions for me: What do we really have control over? What is our true home, our realm, our sphere of influence?

So, I considered the possibility that *Blood and the Dominion* could represent the link, or the union, between the world of matter (the material world) and the world of spirit (the world of transcendence and transformation).

With this new, tentative understanding of my proposed title, I was off to the races, and I began to write my book. Once the book was almost finished, I started sending query letters to various agents. One agent said that she was interested in my project, but she didn't like the title *Blood and the Dominion* because it didn't tell readers what the book was about. Also, the connotations of the words *blood* and *dominion* in the title would be off-putting to readers. A friend of mine had said the same thing, and I decided they were probably right. After many years of carrying that title around in my head, I let it go.

As I was lying in bed that night, a new title popped into my head: *SHAZAM!* It's short. It's punchy. The subject of the book could be explained in the subtitle. I ran the new title by a few friends. They liked it. I ran the title by the agent. She liked it. So that was that, I had a new title.

Now here's the thing. The day after I let go of my title *Blood and the Dominion* I finally found out what it meant. As I was watching a political talk show on TV, the interviewer introduced his next guest as a state senator from the Old Dominion. I had never heard of the Old Dominion. I immediately Googled it. I learned that the Old Dominion is another name for the Commonwealth of Virginia. I just about fell off my chair. As fate would have it, Virginia is the state where my stem cell donor lives.

After 55 years of searching for the meaning of *Blood and the Dominion*, it was finally revealed to me the very day after I let go of the title.

Blood was the problem (leukemia); Dominion was the solution (the state where my stem cell donor lived). Blood was the question; Dominion was the answer. In a sense, then, my illness and my recovery were foretold through the original title of my book, *Blood and the Dominion*.

The remarkable thing was the timing. I had spent decades looking for something and did not find it until I stopped looking. Only when I dropped the title I had held onto for 55 years did I discover what it meant. And the funny thing is, within a few months of the agent's telling me that the words "blood" and "dominion" in the title wouldn't sell books, there was a book on the bestseller list called *Blood*, by Lawrence Hill, and about a month later, another book on the bestseller list called *Dominion*, by C. J. Sansom. The whole series of events unfolded like a running cosmic joke.

One year after my transplant, I was given permission to contact my donor, if he was agreeable. My donor graciously gave his consent, and I wrote to him to thank him for his kind and generous decision to become a stem cell donor.

I learned that my donor was in the U.S. Navy. In 2003, he was stationed on a naval base where they were conducting a stem cell donor drive. He got in line with his buddies, gave a cheek swab, and didn't give it a second thought. He said that when he was informed in 2010 that he was a compatible match for me, he had completely forgotten that he had volunteered to be a donor.

When his name came up on the computer, he was stationed on an aircraft carrier in the Persian Gulf. This was during the Iraq War. He said that the donor center in D.C. does not, as a rule, fly people in from outside the country, but the captain of his ship agreed to pay for his airfare so that he could be a donor for me. Once back in the U.S. he was given injections for five days to stimulate his bone marrow, then his stem cells were harvested from his blood. A medical team from my home city flew down to Washington, D.C., to pick up the sample that was to save my life. Of course, I remain eternally grateful.

SHAZAM is a word used by magicians and conjurers to herald an amazing feat of prestidigitation, an unexpected event, an instantaneous appearance, or a transformation. The word originated in Captain Marvel comics, but it has since morphed into much wider usage and meaning, including the name of a rather "magical" phone app that listens to and identifies songs its owner hears.

For me, it represented the intersection of parallel worlds. In the movie *Runaway Bride*, Richard Gere, playing a New York City reporter, says,

"Shazam! I'm in Mayberry!" when he finds himself in a small town as he pursues Julia Roberts, the eponymous runaway bride. In the movie, which itself is fictional, Gere imagines himself in another fictional community, Mayberry, which was the setting for the Andy Griffiths television show.

As I was sitting in my living room, watching the movie on TV with my family, three worlds collided – the real world, the movie world, and the TV world.

Just as we know the TV world is out there, even though the TV is not turned on, and we know that ultraviolet and infrared light exist even though they are not visible to the naked eye, we also occasionally sense that there are other worlds out there calling to us, if only we had the eyes to see, the ears to hear, and the minds to comprehend the subtle bodies and celestial music just beyond the boundaries of our conscious awareness.

SHAZAM is an acronym.

S is for Solomon, the wisdom of Solomon, the Biblical king and prophet of Israel;

H is for Hercules, the strength of Hercules, the strongest of all mortals;

A is for Atlas, the stamina of Atlas, a Titan who holds the world on his shoulders;

Z is for Zeus, the power of Zeus, king of the gods and god of sky and thunder;

A is for Achilles, the courage of Achilles, Greek hero of the Trojan War in Homer's *Iliad*;

M is for Mercury, the speed of Mercury, the Roman god of communication who carried messages between the world of gods and the world of men.

Wisdom, strength, stamina, power, courage, and speed, as well as the capacity to carry messages back and forth between the sacred and mundane worlds – these were all qualities I needed to nourish in myself as

I wrote this book, as well as attributes we all need in order to find meaning, purpose, solace, and transformation in our own lives.

We don't need to be conjurers or magicians to move from one dimension to the next. We all do it when we die! Why wait until then? Many of us move easily from one dimension to another if and when we have spiritually transformative experiences, but we often don't know what to make of these experiences, how to process them, or even how to talk about them. What was needed was a framework. With a psychiatric filter and a mind/body/spirit paradigm, we have explored paranormal phenomena in order to provide a framework and a new way of looking at the world that we see and the worlds that we don't see.

SHAZAM! was my working title for a number of months, then I went back to my original title – *Blood and the Dominion*. Whether it was nostalgia, difficulty letting go, or my wish not to abandon my childhood dream, I wanted to hang on to my original title for a little while longer.

I thought of the Zen koan:

First there is a mountain, then there is no mountain, then there is.

In the end, however, *Blood and the Dominion* didn't fit. It no longer served my purpose. The riddle had been solved. It was time to let it go, but not without a tinge of sadness and regret. Still, one finds consolation in the oddest of places.

I will leave you with the words of the great Norwegian writer Knausgaard, our modern-day Proust.

Meaning is not something we are given but which we give.

Further Reading

Chapter 1:

1. Barrett, Sir William. *Deathbed Visions: The Psychical Experiences of Dying.* The Aquarian Press, 1986. (Reprint of 1926 edition).

2. Geiger, John. *The Third Man Factor: Surviving the Impossible.* New York: Weinstein Books, 2009.

3. Osis, K, and E. Haraldsson. *At the Hour of Death.* New York: Avon, 1977.

4. Rees, W. Dewi. "The hallucinations of widowhood." *British Medical Journal,* 4 (1971):37–41.

5. Sacks, Oliver. *Hallucinations.* New York: Knopf, 2012.

6. Stip, Emmanuel, and Genevieve Letourneau. "Psychotic symptoms as a continuum between normality and pathology." *Canadian Journal of Psychiatry* 54 (2009): 140–151.

Chapter 2:

1. Holden J. M., B. Greyson, and D. James (eds.) *The Handbook of Near-Death Experiences: Thirty Years of Investigation.* Westport, CT: Praeger, 2009.

2. Botkin A. L., R. C. Hogan, and R. A. Moody. *Induced After-Death Communication: A New Therapy for Healing Grief and Trauma.* Charlottesville, VA: Hampton Roads Publishing, 2005.

3. Moody, Raymond. *Life after Life: the investigation of a phenomenon - survival of bodily death.* St. Simons, GA: Mockingbird Books, 1975.

4. Morse, Melvin et al. "Near-death experience in a pediatric population." *Amer J Dis Children* 139 (1985): 595–600.

5. Parnia, Sam. *Erasing Death: The Science That Is Rewriting the Boundaries between Life and Death.* New York: HarperOne, 2014.

6. Ring, Kenneth. "Near-death and out-of-body experiences in the blind: A study of apparent eyeless vision." *Journal of Near-Death Studies* 16 (Winter 1997).

Chapter 3:

1. Feyerabend, Paul. *Against Method: Outline of an anarchistic theory of knowledge.* New York: Verso, 1975.

2. Putnam, Hilary. *Mathematics, Matter and Method.* Cambridge, UK: Cambridge University Press, 1975.

3. Radin, Dean. *The Conscious Universe: The Scientific Truth of Psychic Phenomena.* New York: HarperOne, 1997.

4. Shermer, Michael. "Anomalous Events That Can Shake One's Skepticism to the Core." *Scientific American*, Sept. 16, 2014.

5. Talbot, Michael. *The Holographic Universe: The Revolutionary Theory of Reality.* New York: Harper Perennial, 2011.

Chapter 4:

1. Dossey, Larry. *The Power of Premonitions: How Knowing the Future Can Shape Our Lives.* New York: Dutton, 2009.

2. Mitchell, Edgar, with Dwight Williams. *The Way of the Explorer: An Apollo Astronaut's Journey through the Material and Mystical Worlds.* New York: G. P. Putnam's Sons, 1996.

3. Rhine, J. B., and William McDougall. *Extra-Sensory Perception* (4th ed.) Boston: Branden Publishing, 1997.

4.   Ullman, M., S. Krippner, and A. Vaughan. *Dream Telepathy.* New York: Macmillan, 1973.

Chapter 5:

1.   Ader, Robert, David L. Felten, and Nicholas Cohen (eds.) *Psychoneuroimmunology Second Edition.* London: Academic Press, 1991.

2.   Chalmers, David. *The Conscious Mind: In Search of a Fundamental Theory.* New York: Oxford University Press, 1996.

3.   Gershon, Michael. *The Second Brain.* New York: HarperCollins, 1998.

4.   McGinn, Colin. "Can we solve the mind-body problem?" *Mind* 98 (1989): 349–366.

5.   Nagel, Thomas. *Mind and Cosmos: Why the Materialist Neo-Darwinian Conception of Nature is Almost Certainly False.* New York: Oxford University Press, 2012.

6.   Pert, Candace. *Molecules of Emotion: The Science behind Mind-Body Medicine.* New York: Touchstone, 1999.

Chapter 6:

1.   James, William. *The Varieties of Religious Experience: A Study in Human Nature.* New York: Longman, Green, 1902.

2.   Cardena, Etzel, Steven Jay Lynn, and Stanley Krippner. *Varieties of anomalous experience: Examining the scientific evidence.* Second edition. Washington DC: American Psychological Association Press, 2013.

3.   Kason, Yvonne, and Teri Degler. *Farther Shore: How near-death and other extraordinary experiences can change ordinary lives.* Toronto: HarperCollins, 1994.

4.   Lukoff, David. "Diagnosis of mystical experiences with psychotic features." *J Transpersonal Psych,* 17 (1987):173–181.

Chapter 7:

1.   Grinspoon, L, and J. B. Bakalar. *Psychedelic Drugs Reconsidered.* New York: The Lindesmith Center, 1997.

2.   Hofmann, Albert. *LSD: My Problem Child.* Oxford, UK: Oxford University Press, 2013.

3.   Huxley, Aldous. *The Doors of Perception.* London: Chatto & Windus, 1954.

4.   Tupper, K.W. et al. "Psychedelic medicine: a re-emerging therapeutic paradigm." *Canadian Medical Association Journal* 187 (2015): 1054–59. doi:10.1503/cmaj.141124.

5.   Schultes R. E., A. Hofmann, and C. Ratsch. *Plants of the Gods: Their Sacred, Healing, and Hallucinogenic Powers.* Second edition. New York: Healing Arts Press, 2001.

Chapter 8:

1.   Beveridge, W. I. B. *Seeds of Discovery.* New York: Norton, 1980.

2.   Bowman, Carol. *Children's Past Lives: How Past Life Memories Affect Your Child.* New York: Bantam Books, 1997.

3.   Kandinsky, Wassily. *Concerning the Spiritual in Art.* trans. by M. T. H. Sadler, New York: Dover Publications, 1997.

4.   Moorjani, Anita. *Dying to be me: my journey from cancer, to near death, to true healing.* Carlsbad, California: Hay House, 2012.

5.   Newton, Michael. *Journey of Souls: Case Studies of Life between Lives.* St. Paul, MN: Llewellyn Publications, 1994.

6.   Tucker, Jim B., and Ian Stevenson. *Life Before Life: A Scientific Investigation of Children's Memories of Previous Lives*. New York: St. Martin's Press, 2005.

Chapter 9:

1.   Laing, R. D. *The Divided Self: An Existential Study of Sanity and Madness*. London, UK: Tavistock Publications, 1960.

2.   Pearce, Joseph Chilton. *The Crack in the Cosmic Egg: New Constructs of Mind and Reality*. Rochester, VT: Park Street Press, 2002.

3.   Schnider, Armin. *The Confabulating Mind: How the Brain Creates Reality*. New York: Oxford University Press, 2008.

4.   Turok, Neil. *From Quantum to Cosmos: The Universe Within*. London, UK: Faber & Faber, 2013.

Epilogue:

Knausgaard, Karl Ove. *A Man in Love: My Struggle Book 2*, translated by Don Bartlett, London: Vintage Books, 2014.

Bibliography

1. Adam Dreamhealer. *Dream Healer: A True Story of Miracle Healings.* New York: Penguin, 2006.

2. Adams, D. J. *Scenting Evil: Based on the Case Files of a Crime-Solving Clairvoyant.* Herndon, Virginia: Capital Books, 2002.

3. Ader, Robert, and Nicholas Cohen. "Behaviorally conditioned immunosuppression." *Psychosomatic Medicine* 37 (July–August 1975): 333–340.

4. Ader, Robert, David L. Felten, and Nicholas Cohen (eds.) *Psychoneuroimmunology Second Edition.* London: Academic Press, 1991.

5. Alcock, J. E. *Parapsychology: Science or Magic?* Elmsford, NY: Pergamon Press, 1981.

6. Alexander, Eben. *Proof of Heaven: A Neurosurgeon's Journey into the Afterlife.* New York: Simon and Schuster, 2012.

7. Alexander, Franz. "Fundamental Concepts of Psychosomatic Research: Psychogenesis, Conversion, Specificity." *Psychosomatic Medicine* 5 (July 1943.)

8. _____. *Psychosomatic Medicine: Its Principles and Applications.* New York: W. W. Norton & Co., 1965.

9. Ananthaswamy, Anil. "Quantum teleportation over 7 kilometers of cables smashes record." *New Scientist*, Sept. 19, 2016. www.newscientist.com/article/2106326

10. Anderson, Greg. *Cancer: 50 Essential Things to Do*. New York: Penguin Books, 1999.

11. Atwater, P. M. H. *The Big Book of Near-Death Experience: the ultimate guide to what happens when we die*. Charlottesville, VA: Hampton Roads Publishing, 2007.

12. Autry, Anita E. et al. "NMDA receptor blockade at rest triggers rapid behavioral antidepressant responses." *Nature* 476 (07 July 2011): 91–5.

13. Bach, Richard. *Illusions: The Adventures of a Reluctant Messiah*. New York: Dell Publishing, 1977.

14. Baethge, Christopher. "Grief hallucinations: True or pseudo? Serious or not? An inquiry into psychopathological and clinical features of a common phenomenon." *Psychopathology* 35 (2002):296–302.

15. Baetz, Marilyn et al. "Spirituality and Psychiatry in Canada: Psychiatric Practice Compared with Patient Expectations." *Can J Psychiatry* 49 (2004):265–71.

16. Baldwin, C. "Interview with Dr. Wilder Penfield." *Maclean's,* April 19, 1976.

17. Barnes, Julian. *The Sense of an Ending*. New York: Knopf, 2011.

18. Barnett, Lisa. *The Infinite Wisdom of the Akashic Records*. Wayne, NJ: New Page Books, 2015.

19. Barrett, Sir William. *Deathbed Visions: The Psychical Experiences of Dying*. The Aquarian Press, 1986. (Reprint of 1926 edition).

20. Bateson, Gregory. *Steps to an Ecology of Mind*. New York: Chandler, 1972.

21. Beauregard, Mario, and Denyse O'Leary. *The Spiritual Brain: A Neuroscientist's Case for the Existence of the Soul.* Toronto: HarperCollins, 2007.

22. _____. *Brain Wars: The Scientific Battle over the Existence of the Mind and the Irrefutable Proof That Will Change the Way We Live Our Lives.* New York: HarperCollins, 2012.

23. Becker, Ernest. *The Denial of Death.* New York: The Free Press, 1973.

24. Bell, J. S. *Speakable and Unspeakable in Quantum Mechanics: Collected Papers on Quantum Philosophy.* Cambridge, UK: Cambridge University Press, 2004.

25. Benner, David. *Spirituality and the Awakening Self: The Sacred Journey of Transformation.* Grand Rapids, MI: Bazos Press, 2012.

26. Bennett, C. H. et al. "Teleporting an unknown quantum state via dual classical and Einstein-Podolsky-Rosen channels." *Physical Review Letters* 70 (1993): 1895–99.

27. Benson, Herbert, and Miriam Z. Klipper. *The Relaxation Response.* New York: William Morrow, 1975.

28. Berlyne, N. "Confabulation." *Brit J Psychiatry* 120 (1972): 31–9.

29. Bern, David, and Charles Honorton, "Does Psi Exist?" *Psychological Bulletin* 115 (1994): 4–18.

30. Bettelheim, Bruno. *Freud and Man's Soul.* New York: Vintage, 1984.

31. Bethune, Brian. "Why so many people – including scientists – suddenly believe in an afterlife." *Maclean's,* May 7, 2013.

32. Beveridge, W. I. B. *The Art of Scientific Investigation.* Portsmouth, NH: Heinemann, 1950.

33. _____. *Seeds of Discovery.* New York: Norton, 1980.

34. Beyer, Stephen V. *Singing to the Plants: A Guide to Mestizo Shamanism in the Upper Amazon.* Albuquerque: University of New Mexico Press, 2009.

35. Blackmore, Susan. "Out-of-body experience." In: *The Encyclopedia of the Paranormal.* Edited by Gordon Stein. Amherst, NY: Prometheus, 1986.

36. _____. *Dying to Live: Near-Death Experience*. Amherst, NY: Prometheus Books, 1993.

37. _____, and R. Moore. "Seeing things: visual recognition and belief in the paranormal." *European Journal of Parapsychology* 10 (1994): 91–103.

38. Blake, William. *Selected Poetry and Prose*. New York: Random House, 1958.

39. Bleuler, Eugen. *Dementia Praecox or the Group of Schizophrenias*, trans. by Joseph Zinkin, New York: International Universities Press, 1950.

40. Bohm, David. *Wholeness and the Implicate Order*. London: ARK Paperbacks, 1983.

41. Bohm, David, and Basil Hiley. *The Undivided Universe*. London: Routledge, 1993.

42. Bonelli, R. M., and Harold G. Koenig. "Mental disorders, religion and spirituality 1990 to 2010: a systematic evidence-based review." *J Relig Health* 52 (2013), 657–73. doi:10.1007/s10943-013-9691-4.

43. Botkin, Allan L., R. Craig Hogan, and Raymond A. Moody. *Induced After-Death Communication: A New Therapy for Healing Grief and Trauma*. Charlottesville, Virginia: Hampton Roads Publishing, 2005.

44. Bouchard, Thomas J. et al. "Sources of human psychological differences: the Minnesota Study of Twins Reared Apart." *Science* 250 (1990): 223–8.

45. Bowler, Kate. "God knows who'll win Super Bowl." *Globe and Mail*, Feb. 1, 2013.

46. Bowman, Carol. *Children's Past Lives: How Past Life Memories Affect Your Child*. New York: Bantam Books, 1997.

47. Breedlove, Ally, and Ken Abraham. *When Will Heaven Begin? This is Ben Breedlove's Story*. New York: New American Library, 2013.

48. Brinkley, Dannion, with Paul Perry. *Saved by the Light: The True Story of a Man Who Died Twice and the Profound Revelations He Received.* New York: Villard Books, 1994.

49. Brodie, Benjamin. *The Works of Sir Benjamin Collins Brodie.* Neuilly sur Seine: Ulan Press, 2012.

50. Browne, Sylvia, with Lindsay Harrison. *Life on the Other Side: A psychic's tour of the afterlife.* New York: New American Library, 2001.

51. Bruner, Jerome. *In Search of Mind: Essays in Autobiography.* New York: HarperCollins, 1983.

52. Buber, Martin. *The Tales of Rabbi Nachman.* New York: Horizon, 1956.

53. Buckley, Carol. *Just for Elephants.* Gardiner, Maine: Tilbury House, 2006.

54. Burpo, Todd, with Lynn Vincent. *Heaven Is For Real: A Little Boy's Astounding Story of his Trip to Heaven and Back.* Nashville, Tennessee: Thomas Nelson, 2010.

55. Calabrese, J. R. et al. "Alterations in Immunocompetence During Stress, Bereavement, and Depression: Focus on Neuroendocrine Regulation." *Am J Psychiatry* 144 (1987): 1123–34.

56. Camus, Albert. *The Myth of Sisyphus.* Harmondsworth, UK: Penguin Books, 1975.

57. Cannon, Walter B. *The Wisdom of the Body.* New York: W. W. Norton & Company, 1932.

58. Capra, Fritjof. *The Tao of Physics: An Exploration of the Parallels between Modern Physics and Eastern Mysticism.* 5th ed. Boulder, CO: Shambhala, 2010.

59. Cardena, E., S. J. Lynn, and S. Krippner. *Varieties of anomalous experience: Examining the scientific evidence.* Second edition. Washington DC: American Psychological Association Press, 2013.

60. Carlson, K. B. "Meet astrophysicist Sara Seager, a Canadian 'genius.'" *Globe and Mail*. Sept. 26, 2013.

61. Carr, Christopher. "Death and near-death: a comparison of Tibetan and Euro-American experiences." *J Transpersonal Psych*, 25 (1993): 59–110.

62. Casey, Hugh Lynn. *Venture Inward: Edgar Casey's Story and the Mysteries of the Unconscious Mind.* New York: HarperCollins, 1985.

63. Castaneda, Carlos. *The Teachings of Don Juan: a Yaqui way of knowledge.* Berkeley, California: University of California Press, 1968.

64. Caterine, Darryl V. *Haunted Ground: Journeys through a Paranormal America.* Santa Barbara, California: Praeger, 2011.

65. Cecil, Lord David. *A Choice of Tennyson's Verse.* London: Faber and Faber, 1971.

66. Celona, Marjorie. "Bumps in the night: Claire Mulligan's new novel traces the history of the Spiritualist movement through the lives of the three sisters who founded it." Review of *The Dark*, by Claire Mulligan. *Globe and Mail*, May 25, 2013.

67. Chalmers, David. *The Conscious Mind: In Search of a Fundamental Theory.* New York: Oxford University Press, 1996.

68. Chaney, Warren. *Dynamic Mind.* Las Vegas: Houghton-Brace, 2007.

69. Chaney, Robert. *Akashic Records: Past Lives & New Directions.* Upland, CA: Astara, 1996.

70. Chowdry, Affan. "Angels exist but don't have wings, senior priest says." *Globe and Mail*, Dec. 21, 2013.

71. Claudii Galeni Pergamoni (ed.), Odysseas Hatzopoulos, "That the Best Physician is also a Philosopher." Athens, Greece: Odysseas Hatzopoulos & Company, 1992.

72. Cohen, Andrew. "Martyr or Satyr – Which One Was Real?" *Globe and Mail*. Nov. 16, 2013.

73. Cohen, Leonard. *Book of Longing*. Toronto: McClelland & Stewart, 2006.

74. Cohen, Sidney. *The Beyond Within*. New York: Atheneum, 1965.

75. Collins, Anne. *In the Sleep Room: The Story of the CIA Brainwashing Experiments in Canada*. Toronto: Key Porter Books, 1988.

76. Conradt, Stacy. "Edgar Allen Poe's Eerie Richard Parker Coincidence." *Mental Floss*, Feb. 27, 2012.

77. Cooper, David A. *God is a Verb: Kabbalah and the Practice of Mystical Judaism*. New York: The Berkley Publishing Group, 1997.

78. Cressy, Judith. *The Near-Death Experience: Mysticism or Madness?* Boston: Christopher, 1994.

79. CTV News.ca staff. "Prof reunites with father in Cambodia after 36 years." *CTV News*, online edition, July 14, 2011.

80. Davies, Paul. *About Time: Einstein's Unfinished Revolution*. New York: Simon & Schuster, 1996.

81. Dawkins, Richard. *The God Delusion*. Boston: Houghton Mifflin, 2006.

82. Dean, Stanley R. (ed.), *Psychiatry and Mysticism*. Chicago: Nelson-Hall, 1975.

83. Dennett, Daniel C. *Breaking the Spell: Religion as a Natural Phenomenon*. New York: Penguin Books, 2006.

84. Devlin, Hannah. "Radical ketamine therapy could treat alcohol addiction." *Guardian*. Jan. 24, 2017.

85. DeWaal, Frans. Review of *Being a Dog: Following the dog into a world of smell*, by Alexandra Horowitz, *New York Times*, Nov. 13, 2016, Sunday Book Review.

86. DeWitt, Bryce Seligman, and Neill R. Graham (eds.) *The Many-Worlds Interpretation of Quantum Mechanics*. Princeton, NJ: Princeton University Press, 1973.

87. Diazgranados, N. et al. "A randomized add-on trial of an N-methyl-d-aspartate antagonist in treatment-resistant bipolar depression". *Arch Gen Psychiatry* 67 (2010):793-802.doi:10.1001/archgenpsychiatry.2010.90

88. Doblin, Rick. "A Clinical Plan for MDMA (Ecstasy) in the Treatment of Post-traumatic Stress Disorder (PTSD): Partnership with the FDA. Santa Cruz, CA: *MAPS Bulletin* 12 (3), 2002: 5–18.

89. Dossey, Larry. *The Power of Premonitions: How Knowing the Future Can Shape Our Lives.* New York: Dutton, 2009.

90. Doyle, Arthur Conan. *The Vital Message.* Charleston, SC: BiblioLife, 2009.

91. Dyer, Wayne W. *I Can See Clearly Now.* Carlsbad, CA: Hay House, 2014.

92. Dyson, Freeman. "One in a million." Review of *Debunked! ESP, Telekinesis and Other Pseudoscience by G. Charpak and H. Broch, New York Review of Books*, March 25, 2004.

93. Dyson, Freeman, and Paul Davis. "Einstein's God." Transcript. *Speaking of Faith*, American Public Media, Feb. 25, 2010.

94. Eadie, Betty J. *Embraced by the Light.* Placerville, CA: Gold Leaf Press, 1992.

95. Ecklund, Elaine Howard. *Science vs. Religion: What Scientists Really Think.* New York: Oxford University Press, 2010.

96. Edward, John. *One Last Time: A psychic medium speaks to those we have loved and lost.* New York: The Berkley Publishing Group, 1998.

97. Eells, Josh. "A League of His Own." *Rolling Stone*, Nov. 8, 2012.

98. Ehrenreich, Barbara. *Living with a Wild God: A Non-believer's Search for the Truth about Everything.* New York: Twelve, 2014.

99. Einstein, Albert. *Living Philosophies.* New York: Simon & Schuster, 1931.

100. Elber, Lynn. "Last words: 'I want to be with Carrie': Reynolds remembered for star power, resilience" *The Associated Press, Winnipeg Free Press*, Dec. 29, 2016.

101. Eliot, T. S. *The Complete Poems and Plays 1909 – 1950*. New York: Harcourt, Brace & World, 1952.

102. Engel, George. "The need for a new medical model: a challenge for biomedicine." *Science* 196 (1977): 129–136.

103. Epictetus. *A Manual for Living: A New Interpretation by Sharon Lebell*. New York: HarperCollins, 1994.

104. Erdrich, Louise. "Nero." *New Yorker*, May 7, 2012.

105. *Ethics of the Fathers (Pirkei Avot)* 4:21, trans. by Ben Zion Bokser, New York: Hebrew Publishing Company, 1962.

106. Everett, Hugh. " 'Relative state' formulation of quantum mechanics." *Reviews of Modern Physics* 29 (1957): 454–62.

107. Feyerabend, Paul. *Against Method: Outline of an anarchistic theory of knowledge*. New York: Verso, 1975.

108. Feynman, Richard. *Surely You're Joking, Mr. Feynman! : Adventures of a Curious Character*. New York: Bantam, 1986.

109. Forman, R. K. C. (ed.) *The Innate Capacity: Mysticism, Philosophy and Psychology*. New York: Oxford University Press, 1998.

110. Frankl, Viktor E. *Man's Search for Meaning*. Boston: Beacon Press, 1959.

111. French, C. "Dying to know the truth: visions of a dying brain, or false memories?" *Lancet* 358 (2001 Dec. 15):2010–11.

112. Freud, S. Civilization and Its Discontents. (1930). *Standard Edition of the Complete Psychological Works of Sigmund Freud*. Vol. 21, London: Hogarth Press, 1956–1974.

113. _____. The Future of an Illusion. (1927). *Standard Edition of the Complete Psychological Works of Sigmund Freud*. Vol. 21, London: Hogarth Press, 1956–1974.

114. _____. Formulations on the Two Principles of Mental Functioning. (1911). *Standard Edition of the Complete Psychological Works of Sigmund Freud.* Vol. 12, London: Hogarth Press, 1956–1974.

115. _____. The Interpretation of Dreams. (1900). *Standard Edition of the Complete Psychological Works of Sigmund Freud.* Vol. 4, London: Hogarth Press, 1956–1974.

116. _____. Dreams and the Occult. (1922) in *New Introductory Lectures on Psychoanalysis.* New York: W. W. Norton, 1933.

117. Fuller, Elizabeth. *Everyone is Psychic.* New York: A Berkley Book, 1989.

118. Gardner, Martin. *Fads and Fallacies In the Name of Science.* 2nd ed. Mineola, New York: Dover Publications, 1957.

119. Gasser, P. et al. "Safety and efficacy of LSD-assisted psychotherapy in subjects with anxiety associated with life-threatening diseases: a randomized active placebo-controlled phase 2 pilot study." *J Nerv Ment Dis* 202 (2014):513–20.

120. Gawain, Shakti. *Creative Visualization.* San Rafael, CA: New World Library, 1979.

121. Geiger, John. *The Third Man Factor: Surviving the Impossible.* New York: Weinstein Books, 2009.

122. _____. *The Angel Effect: The Powerful Force That Ensures We Are Never Alone.* New York: Weinstein Books, 2013.

123. Gershon, Michael. *The Second Brain.* New York: HarperCollins, 1998.

124. Global News Hour at 6 online, "B.C. psychic finds body of missing man." July 31, 2014.

125. Goodman, Aviel. "Organic Unity Theory: The Mind-Body Problem Revisited." *Amer J Psychiatry* 148 (May 1991):553–563. doi.org/10.1176/ajp.148.5.553.

126. Gordon-Reed, Annette. "The persuader: what Harriet Beecher Stowe wrought." *New Yorker*, June 13 & 20, 2011.

127. Goswami, Amit. *The Self-Aware Universe. How Consciousness Creates the Material World.* Los Angeles: Tarcher, 1993.

128. Govinda, A. *Creative Meditation and Multidimensional Consciousness.* Wheaton, IL: Theosophical Publishing House, 1976.

129. Greeley, Andrew. "The 'impossible': it's happening." *Noetic Sciences Review* 1(1987):7–9.

130. Green, Celia. *Out-of-the-body experiences.* London: Hamish Hamilton, 1968.

131. _____ and Charles McCreery. *Lucid Dreaming: The Paradox of Consciousness during Sleep.* London: Routledge, 1994.

132. Greene, Brian. *The Elegant Universe: Superstrings, Hidden Dimensions, and the Quest for the Ultimate Theory.* New York: W. W. Norton & Company, 1999.

133. Grey, Alex. *The Mission of Art.* Boston: Shambhala, 1998.

134. Greyson, Bruce. "Near-death experiences and spirituality." *Zygon* 41 (June 2006), 393–414.

135. Griffiths, R. R. et al. "Psilocybin can occasion mystical-type experiences having substantial and sustained personal meaning and spiritual significance." *Psychopharmacology* 187 (2006): 268–83.

136. Grinspoon, L., and J. B. Bakalar. *Psychedelic Drugs Reconsidered.* New York: The Lindesmith Center, 1997.

137. Griscom, Chris, with Wulfing von Rohr. *Time Is an Illusion.* New York: Simon & Schuster Inc., 1986.

138. Grob, C. S. et al. "Pilot study of psilocybin treatment for anxiety in patients with advanced-stage cancer." *Arch Gen Psych* 68 (2011): 71–8.

139. Grof, S., and J. Halifax. "The human encounter with death." In *Psychedelic Biographies.* New York: E. P. Dutton, 1963.

140. Haberman, Clyde. "LSD-Like drugs are out of the haze and back in the labs." *New York Times*, May 15, 2016.

141. Hadhazy, Adam. "Think twice: how the gut's 'second brain' influences mood and well-being." *Scientific American*, Feb. 12, 2010.

142. Halpern, J. H. et al. "Evidence of health and safety in American members of a religion who use a hallucinogenic sacrament." *Med Sci Monit* 14 SR (2008): 15-22.

143. Hamilton, Allan J. *Zen Mind, Zen Horse: The Science and Spirituality of Working with Horses*. North Adams, MA: Storey Publishing, 2011.

144. _____. *The Scalpel and the Soul*. London: Penguin, 2008.

145. Hamilton, David R. *It's The Thought That Counts: Why Mind Over Matter Really Works*. Carlsbad, CA: Hay House, 2005.

146. Hamilton, Edith. *Mythology*. Boston: Little, Brown & Company, 1942.

147. Harris, Sam. *Letter to a Christian Nation*. New York: Knopf, 2006.

148. _____. *The End of Faith: Religion, Terror, and the Future of Reason*. New York: W. W. Norton & Company, 2004.

149. Hay, Louise. *You Can Heal Your Life*. Santa Monica, CA: Hay House, 1984.

150. Heim, A. "Uber den Tod durch Absturz". *Jahrbuch des Schweizer Alpenclub*. 27 (1892): 327–37, trans. by Noyes R, Kletti R, "The experience from dying from falls." *Omega* 3 (1972): 45–52.

151. Helling, Steve, Jill Smolowe, Kristen Mascia. "With a strong belief, she beat the odds." *People*, Mar. 12, 2012.

152. Hill, Lawrence. *Blood: The Stuff of Life*. Toronto: House of Anansi Press, 2013.

153. Hitchens, Christopher. *God Is Not Great: How Religion Poisons Everything*. New York: Twelve Books, Hachette Book Group, 2007.

154. Hoffman, Jan. "A dose of a hallucinogen from a 'magic mushroom' and then lasting peace." *New York Times*, Dec. 1, 2016.

155. Hofmann, Albert. *LSD: My Problem Child.* Oxford, UK: Oxford University Press, 2013.

156. His Holiness the Dalai Lama and Howard C. Cutler. *The Art of Happiness.* New York: Riverhead Books, 1998.

157. _____. *The Dalai Lama's little book of inner peace: the essential life and teachings.* Charlottesville, VA: Hampton Roads, 2009.

158. Holden, J. M., B. Greyson, and D. James (eds.) *The Handbook of Near-Death Experiences: Thirty Years of Investigation.* Westport, CT: Praeger, 2009.

159. Hollander, John (ed.), *Committed to Memory: 100 Best Poems to Memorize.* New York: Riverhead Books, 1996.

160. Holt, Henry. *On the Cosmic Relations Volumes 1 & 2 (1914).* Whitefish, Montana: Kessinger Publishing Co.

161. Honorton, Carol, and D. C. Ferrari. "Future telling: A meta-analysis of forced-choice precognition experiments, 1935-1987." *Journal of Parapsychology* 53 (1989):281-308.

162. Hood, Bruce. *The Self Illusion: How the Social Brain Creates Identity.* New York: Oxford University Press, 2012.

163. Hook, R., and W. P. Williamson. *Them That Believe: The Power and Meaning of the Christian Serpent-Handling Tradition.* Berkeley and Los Angeles: University of California Press, 2008.

164. Horgan, John. "Peyote on the brain: Is the secret to alcoholism and other addictions locked up in hallucinogenic drugs?" *Discover Magazine*, February 2003.

165. _____. "Brilliant Scientists are Open-Minded about Paranormal Stuff, So Why Not You?" *Scientific American.* July 20, 2012.

166. Hu, H., and M. Wu. "Human Consciousness as Limited Version of Universal Consciousness." *Journal of Consciousness Exploration & Research.* 4 (2013): 51–68.

167. Huxley, Aldous. *The Doors of Perception*. London: Chatto & Windus, 1954.

168. Isaacson, Walter. *Steve Jobs*. New York: Simon and Schuster, 2011.

169. _____. *Einstein: His Life and Universe*. New York: Simon and Schuster, 2007.

170. Jackovich, Karen G. "Sex, Visitors from the Grave, Psychic Healing: Kubler-Ross is a Public Storm Center Again." *People*, Oct. 29, 1979.

171. Jahn, R.G., and B. J. Dunne. *Margins of Reality: The Role of Consciousness in the Physical World*. San Diego: Harcourt Brace Janovich, 1987.

172. James, William. *The Varieties of Religious Experience: A Study in Human Nature*. New York: Longman, Green, 1902.

173. Jaspers, Karl. *General Psychopathology* (1913), trans. by Hoenig, J., and Hamilton M.W., Manchester: Manchester University Press, 1962.

174. Jaynes, Julian. *The Origin of Consciousness in the Breakdown of the Bicameral Mind*. New York: Houghton Mifflin, 1976.

175. Johnson, Steven. *Where Good Ideas Come From: The Natural History of Innovation*. New York: Riverhead Books, 2010.

176. Jovanovic, Pierre. *An Inquiry into the Existence of Guardian Angels: A Journalist's Investigative Report*. trans. by Stephen Becker, New York: M. Evans and Co., 1995.

177. Jung, C. G. *Synchronicity: An acausal connecting principle*. Bollingen, Switzerland: Bollingen Foundation, 1952.

178. _____. *Memories, Dreams and Reflections*. New York: Vintage, 1989.

179. _____. *Psychology and the East*. Princeton, NJ: Princeton University Press, 1978.

180. _____. "Psychological types." *Collected Works of C. G. Jung* Vol. 6, Princeton, NJ: Princeton University Press, 1971.

181. _____. "The structure of the unconscious." (1916), *Collected Works of C. G. Jung* Vol. 7, Princeton, NJ: Princeton University Press, 1963.

182. _____. "The archetypes and the collective unconscious." *Collected Works of C. G. Jung*, Vol. 9, Princeton, NJ: Princeton University Press, 1971.

183. Kabat-Zinn, Jon. *Full Catastrophe Living: Using the Wisdom of Your Body and Mind to Face Stress, Pain, and Illness.* New York: Delta, 1991.

184. Kandinsky, Wassily. *Concerning the Spiritual in Art.* trans. by M. T. H. Sadler, New York: Dover Publications, 1997.

185. Kantrowitz, Barbara. "In search of the sacred." *Newsweek*, Nov. 28, 1994.

186. Kaprio, J. et al. "Mortality after bereavement: a prospective study of 95,647 widowed persons." *Am J Pub Health* 77 (1987): 283-7.

187. Kaptchuk, T. et al. "Components of the placebo effect: a randomized controlled trial in irritable bowel syndrome." *BMJ* 336 (2008):998–1003.

188. Kason, Yvonne, and Teri Degler. *Farther Shore: How near-death and other extraordinary experiences can change ordinary lives.* Toronto: HarperCollins, 1994.

189. Kerr C.W. et al. "End-of-life dreams and visions: A longitudinal study of hospice patients' experiences." *J Palliat Med.* 17 (2014): 296–303.

190. Khatchadourian, Raffi. "Operation delirium: decades after a risky Cold War experiment, a scientist lives with his secrets." *New Yorker*, Dec. 17, 2012.

191. Kirsch, Adam. "The dawn of modern philosophy." *New Yorker*, Sept. 5, 2016.

192. Koenig, H. G. "Research on religion, spirituality, and mental health: A review." *Can J Psychiatry* 54 (2009): 283–91.

193. Koenig, X., and K. Hilber. "The anti-addictive drug ibogaine and the heart: a delicate relation." *Molecules.* 20 (2015):2208-28. doi:10.3390/molecules20022208.

194. Koestler, Arthur. *The Roots of Coincidence.* London: Hutchinson, 1972.

195. Korsakoff, S. S. "Étude medico-psychologique sur une forme des maladies de la memoire." *Revue Philosophique* 20 (1889): 501–30.

196. Krauss, L. M., and Richard Dawkins. *A Universe from Nothing: Why There is Something Rather than Nothing.* New York: Free Press, 2012.

197. Krishna, Gopi. *Higher Consciousness.* New York: Julian Press, 1974.

198. Krupitsky, E. M., and A.Y. Grinenko. "Ketamine psychedelic therapy (KPT): a review of the results of ten years of research." *J Psychoactive Drugs* 29 (1997):165–83.

199. Kubler-Ross, Elisabeth. *On Life after Death.* Berkeley, CA: Celestial Arts, 1991.

200. _____. *On Death and Dying.* New York: Scribner, 1997.

201. LaBarre, Weston. "Stinging criticism from the author of *The Peyote Cult.*" in *Seeing Castaneda*, ed. Daniel C. Noel, New York: G. P. Putnam's Sons, 1976: 40–42.

202. Lahr, John. "Varieties of Disturbance: Claire Danes's volcanic performances." *New Yorker*, Sept. 9, 2013.

203. Laing, R. D. *The Divided Self: An Existential Study of Sanity and Madness.* London, UK: Tavistock Publications, 1960.

204. Laszlo, Ervin. *Science and the Akashic Field: An Integral Theory of Everything.* Rochester, Vermont: Inner Traditions, 2004.

205. Lazar, S. et al. "Meditation experience is associated with increased cortical thickness." *NeuroReport* 16 (Nov. 28, 2005):1893–97.

206. Leary, Timothy, Ralph Metzner, and Richard Alpert. *The Psychedelic Experience: A Manual Based on the Tibetan Book of the Dead.* Secaucus, NJ: Citadel Press, 1964.

207. Light, Alan. *The Holy or the Broken: Leonard Cohen, Jeff Buckley, and the Unlikely Ascent of Hallelujah*. New York: Atria Books, 2012.

208. Lindeman, Marjaana et al. "Is it just a brick wall or a sign from the universe? An fMRI study of supernatural believers and skeptics." *Soc Cogn Affect Neurosci* (2012) first published online: Sept. 5, 2012.

209. Litchman, J. H. et al. "Depression and coronary heart disease: Recommendations for screening, referral and treatment." *Circulation* 118 (2008). 1768–75.

210. Luhrmann, T. M. *When God Talks Back: Understanding the American Evangelical Relationship with God*. New York: Knopf, 2012.

211. Lukoff, David. "Diagnosis of mystical experiences with psychotic features." *J Transpersonal Psych,* 17 (1987):173–81.

212. MacKinnon, Mark. "Banned on Tiananmen anniversary: 6, 4, 89 and 'today'." *The Globe and Mail* June 5, 2012.

213. MacLaine, Shirley. *Out on a Limb*. New York: Bantam Books, 1983.

214. Malarkey, Kevin, and Alex Malarkey. *The Boy Who Came Back From Heaven: A remarkable account of miracles, angels, and life beyond this world*. Carol Stream, Illinois: Tyndale House Publishers, 2010.

215. Manco, Tristan, and Caleb Neelson. "Lost Art." (October/05) *Graffiti Brasil*. Thames and Hudson, p. 64.

216. Marlatt, G.A., and J.L. Kristeller. "Mindfulness and meditation." In *Integrating spirituality into treatment: resources for practitioners,* edited by W. R. Miller. (Washington, DC: American Psychological Association, 1999), 67–84.

217. Martel, Yann. *Life of Pi*. New York: Mariner Books, 2003.

218. Martin, Joel, and Patricia Romanowski. *We Don't Die: George Anderson's Conversations with the Other Side*. New York: Berkley Books, 1989.

219. Martino, Joe. "Founder of skeptic society rattled after witnessing a paranormal event." www.collective-evolution.com/ Nov. 8, 2014.

220. Maslow, A.H. "A theory of human motivation." *Psychological Review* 50 (1943): 370-96.

221. Mayer, Elizabeth Lloyd. *Extraordinary Knowing: Science, Skepticism, and the Inexplicable Powers of the Human Mind.* New York: Bantam Books, 2007.

222. McCauley, Janie. "Giants capitalize on 49ers fumbles." *Winnipeg Free Press*, Jan. 23, 2012.

223. McGinn, Colin. "Can we solve the mind-body problem?" *Mind* 98 (1989): 349-66.

224. McLuhan, Marshall. *Understanding Media: The Extensions of Man.* New York: McGraw Hill, 1964.

225. Messadié, Gerald. *A History of the Devil.* New York: Kodansha America, 1996.

226. Miles, Barry. *Call Me Burroughs: A Life.* New York: Twelve, 2013.

227. Miller, P. "A thing or two about twins." *National Geographic*, 221 (January 2012).

228. Mitchell, Edgar, with Dwight Williams. *The Way of the Explorer: An Apollo Astronaut's Journey through the Material and Mystical Worlds.* New York: G. P. Putnam's Sons, 1996.

229. Monroe, Robert A. *Journeys out of the Body.* New York: Doubleday, 1971.

230. Moody, Raymond. *Life after Life: the investigation of a phenomenon – survival of bodily death.* St. Simons, GA: Mockingbird Books, 1975.

231. Moody, Raymond, and Paul Perry. *The Light Beyond.* New York: Bantam, 1988.

232. Morehouse, David. *Psychic Warrior: Inside the CIA's Stargate Program: The True Story of a Soldier's Espionage and Awakening.* New York: St. Martin's Press, 1996.

233. Moorjani, Anita. *Dying to be me: my journey from cancer, to near death, to true healing.* Carlsbad, CA: Hay House, 2012.

234. Morrissey, Dianne. *Anyone Can See the Light: The Seven Keys to a Guided Out-of-Body Experience.* Walpole, NH: Stillpoint Publishing, 1996.

235. Morse, Melvin et al. "Near-death experience in a pediatric population." *Amer J Dis Children* 139 (1985): 595-600.

236. Morse, Melvin, and Paul Perry. *Closer to the Light.* New York: Ivy Books, 1990.

237. _____. *Parting Visions: Uses and Meanings of Pre-Death, Psychic and Spiritual Experiences.* New York: Villard Books, 1994.

238. Mukherjee, S. "Same but different." *New Yorker.* May 2, 2016.

239. Musella, D. P. "Gallup poll shows that Americans' belief in the paranormal persists." *Skeptical Inquirer* 29 (2005): 5.

240. Nagel, Thomas. "What is it like to be a bat?" *Philosophical Review* 83 (1974): 435–50.

241. _____. *Mind and Cosmos: Why the Materialist Neo-Darwinian Conception of Nature is Almost Certainly False.* New York: Oxford University Press, 2012.

242. Nhat Hanh, Thich. *Peace is Every Step: The Path of Mindfulness in Everyday Life.* New York: Bantam, 1991.

243. _____. *The Miracle of Mindfulness: An Introduction to the Practice of Meditation.* New York: Beacon Press, 1996.

244. Neal, Mary C. *To Heaven and Back: A Doctor's Extraordinary Account of Her Death, Heaven, Angels, and Life Again: A True Story.* Colorado Springs, Colorado: WaterBrook Press, 2012.

245. Nelson, Kevin. *The Spiritual Doorway in the Brain: A Neurologist's Search for the God Experience.* New York: Dutton, 2011.

246. Neugroschel, Joachim, ed., *Yenne Velt: The Great Works of Jewish Fantasy & Occult.* New York: Stonehill Publishing Company, 1976.

247. Newman, Tim. "Psychoneuroimmunology: laugh and be well." www. medicalnewstoday.com Feb. 3, 2016.

248. Newton, Michael. *Journey of Souls: Case Studies of Life between Lives.* St. Paul, MN: Llewellyn Publications, 1994.

249. _____. *Destiny of Souls: New Case Studies of Life between Lives.* St Paul, MN: Llewellyn Publications, 2001.

250. Nichols, Sally. *Jung and Tarot: An Archetypal Journey.* York Beach, Maine: Samuel Wiser, Inc., 1980.

251. Noble, Denis. *The Music of Life: Biology beyond Genes.* New York: Oxford University Press USA, 2006.

252. _____. *Dance to the Tune of Life: Biological Relativity.* Cambridge: Cambridge University Press, 2016.

253. Noyes, Russell. "Attitude change following near-death experiences." *Psychiatry* 43 (1980): 234–42.

254. Nussbaum, Emily. "Fantastic voyage: *Doctor Who, Community*, and the passionate fan." *New Yorker*, June 4 & 11, 2012.

255. Osis, K. and E. Haraldsson. *At the Hour of Death.* New York: Avon, 1977.

256. Pahnke, W. N. "Drugs and mysticism." *International Journal of Parapsychology.* 8 (1966): 295-315.

257. Parnia, Sam. *Erasing Death: The Science That Is Rewriting the Boundaries between Life and Death.* New York: HarperOne, 2014.

258. Pascual-Leone, A. et al. "The plastic human brain cortex." *Ann R Neuroscience* 28 (2005):377-401.

259. Paumgarten, Nick. "Magic Mountain: Among the great and the good at Davos." *New Yorker*, Mar. 5, 2012.

260. Pearce, Joseph Chilton. *The Crack in the Cosmic Egg: New Constructs of Mind and Reality.* Rochester, Vermont: Park Street Press, 2002.

261. Pearson, Patricia. *Opening Heaven's Door: What the Dying May Be Trying to Tell Us about Where They're Going.* Toronto: Random House Canada, 2014.

262. Peat, F. David. *Synchronicity: The Bridge between Matter and Mind.* New York: Bantam Books, 1987.

263. Penfield, W. "The role of temporal cortex in certain psychical phenomena." *J Ment Sci* 101 (1955): 451-65.

264. Perry, Ralph Barton. *The Thought and Character of William James.* Boston: Little, Brown, 1935.

265. Pert, Candace. *Molecules of Emotion: The Science behind Mind-Body Medicine.* New York: Touchstone, 1999.

266. Pert, C. B. et al. "Neuropeptides and their receptors: a psychosomatic network." *J. Immunol* 1985 August: 135 (2 Suppl): 820s–826s.

267. Piper, Don, with Cecil Murphey. *90 Minutes in Heaven.* Grand Rapids, MI: Revell, 2004.

268. Playfair, Guy. *Twin Telepathy: The Psychic Connection.* London: Vega Books, 2002.

269. Plato and Jowett B. *Plato's The Republic.* New York: Modern Library, 1941.

270. Poe, Edgar Allan. *The Narrative of Arthur Gordon Pym of Nantucket, and Related Tales.* Oxford: Oxford University Press, 2008.

271. Pollan, Michael. "The trip treatment: a renaissance in psychedelic research." *New Yorker*, February 9, 2015.

272. Polster, E., and M. Polster. *Gestalt Therapy Integrated.* New York: Brunner/Mazel, 1973.

273. Posner, Michael. "Plants with soul." *The Walrus*, July/August 2006.

274. _____. "B.C. doctor agrees to stop using Amazonian plant to treat addictions." *Globe and Mail*, Nov. 9, 2011.

275. _____. "A brief mystery of time." *Globe and Mail*, Nov. 10, 2012.

276. Potter, Linda M. "The Golden Motorcycle Gang: Jack 'Chicken Soup for the Soul' Canfield on the inspiration for his autobiographical new book." *The Aquarian*, 19. (Winter 2011).

277. Powell, Diane Hennacy. *The ESP Enigma: The Scientific Case for Psychic Phenomena*. New York: Walker & Company, 2009.

278. Putnam, Hilary. *Renewing Philosophy*. Cambridge, MA: Harvard University Press, 1992.

279. _____. *Mathematics, Matter and Method*. Cambridge, UK: Cambridge University Press, 1975.

280. Radin, Dean. *The Conscious Universe: The Scientific Truth of Psychic Phenomena*. New York: HarperOne, 1997.

281. _____, and R. D. Nelson. "Repeatable evidence for anomalous human-machine interaction." in *Paranormal Research*, ed. M. L. Albertson et al. (Fort Collins, CO: Rocky Mountain Research Institute, 1988), 303–17.

282. Ram Dass. *Still Here: Embracing Aging, Changing, and Dying*. New York: Riverhead Books, 2000.

283. _____. *Be Here Now*. San Cristobal, NM: Lama Foundation, 1971.

284. Randi, James. *An Encyclopedia of Claims, Frauds, and Hoaxes of the Occult and Supernatural*. New York: St. Martin's Press, 1995.

285. Rees, W. Dewi. "The hallucinations of widowhood." *Br Med J*, 4 (1971):37-41.

286. Reik, Theodor. *Listening With the Third Ear*. New York: Farrar, Strauss & Co., 1948.

287. Remnick, David. "Leonard Cohen makes it darker." *New Yorker*, Oct. 17, 2016.

288. Rhine, J .B. *New Frontiers of the Mind: The Story of the Duke Experiments*. New York: Farrar & Rinehart, 1937.

289. _____. *Extra-Sensory Perception after Sixty Years*. Boston: Branden Publishing Company, 1981.

290. _____, and William McDougall. *Extra-Sensory Perception* (4th ed.) Boston: Branden Publishing Company, 1997.

291. Ring, Kenneth. "Near-death and out-of-body experiences in the blind: A study of apparent eyeless vision." *Journal of Near-Death Studies* 16 (Winter 1997).

292. _____. "Religiousness and Near-Death Experiences: An Empirical Study." *Theta* 8 (1980): 3–5.

293. _____. *Heading Toward Omega: In Search of the Meaning of the Near-Death Experience*. New York: Morrow, 1984.

294. _____. *The Omega Project*. New York: William Morrow, 1992.

295. Rinpoche, S. *The Tibetan book of living and dying*. San Francisco: HarperOne, 1992.

296. Roberts, Jane. *The Seth Material: The Spiritual Teacher That Launched the New Age*. Cutchogue, New York: Buccaneer Books, Inc., 1970.

297. Robertson, Morgan. *The Wreck of the Titan: Or, Futility 1912*. Delhi, India: Gyan Books, 2016.

298. Rosenhan, D. L. "On being sane in insane places." *Science* 179 (1973): 250–8.

299. Russell, Bertrand. *Religion and Science*. London: Oxford University Press, 1935.

300. _____. *Skeptical Essays*. London: George Allen & Unwin Ltd., 1928.

301. Ryback, David. *Dreams That Come True*. New York: Bantam, 1988. Sacks, Oliver. "Altered states: Self-experiments in chemistry." *New Yorker*, August 27, 2012.

302. _____. *Hallucinations*. New York: Knopf, 2012.

303. _____. *On the Move: A Life*. New York: Knopf, 2015.

304. Sagan, Carl. *The Demon Haunted World*. New York: Random House, 1995.

305. Sansom, C. J. *Dominion*. Toronto: Random House Canada, 2014.

306. Sartre, Jean-Paul. *Existentialism and Humanism*. London: Methuen & Co., 1946.

307. _____. *Being and Nothingness*. Third Paperbound Edition. New York: Citadel Press, 1965.

308. Schiffman, Richard. "Psilocybin: a journey beyond the fear of death?" *Scientific American*, Dec. 1, 2016.

309. Schmale, Arthur H. Jr. "Relationship of Separation and Depression to Disease: 1. A Report on a Hospitalized Medical Population." *Psychosomatic Medicine* 20 (1958):259–77.

310. Schmeidler, G. R. "Predicting good and bad scores in a clairvoyance experiment: A preliminary report." *JASPR* 37 (1943):103–10.

311. Schnider, Armin. *The Confabulating Mind: How the Brain Creates Reality*. New York: Oxford University Press, 2008.

312. Schultes R.E., A. Hofmann, and C. Ratsch. *Plants of the Gods: Their Sacred, Healing, and Hallucinogenic Powers*. 2nd edition. New York: Healing Arts Press, 2001.

313. Schulz, Mona Lisa. *Awakening Intuition: Using Your Mind-Body Network for Insight and Healing*. New York: Three Rivers Press, 1998.

314. Selye, Hans. *The Stress of Life*. New York: McGraw-Hill, 1956.

315. Semeniuk, Ivan. "Thinking big: hacking the brain." *Globe and Mail*, Jan. 12, 2013.

316. Shakespeare, William. *The Tragedy of Hamlet, Prince of Denmark*. In *The Complete Works of William Shakespeare*. London: Octopus Books, 1983.

317. _____. *Julius Caesar*. In *The Complete Works of William Shakespeare*. London: Octopus Books, 1983.

318. _____. *As You Like It*. In *The Complete Works of William Shakespeare*. London: Octopus Books, 1983.

319. Shermer, Michael. *The Believing Brain: From Ghosts and Gods to Politics and Conspiracies – How We Construct Beliefs and Reinforce Them as Truths*. New York: Time Books, 2011.

320. _____. *Why People Believe Weird Things: Pseudoscience, Superstition, and Other Confusions of our Time*. New York: Henry Holt and Company, 1997.

321. _____. "Anomalous Events That Can Shake One's Skepticism to the Core." *Scientific American*, Sept. 16, 2014.

322. Shomrat, Tal, and Michael Levin. "An automated training paradigm reveals long-term memory in planaria and its persistence through head regeneration." *Journal of Experimental Biology* 216 (2013): 3799–3810: doi: 10.1242/jeb.087809.

323. Silver, Nate. *The Signal and the Noise: Why So Many Predictions Fail – but Some Don't*. New York: The Penguin Press, 2012.

324. Sims, Andrew. *Symptoms in the Mind: An introduction to descriptive psychopathology*. Second Edition. London: W. B. Saunders, 1995.

325. Singer, Isaac Bashevis. *Meshugah*. New York: Plume/Penguin, 1995.

326. Slater, Joanna. "It's okay to hallucinate." *Globe and Mail*, November 17, 2012.

327. Slater, Lauren. "How Psychedelic Drugs Can Help Patients Face Death." http://www.nytimes.com/2012/04/22/magazine.

328. Smith, Daniel B. *Muses, Madmen and Prophets: Rethinking the History, Science, and Meaning of Auditory Hallucination*. New York: Penguin, 2007.

329. Smith, Russell. "Dubstep's fall from club beat to news ditty." *Globe and Mail*, Nov. 29, 2012.

330. Smith, Susy. *The Enigma of Out-of-Body Travel*. New York: Signet Books, 1965.

331. Snowdon, David. *Aging with Grace: What the Nun Study Teaches Us About Leading Longer, Healthier, and More Meaningful Lives.* New York: Bantam, 2001.

332. Solomon, G.F., and R.H. Moos. "Emotions, immunity, and disease: A speculative theoretical integration." *Arch Gen Psychiatry* 11 (Dec. 1964): 657–74.

333. Specter, Michael. "The Power of Nothing." *New Yorker,* Dec. 12, 2011.

334. Spitz, Elie Kaplan. *Does the Soul Survive? A Jewish Journey to Belief in Afterlife, Past Lives & Living with Purpose.* Woodstock, Vermont: Jewish Lights Publishing, 2000.

335. Stenger, Victor. "Meta-Analysis and the File Drawer Effect." *Skeptical Briefs* 12 (December 2002).

336. Stevenson, Ian. *Children Who Remember Previous Lives: A Question of Reincarnation.* Charlottesville, VA: University of Virginia Press, 1988.

337. _____. *Twenty Cases Suggestive of Reincarnation.* Charlottesville, VA: University of Virginia Press, 1980.

338. _____. *Unlearned Language: New Studies in Xenoglossy.* Charlottesville, VA: University of Virginia Press, 1984.

339. Stip, Emmanuel, and Genevieve Letourneau. "Psychotic symptoms as a continuum between normality and pathology." *Can J Psychiatry* 54 (2009): 140–51.

340. Storm, Howard. *My Descent into Death: A Second Chance in Life.* New York: Doubleday, 2005.

341. Strand, Mark. *The Story of Our Lives, with The Monument and The Late Hour.* New York: Knopf, 2002.

342. Sugrue, Thomas. *There Is A River: The Story of Edgar Cayce.* New York: Holt, Rinehart and Winston, 1942.

343. Sykes, J. B. (ed.) *Concise Oxford Dictionary, Seventh Edition.* New York: Oxford University Press, 1982.

344. Talbot, Michael. *Mysticism and the New Physics.* London: Penguin Arkana, 1993.

345. _____. *The Holographic Universe: The Revolutionary Theory of Reality.* New York: Harper Perennial, 2011.

346. Targ, Russell. *The Reality of ESP: A Physicist's Proof of Psychic Abilities.* Wheaton, Il: Quest Books Theosophical Publishing House, 2012.

347. _____, and H. E. Puthoff. "Information transmission under conditions of sensory shielding." *Nature,* 251 (1974):602-7.

348. Taylor, Kate. "What happens when an atheist sees God?" *Globe and Mail,* April 5, 2014.

349. Taylor, Paul. "Grey mattered." *Globe and Mail,* Dec. 31, 2012.

350. Teunisse, R.J. et al. "Visual hallucinations in psychologically normal people: Charles Bonnet syndrome." *Lancet* 347 (1996):794–97.

351. *The Holy Scriptures: A New Translation.* Philadelphia: The Jewish Publication Society of America, 1957.

352. Tolle, Eckhart. *The Power of Now: A Guide to Spiritual Enlightenment.* Novato, CA: New World Library, 1999.

353. Trachtman, P. "Review of '*Molecules of Emotion*'." by Candace B. Pert. *Smithsonian Magazine,* Sept. 1998.

354. Tucker, Jim B. and Ian Stevenson. *Life Before Life: A Scientific Investigation of Children's Memories of Previous Lives.* New York: St. Martin's Press, 2005.

355. _____. *Return to Life: Extraordinary Cases of Children Who Remember Past Lives.* New York: St. Martin's Press, 2013.

356. Tupper K. W. et al. "Psychedelic medicine: a re-emerging therapeutic paradigm." *CMAJ,* 187 (2015): 1054–59. doi:10.1503/cmaj.141124.

357. Turok, Neil. *From Quantum to Cosmos: The Universe Within.* London, UK: Faber & Faber, 2013.

358. Tye, Michael. "Qualia." *The Stanford Encyclopedia of Philosophy* (Summer 2009), edited by N. Zalta.

359. Tymoczko, Dmitri. "The nitrous oxide philosopher." *Atlantic Monthly*, 277 (May 1996), 93–101.

360. Tyrrell, G. N. H. *Apparitions.* London: Gerald Duckworth and Co. Ltd., 1943.

361. Ullman, M., S. Krippner, and A. Vaughan. *Dream Telepathy.* New York: Macmillan, 1973.

362. Van Lommel P. et al. "Near-death experience in survivors of cardiac arrest: a prospective study in the Netherlands." *Lancet* 358 (2001):2039-45.

363. Van Praagh, James. *Ghosts among Us: Uncovering the Truth about the Other Side.* New York: HarperCollins, 2009.

364. Vaughan W. T. et al. "Immunity and schizophrenia." *Psychosomatic Medicine* 11 (1949):327–33.

365. Watson, James D. *The Double Helix: A personal account of the discovery of the structure of DNA.* London: Weidenfeld and Nicolson, 1968.

366. Watts, Alan W. *The Way of Zen.* New York: Vintage Books, 1957.

367. _____, Timothy Leary, and Richard Alpert. *The Joyous Cosmology: Adventures in the Chemistry of Consciousness.* New York: Random House, 1962.

368. Weil, Andrew. *Spontaneous Healing.* New York: Ballantine Books, 1995.

369. Weiler, Craig. "Scientific skeptic organization." *Parapsychology Journalism: The People, The Theory, The Science, The Skeptics.* Posted Aug. 30, 2011.

370. Ibid. "A critical look at Randi's million dollar challenge." updated Jan. 2, 2011.

371. Weiss, Brian L. *Many Lives, Many Masters*. New York: Simon & Schuster, 1988.

372. Whelan, Matt. "Hallucinating in the Himalayas." *Globe and Mail*, Dec. 4, 2012.

373. Whitton, Joel, and Joe Fisher. *Life between Life*. New York: Warner Books, 1986.

374. Wiese, Bill. *23 Minutes in Hell: One Man's Story about What He Saw, Heard, and Felt in that Place of Torment*. Lake Mary, Florida: Charisma House, 2006.

375. Wiesel, Elie. "Why I write: making no become yes." *New York Times Book Review*. April 14, 1985.

376. Wills-Brandon, Carla. *Heavenly Hugs: Comfort, Support and Hope from the Afterlife*. Pompton Plains, NJ: Career Press, 2013.

377. Wilson, Colin. *The Occult: A History*. New York: Random House, 1974.

378. Wiseman, Richard. *Paranormality: Why We See What Isn't There*. London: Macmillan, 2011.

379. Witt, Emily. "Letter from California: The trip planners: The unusual couple behind an online encyclopedia of psychoactive substances." *New Yorker*, November 23, 2015.

380. Wittgenstein, L. *Philosophical Investigations*. Oxford: Blackwell, 1953.

381. Woolger, Roger J. *Other Lives, Other Selves: A Jungian Psychotherapist Discovers Past Lives*. New York: Doubleday, 1987.

Acknowledgments

I wish to thank my editor, Toby Macklin, without whose help this book would have been much longer and less erudite.

I wish to thank numerous family, friends, teachers, guides, and mentors, who have been nothing but kind, generous, loving, and supportive throughout the years. You know who you are. But just in case you don't, here are a few names.

Some are gone, but not forgotten. In my life, I've loved them all.

Harry Matas, Esther Matas, Anna Matas, Sylvia Matas, David Matas, Robert Matas, Alicia Matas, David McCleary, Mike Brown, Carol Matas, Lewis Pullmer, Mary Marantz, Sylvia Pullmer, Rose Steiman, Maria Gomori, Cynthia Powell, Eleanor Adaskin, Andrea Moore, Doug Staley, Dano Demaré, Carole Ladocha, Jiri Ladocha, Sid Robinovitch, Roger Fournier, Ben Wong, Jock McKeen, Lynn Petrie, Marilyn Rossner, Maggie Dwyer, Mallory Tabah, Miriam Russell, Chester Duncan, Rabbi Joseph Schachter, Stephanie Ballard (my manager), Catherine Holmes, and Miss Prucyk, my grade three teacher.

I can't thank you enough.

I would be remiss if I did not express my appreciation to the hard-working team at Friesen Press; my brilliant hematologist, Dr. James Johnston; and my selfless, compassionate, anonymous stem cell donor, without whose kindness I would not have been able to write this book.

CPSIA information can be obtained
at www.ICGtesting.com
Printed in the USA
LVOW11s0340050418
572393LV00001B/87/P

9 781525 504563